The Impression of Influence

The Impression of Influence

LEGISLATOR COMMUNICATION,
REPRESENTATION, AND DEMOCRATIC
ACCOUNTABILITY

Justin Grimmer
Sean J. Westwood
Solomon Messing

PRINCETON UNIVERSITY PRESS

Princeton and Oxford

Published by Princeton University Press, 41 William Street,
Princeton, New Jersey 08540
In the United Kingdom: Princeton University Press, 6 Oxford Street,
Woodstock, Oxfordshire OX20 1TW

press.princeton.edu

Library of Congress Cataloging-in-Publication Data
Grimmer, Justin.
  The impression of influence : legislator communication, representation, and democratic
accountability / Justin Grimmer, Sean J. Westwood, and Solomon Messing.
      pages cm
  Includes bibliographical references and index.
  ISBN 978-0-691-16261-4 (hardcover : alk.paper) – ISBN 0-691-16261-1
(hardcover : alk.paper) – ISBN 978-0-691-16262-1 (pbk. : alk. paper) –
ISBN 0-691-16262-X (pbk. : alk. paper) 1. Legislators–United States–Public opinion.
2. Government spending policy–United States–Public opinion. 3. Communication in
politics–United States. I. Title.
  JK1726.G755 2015
  328.73–dc23
                              2014010921

British Library Cataloging-in-Publication Data is available

This book has been composed in Sabon

Printed on acid-free paper ∞

Typeset by S R Nova Pvt Ltd, Bangalore, India
Printed in the United States of America

10 9 8 7 6 5 4 3 2 1

To Terese, Izzy, Eli, and Holden
  —JG

To Debbie Seltzer-Kelly
  —SJW

To Kathryn and our child, whose arrival we eagerly await
  —SM

Contents

List of Illustrations   ix

List of Tables   xi

Acknowledgments   xiii

1 Representation, Spending, and the Personal Vote   1

2 Solving the Representative's Problem and Creating the
   Representative's Opportunity   15

3 How Legislators Create an Impression of Influence   32

4 Creating an Impression, Not Just Increasing Name
   Recognition   64

5 Cultivating an Impression of Influence with Actions and
   Small Expenditures   81

6 Credit, Deception, and Institutional Design   121

7 Criticism and Credit: How Deficit Implications Undermine
   Credit Allocation   148

8 Representation and the Impression of Influence   174

9 Text as Data: Methods Appendix   186

Bibliography   189

Index   203

List of Illustrations

FIGURE 3.1: Substantial Variation in Credit Claiming
Propensity 40

FIGURE 3.2: Proportion of Credit Claiming Press Releases Are
Responsive to District Characteristics 43

FIGURE 3.3: The Decline of Republican Credit Claiming 46

FIGURE 3.4: Proportion of Credit Claiming Press Releases Are
Correlated with Partisan Composition 50

FIGURE 3.5: Proportion of Credit Claiming Press Releases Are
Correlated with Legislator Ideology 52

FIGURE 3.6: Legislators Regularly Claim Credit for Small
Expenditures 60

FIGURE 4.1: The Reach of Congressional Facebook Posts 72

FIGURE 4.2: Example Message from Our Facebook
Application, Compared to Actual Credit Claiming on
Facebook 77

FIGURE 5.1: Massive Increases in Expenditures Cause Only a
Small Increase in Support 93

FIGURE 5.2: The Limited Responsiveness to Increases in Dollar
Amount 96

FIGURE 5.3: Constituents Allocate Credit throughout the
Appropriations Process and Are Unresponsive to Money 100

FIGURE 5.4: Constituents Are Responsive to the Type of Project
Allocated 102

FIGURE 5.5: Constituents Allocate Credit to Opposing
Partisans, but Reward Copartisans More 105

FIGURE 5.6: Number of Messages Dominates the Amount
Claimed 110

FIGURE 5.7: Constituents Only Loosely Recall Total
Expenditures 113

FIGURE 6.1: Implications Lead to Constituent Credit
Allocation 132

FIGURE 6.2: The Assistance to Firefighter Grant Application
Process, as described in the Code of Federal Regulations 135

FIGURE 6.3: Congressional Press Releases Are Released before
Agency Press Releases 139

FIGURE 7.1: Zach Wamp (R-TN) and the Abandoning of
Credit Claiming 153

FIGURE 7.2: The Rise of Antispending Rhetoric 155
FIGURE 7.3: The Rise of Antispending Rhetoric among
Republicans 158
FIGURE 7.4: Heterogeneity in Response to Credit Claiming 168

List of Tables

TABLE 3.1: Credit Claiming Topics   57

TABLE 4.1: Example Templates for Facebook Posts   75

TABLE 4.2: The Effect of Credit Claiming and Advertising on Constituents   78

TABLE 5.1: Article Content across Conditions   85

TABLE 5.2: Constituents Respond to the Mere Report of an Action, but Are Unresponsive to the Type of Action   86

TABLE 5.3: Measuring Constituent Responsiveness to the Dollar Amount Claimed   92

TABLE 5.4: Measuring Constituent Responsiveness to Dollar Amounts and Comparing to Advertising Condition   95

TABLE 5.5: Examining the Effects of Credit Claiming Statements on Constituent Credit Allocation   99

TABLE 5.6: Total Amount Claimed across Experiment Conditions   108

TABLE 5.7: Example Credit Claiming Manipulation   108

TABLE 5.8: Number of Messages Dominates the Amount Claimed   109

TABLE 5.9: The Observational Effect of Legislator Credit Claiming   116

TABLE 6.1: Article Content across Conditions   130

TABLE 6.2: Legislators Who Claim Credit for Fire Grants Vote to Restore Agency Funding   142

TABLE 7.1: Content across Conditions, Experiment 1   162

TABLE 7.2: Budget Information Undermines Support from Credit Claiming   163

TABLE 7.3: Content across Conditions, Experiment 2   165

TABLE 7.4: Regardless of Source, Budget Information Undermines the Impression of Influence   166

TABLE 7.5: Budget Information Erodes Support for the Spending Program   167

TABLE 7.6: The Consequences of Budget Criticism for Legislators' Credit Claiming Efforts   169

Acknowledgments

WHEN SCHOLARS WRITE BOOKS, THEY AMASS DEBTS. WE ARE NO EX-
ception. We owe much to our wonderful research university, our patient
colleagues, dedicated reviewers, studious research assistants, and loving
families. Our acknowledgments are a step in settling this debt, but only a
small step. Like other scholars before us, we recognize that we still owe
much to everyone who contributed to this book.

We wrote this book while at Stanford University, an incredible
research environment. Our colleagues' steady encouragement, earnest
criticism, and sharp insights made this book possible and improved its
content. Lisa Blaydes, Adam Bonica, David Brady, David Broockman,
Daniel Butler, Gary Cox, Lauren Davenport, Kyle Dropp, Jim Fearon,
Mo Fiorina, Judy Goldstein, Jessica Gottlieb, Robert Gulloty, Steve
Haber, Shanto Iyengar, Simon Jackman, Karen Jusko, Jon Krosnick,
David Laitin, Phil Lipscy, Alison McQueen, Clayton Nall, Kristi Olson,
Amanda Robinson, Jonathan Rodden, Gary Segura, Paul Sniderman,
Jonathan Wand, Rebecca Weiss, Barry Weingast, Arjun Wilkins, and
Frannie Zlotnick all deserve special mention for their contributions. The
staff in the Department of Political Science were wonderfully helpful.
We are especially indebted to Jackie Sargent, Kelly Rosellen, and Eliana
Vasquez for their hard work.

We received generous funding from organizations throughout Stan-
ford and beyond to fund our research. This includes support from the
Hoover Institution, the Institute for Research in the Social Sciences, the
Lab for the Study of American Values, the United Parcel Service Endow-
ment Fund Grant, the Chair's Fund for New Faculty Development, a
Google Research Gift, and the Victoria Schuck Faculty Scholar Fund.

Our team of content analysts was fantastic. Molly Cain, Sara Ramsey,
and Jack Weller were diligent, thoughtful, hardworking, and patient.
This manuscript would not have been possible without them.

Perhaps one of the most productive, and fun, steps in producing a
manuscript is presenting nascent ideas to other scholars. The Department of Political Science generously hosted a book conference for our
manuscript, and Josh Ober's support made the conference possible. The
conference attendees—Chris Berry, Barry Burden, David Lewis, Arthur
Spirling, Mike Tomz, and Rob van Houweling—provided earnest and
productive criticisms that improved our manuscript and refined our
argument. Participants in workshops at other institutions helped us to

shape this manuscript. This includes workshop participants at Harvard University, Oxford University, University of Rochester, University of California Berkeley, University of Chicago Harris School of Public Policy, Yale University, Emory University, and Ohio State University. We also thank conference participants at the Midwest Political Science Association; the American Political Science Association; Political Methodology Summer Conference; the Northeast Political Methods Meeting; and the Politics, Elections, and Data Workshop. Several scholars from other universities were also kind enough to read and engage with our manuscript, including Avidit Acharya, Matt Blackwell, Amber Boydstun, Anthony Fowler, Andrew Hall, Eitan Hersh, Daniel Hopkins, Gabriel Lenz, Michael Peress, Jas Sekhon, Maya Sen, Brandon Stewart, Hanna Wallach, and John Wilkerson.

The editorial staff at Princeton University Press and the anonymous reviewers contributed greatly to the manuscript. Eric Crahan was extremely supportive of our project. The anonymous reviewers offered careful and fair criticisms of our manuscript. Anonymous reviewers at the *American Political Science Review* and the editorial team contributed further to our argument. And we thank Cambridge University Press for allowing us to reprint some of the content of "How Words and Money Cultivate a Personal Vote: The Effect of Legislator Credit Claiming on Constituent Credit Allocation."

In producing this manuscript, and in our careers, we also amassed our own personal debts to family, mentors, and friends. We dedicate this book to those to whom we owe the greatest debts. Justin can never repay the debt he owes Terese Grimmer, who has been a paragon of dedication, support, and patience, as well as to Izzy, Eli, and Holden, who are a source of constant joy and inspiration. Sean is indebted to Debbie Seltzer-Kelly, a friend and mentor. Solomon owes a tremendous debt to Kathryn, who has been a source of consultation, support, and encouragement, and dedicates this book to her and to their child, whose arrival they eagerly await.

The Impression of Influence

CHAPTER 1

Representation, Spending, and the Personal Vote

THIS IS A BOOK ABOUT HOW POLITICAL REPRESENTATION OCCURS on government spending decisions—one of the most consequential powers of government. The Constitution empowers Congress to "pay the Debts and provide for the common Defence and general welfare of the United States." Federal spending has a pervasive influence—impacting nearly every aspect of American life. How Congress allocates money affects the quality of infrastructure in American cities, the availability of health care in rural towns, and the provision of affordable housing across the country. Spending helps guard against harm—helping local governments prepare for natural disasters, protect against crime and fire, and deter terror attacks. It also sustains a powerful military, a network of federal law enforcement officials, and the flow of commerce and citizens across international borders. Government spending buoys local economies and even supports universities with funding for research.

Political representation in Congress is, in large part, about how elected officials decide how to spend federal money. While a large literature analyzes how district expenditures affect support for congressional incumbents it remains unclear how constituents hold legislators accountable for expenditures—how constituents attribute spending to legislators, how constituents evaluate those expenditures, and how constituents reward or punish legislators for spending on projects.[1] One reason for this lack of clarity is that constituents are unlikely to learn about the projects on their own. Constituents' inability to track spending is not an indictment of their democratic competence. Instead, it reflects the many activities representatives perform and the subtle ways that federal expenditures occur. Constituents lack the time, capacity, and incentives to carefully track what their representatives do in Congress to direct spending to the district. Even when spending reaches the district, it is difficult for constituents to attribute that spending to their representative. Projects in the district often do not have an obvious connection to the federal government.[2] And even if constituents do recognize that a project in the

---

[1] Stein and Bickers (1994); Levitt and Snyder (1997); Lazarus (2009).
[2] Mettler (2011).

district comes from the federal government, they may fail to link the project to their representatives.[3]

Constituents' inattention to spending creates a problem for representatives. Legislators want to use spending to bolster their standing in the district, but inattentive constituents are unlikely to learn about expenditures on their own. Political scientists have long argued that legislators use federal expenditures to cultivate support with their constituents and build a personal vote—support based on neither partisan affiliation nor ideological agreement.[4] For spending to have a direct effect on constituent support, constituents must at least know that the spending has occurred in the district. But legislators also want constituents to attribute the spending to the representative and to view the spending as beneficial to the district.

Representatives solve this problem with communication—turning the problem of constituent inattention into an opportunity to receive credit for much more than just spending as it occurs in the district. Legislators use credit claiming messages—statements intended to "generate a belief" that a representative is responsible for spending in the district—as part of a broad marketing campaign to ensure that constituents learn about spending projects in the district and attribute responsibility to their representatives.[5] The goal is to create an impression of influence over expenditures—a reputation of being effective at delivering money to the district. To do this, members of Congress issue press releases announcing new projects, send newsletters to describe work done in Washington to secure expenditures, make appearances at groundbreaking ceremonies as projects begin, and cut ribbons when projects are finished.

We show that this marketing effort is effective. Using a large collection of political texts, a series of experiments, and extensive case studies, we demonstrate that legislators' credit claiming affects constituent credit allocation and leads to a personal vote. To demonstrate how legislators claim credit for spending we analyze a large new collection of House press releases. We show that legislators strategically vary their association with spending, depending on their incentives to cultivate a personal vote. Representatives who need the support of independents and opposing partisans to win elections engage in higher rates of credit claiming than legislators who can rely on the support of copartisans to win election. When claiming credit for spending, legislators lay claim to a broad set of activities and grants. Representatives do claim credit for expenditures as they occur in the district, but members of Congress also

---

[3] Kriner and Reeves (2012).

[4] Fiorina (1977); Fenno (1978); Cain, Ferejohn, and Fiorina (1987).

[5] Mayhew (1974).

claim credit for expenditures they had only an indirect role in securing and expenditures that are unlikely to reach the district soon. And they tend to claim credit for relatively small projects in their district.

Constituents are responsive to legislators' credit claiming efforts. Using a series of experiments, we show that constituents evaluate the actions that legislators report performing and are responsive to who receives the funding. The result is that constituents reward legislators for work throughout the expenditure process—even if the expenditures have yet to be secured, will be delivered only to the district in the distant future, and even if constituents recognize the project has only a small chance of actually occurring. But constituents are largely unresponsive to the amount of money legislators claim credit for securing. Even large increases in the size of expenditures cause only slight increases in support for legislators.

The credit claiming, credit allocation process we characterize helps explain the institutions that disburse federal funds. We show legislators value the mere opportunity to announce expenditures—even if they had only an indirect role in securing the expenditure. Bureaucrats at competitive grant programs recognize this and create opportunities for legislators to announce expenditures. Legislators take advantage of the opportunities, using subtle language to imply that they are responsible for expenditures—even though they never literally claim credit for the project. Constituents allocate credit in response to the messages, inferring that legislators are responsible for the spending. And, in turn, representatives support the grant programs when their budgets are threatened.

We also show that the value of credit claiming is contingent on what other political actors say about spending. We show that after the election of Barack Obama congressional Republicans decreased their credit claiming rate and instead criticized government expenditures. The criticism undermines other legislators' credit claiming efforts— it dampens constituents' response to messages, creates opposition to spending programs, and even affects constituents' attitudes about prior credit claiming efforts.

We demonstrate how representation occurs around federal spending. It occurs through a dynamic process, with legislators anticipating how constituents will react to particular kinds of messages, constituents rewarding legislators for their credit claiming statements, and other actors attempting to affect how legislators cultivate this support.[6] Because legislators are entrepreneurial and anticipate constituents' reactions, constituents are able to exercise indirect control over their legislator,

[6] Mansbridge (2003); Disch (2012).

making it possible for legislators to be responsive to their constituents and creating conditions for democratic accountability.[7] The form of this control, however, is distinct from the usual notions of control and accountability in ideological representation.[8] A large literature seeks to measure how well legislators align with constituents' stated political preferences. This literature provides insights into how well legislators adopt constituent preferences, but is a less useful framework for studying representation around spending. It is less useful because constituents are unlikely to have the strong preferences over spending necessary to be located in ideological space. Rather than reacting to clearly articulated preferences, legislators anticipate constituents' reactions to credit claiming messages. And because legislators want to cultivate support, they will attempt to deliver and claim credit for projects popular with constituents. The result of the process is that constituents can have their underlying preferences enacted in the expenditure process.[9] But the process also creates new challenges for assessing the quality of representation and reveals new risks in representation. The risks arise because legislators may fool constituents, which may make it difficult for constituents to hold legislators accountable for actual spending that occurs in the district. And if we prioritize the reasoned exchange of ideas, we may criticize legislators for deceiving constituents.[10] But the potential benefits may outweigh the risks. Legislators' deceptions of constituents can lead to more efficient spending decisions and create incentives for legislators to work harder throughout the appropriations process.

The findings in this book provide an expansive characterization of how legislators claim credit for spending and how this affects constituent credit allocation. To do this, we make use of new data, introduce new statistical techniques, and deploy new experimental designs. To measure how legislators claim credit for spending, we use a new collection of nearly 170,000 House press releases—every press release from each House office from 2005 to 2010. To measure the content of the press releases, we use text as data methods, providing efficient means for identifying press releases that claim credit for spending. To uncover the effects of the credit claiming statements we introduce new experimental designs that enable us to isolate how features of legislators' credit claiming messages affect constituent credit allocation. We embed the experiments in surveys but also use more realistic settings to replicate how constituents may actually encounter credit claiming messages.

[7] Ashworth (2012).

[8] Miller and Stokes (1963); Achen (1978); Bafumi and Herron (2010).

[9] Arnold (1992).

[10] Kant (1983); Gutmann and Thompson (1996); Applbaum (1999); Mansbridge (2003).

When legislators engage in credit claiming they cultivate an impression of influence over expenditures and build a personal vote with constituents. To illustrate how this process works, and how legislators use credit claiming as part of a broader rhetorical strategy, we examine how one representative, Stephanie Herseth-Sandlin, used credit claiming to bolster support in South Dakota—and how this credit claiming became a liability when she was attacked by an antispending Republican.

1.1 CREATING A PERSONAL VOTE WITH CREDIT CLAIMING

In 2002, Stephanie Herseth-Sandlin—a Democrat from South Dakota—narrowly lost election to the state's lone seat in the House of Representatives to Bill Jankalow, who was serving as governor. But Herseth-Sandlin would soon have an opportunity to claim the seat—Jankalow was forced to resign after a vehicular manslaughter conviction. Herseth-Sandlin ran and won in the June 2004 special election over Larry Diedrich, securing 51% of the vote, and beat Diedrich again in the fall, expanding her support to 53% of the vote. By winning the November election, Herseth-Sandlin would join the 109th Congress as South Dakota's lone representative in the House, equipped with the power of incumbency and a full term in office to expand her electoral base.

To use the office to build support, however, Herseth-Sandlin would need to be responsive to her constituents—and in particular to moderates who supported the Republican Party in national elections. While South Dakota voters tend to elect both Democrats and Republicans to Congress, the state is solidly Republican in presidential elections. Recent elections have seen dismal returns for Democratic presidential candidates—John Kerry carried only 39.1% of the two-party vote in 2004 and Barack Obama won only 45.9% of the vote in 2008 and 39% in 2012. The recent results are in line with a long historical trend: since 1932 only two Democratic presidential candidate have won the state. The election results reflect the ideological views of South Dakota voters, who are known as morally conservative, agrarian, and pragmatic. And polls confirm a sizable Republican advantage in party identification: over 47% of the state identifies as Republican, while 38% identify as Democratic.[11]

Herseth-Sandlin would also need to maintain the support of her Democratic base, many of whom reside on Indian reservations in some

---

[11] Jones (2011).

of the poorest parts of America. For example, Shannon County, which contains the Pine Ridge Indian Reservation, is the most Democratic county in the country, with over 90% of the voters supporting Barack Obama in 2008 and 2012. It is also one of the poorest counties: it has a median household income around $25,000 and over 53% of the residents fall below the federal poverty line.[12] Other Democratic counties in the state have a similar profile. They contain impoverished reservations, full of Democratic voters who reside in towns that need federal funds to sustain local services.

To cultivate support among both the poor Democrats in her base and the independents necessary to bolster her appeal, Herseth-Sandlin cultivated an impression of influence—creating a reputation as effective at delivering money to the district. Herseth-Sandlin would regularly appear in the district, issue statements from her office, and distribute newsletters to make sure that constituents attributed spending to her. To create a reputation for being effective at delivering money to the district, Herseth-Sandlin made use of a broad set of expenditures at many different stages in the appropriations process. She sometimes claimed credit for expenditures as construction on a project began. For example, Herseth-Sandlin attended a groundbreaking ceremony for a $29 million renovation of the South Dakota National Guard Headquarters. At the ceremony, Herseth-Sandlin praised the investment, stating that "it represents an eye towards the future."[13] She also claimed credit for spending that was still far from reaching the state—including a $1.3 million earmark to improve an airfield that had only recently passed in the House,[14] and money for the South Dakota School of Mines in a recently passed House bill.[15] Herseth-Sandlin also claimed credit for projects even further from the district, projects that had been approved only by the Appropriations Committee. For example, she used a press release to announce "that significant funding for several South Dakota priorities has passed the House Appropriations Committee," though they had not yet been voted on by the full House.[16] Other times, Herseth-Sandlin claimed credit for merely requesting that funding be directed to the state. One newspaper story describes how she asked for $150 million in funds to manage forests in South Dakota. Herseth-Sandlin justified the requested expenditure, arguing that "[u]sing even a small portion of the Forests Service's...funds for the timber program will help to create jobs

---

[12] Census (2013).
[13] Kokesh (2009).
[14] Herseth-Sandlin (2009a).
[15] Herseth (2006b).
[16] Herseth (2005b).

in rural areas, cut down on catastrophic wildfires and promote healthy forests."[17]

Herseth-Sandlin also implied that she deserved credit for expenditures that she had only an indirect role in securing, regularly claiming credit for money allocated through executive branch grant programs. This included funds to bolster firefighting at the Rapid City airport[18] and money to "help ensure access to health care in rural communities in South Dakota."[19] Herseth-Sandlin also regularly shared the credit for projects with her Senate colleagues Tim Johnson and John Thune[20] and with high-ranking officials from the presidential administration.[21]

Herseth-Sandlin was particularly attentive to money allocated to Indian reservations, the poorest and most Democratic counties in South Dakota. When claiming credit for projects on reservations, she clarified her goal of improving her constituents' well-being. For example, she claimed credit for $3 million for housing on an Indian reservation, arguing that the expenditure was needed because "affordable housing is a critical component in the development and prosperity of tribal communities."[22] Herseth-Sandlin articulated a similar goal when announcing new highway funds for some Indian reservations—arguing that "the funding for Wakpa Sica and St. Joseph's Indian School, as well as the paving of an important highway through the Cheyenne River Indian Reservation, are key investments in Indian Country."[23] And when claiming credit for securing "critical funding for Indian country" in a bill that passed the House, she argued that "funding in this legislation will improve infrastructure on reservations and assist with economic development efforts by attracting investment to Indian Country."[24]

Herseth-Sandlin also claimed credit for many other types of expenditures in order to cultivate support with residents throughout South Dakota. She claimed credit for law enforcement expenditures, including "more than $5 million to hire, retain 30 police officers"[25] and "$250,000 for Methamphetamine Awareness and Prevention Project."[26] She also claimed credit for infrastructure improvements, including $22 million for the Lewis and Clark Water Project and $32 million for the

---

[17] Staff (2010*b*).
[18] Staff (2009*a*).
[19] Herseth (2005*a*).
[20] Herseth (2006*a*).
[21] Staff and Press (2009).
[22] Herseth-Sandlin (2009*b*).
[23] Herseth (2006*c*).
[24] Herseth-Sandlin (2009*d*).
[25] Herseth-Sandlin (2009*c*).
[26] Herseth (2005*c*).

Mni Wiconi project. Herseth-Sandlin explained that the projects were vital, because "[t]he importance of a clean, reliable source of drinking water to rural economies can not be overstated."[27] She claimed credit for funds that would help her constituents during the winter. In one press release, she "announced...more than $629,000 specifically for heating communities in South Dakota,"[28] and in another she "announced that South Dakota will receive an additional $620,264 in Low Income Home Energy Assistance Program."[29]

Herseth-Sandlin used public statements, appearances, and press releases to make the case that she was an effective advocate for South Dakota. This was part of Herseth-Sandlin's broader strategy in Congress to appeal to independents and moderate Republicans. As a Blue-Dog Democrat she often voted against her party. She declared publicly that "I've worked with both political parties. I've stood up to both political parties to do what's right for South Dakota."[30] After her reelection in 2006 she declared that her win is "an affirmation of the idea that South Dakotans expect and deserve representation from the center, not the ideological extremes."[31] Indeed, Herseth-Sandlin's nonpartisan reputation was so effective that local newspapers would occasionally misidentify her as a Republican.[32]

Herseth-Sandlin's strategy worked for her first two terms in office. Her base of support grew in the 2006 and 2008 elections, capturing over 67% of the vote in both elections. Exit polls in the 2008 election reveal how effectively she grew her support. She maintained her high level of support among Democrats—securing 94% of the vote—while also securing 72% of the independent vote and even 40% of the Republican vote.[33] After she outperformed Obama by almost 23 percentage points in the 2008 election, political pundits viewed Herseth-Sandlin's seat as safe for the upcoming midterm elections.

But Herseth-Sandlin's strength—a reputation for delivering federal money to her state—would become a liability in the 2010 midterm elections. After Barack Obama's election in 2008, the Republican base and political elites mobilized in opposition to stimulus-spending measures and proposed policy reforms—such as the Affordable Care Act, financial reform, and cap-and-trade environmental regulations. Tea Party Republicans attacked Democrats for expenditures arguing that the

---

[27] Herseth (2006a).
[28] Herseth (2006d).
[29] Herseth-Sandlin (2008).
[30] Brokaw (2010).
[31] Lammers (2006).
[32] Staff (2006a).
[33] Staff (2008).

particularistic district spending was wasteful—an attempt to undermine the value of spending to cultivate a personal vote.

In the 2010 midterm elections Herseth-Sandlin faced Kristi Noem, a South Dakota legislator and Tea Party member. Noem's campaign worked to undermine Herseth-Sandlin's reputation as a nonpartisan advocate for South Dakota. Undermining Herseth-Sandlin's image as a moderate legislator, Noem portrayed Herseth-Sandlin as a liberal who supported Nancy Pelosi. At one debate, Noem asked Herseth-Sandlin, "In 2005 you voted for Nancy Pelosi [for speaker], again in 2007, and again in 2009. If you had the opportunity to represent South Dakota again in the House, would you vote for Nancy Pelosi again?" At the same time, Noem attacked Herseth-Sandlin for contributing to "out of control" spending in Washington. Noem's campaign regularly remarked that Herseth-Sandlin was far from a fiscal conservative and that "South Dakotans are frustrated with politicians in Washington spending like there is no tomorrow."[34] Noem's attacks forced Herseth-Sandlin to work even harder to portray herself as a moderate. And this further eroded Herseth-Sandlin's already diminished support among the relatively small group of liberal South Dakotans. At a McGovern Day event—an annual event for the South Dakota Democratic party—several audience members refused to hold Herseth-Sandlin signs, to protest her increasingly moderate positions.[35]

Noem's campaign was successful—securing a narrow 7,000-vote margin of victory over Herseth-Sandlin. Noem's victory—and Herseth-Sandlin's attempts to hold her seat during an election that favored Republicans—reveals trade-offs in how legislators can use particularistic spending to cultivate support. Legislators can engage in credit claiming to cultivate support with poor constituents and opposing partisan voters. But this risks alienating ideological partisans. And claiming credit for spending also creates a risk that a legislator will be portrayed as fiscally irresponsible and undermines her ability to use credit claiming to cultivate support.

1.2 THE IMPRESSION OF INFLUENCE: PREVIEWING OUR ARGUMENT

Herseth-Sandlin's broad credit claiming efforts are indicative of how legislators create an impression of influence over expenditures and how representation occurs around federal spending. Across congressional districts the credit claiming occurs regularly. We characterize legislator

[34] Palmer (2010).
[35] Woster (2010).

credit claiming across all House members—that is, how often legislators claim credit for spending, what they claim credit for obtaining, and how much legislators obtain. We then use a series of experiments to show how constituents allocate credit in response to legislators' credit claiming messages—demonstrating how constituents are responsive to the actions that legislators report, but are less responsive to the amount that legislators claim credit for securing. We show how this process matters for the way the federal government spends money, demonstrating how legislators support grant programs because they provide the opportunity to announce expenditures. We also show how criticism of federal expenditures undermines the value of credit claiming.

Our findings have broad implications for the political economy of government spending, the design of political institutions, and political representation in Congress. In this section we preview our argument and the evidence for our conclusions that legislators cultivate an impression of influence over expenditures with credit claiming messages and this leads to a personal vote.

In Chapter 2 we explain when strategic legislators will associate themselves with spending and how constituents are likely to allocate credit in response to legislators' credit claiming messages. The complicated appropriations process makes it nearly impossible for constituents, on their own, to track their legislators' activities. This complexity creates a need for legislators to explain their work to constituents. Reelection-oriented legislators face a trade-off between adopting a nonpartisan reputation as an effective advocate for the district or cultivating an image as a partisan who effectively advocates for their party. As a result, who legislators represent affects how legislators balance these considerations in their public messages. Constituents are responsive to legislators' credit claiming efforts, but lack both the context and the information necessary to be responsive to the amount legislators claim credit for securing. Instead, constituents will seize on information they are better equipped to evaluate: the action legislators report, the recipient of the expenditure, and the purported benefits.

In Chapter 3 we characterize legislators' credit claiming efforts, demonstrating how often legislators claim credit for spending, what legislators claim credit for securing, and the amount legislators tout. We develop accurate measures of legislators' credit claiming rates and then show how legislators' credit claiming strategies reflect the types of districts they represent. Legislators with the greatest incentive to cultivate a personal vote claim credit more often than colleagues who can win reelection with appeals to their partisan base. We also illuminate how members of Congress claim credit broadly and not just for money that is earmarked during the appropriations process. This behavior includes claiming credit for requests made during the appropriations process even if the expenditures only have a small chance of actually reaching the district. What is more, legislators claim credit for more than funds earmarked during the appropriations process. They also claim credit for grants that executive agencies allocate. And legislators claim credit for relatively small amounts of money—often claiming credit for expenditures that appear inconsequential relative to the federal budget.

We then show the distinct effects of legislators' credit claiming messages. In Chapter 4 we demonstrate that legislators' credit claiming efforts do more than simply bolster name recognition—they also cultivate an impression of influence over federal funds. We report the results of an experiment conducted on a major social media website—a setting where constituents regularly receive messages like the ones we use in our experiment from their member of Congress. Using our experimental design, we show that credit claiming messages do make constituents more familiar with their representative, but the credit claiming messages also lead constituents to infer that their legislator is more effective at delivering money to the district. The result is that credit claiming messages cause a larger increase in overall support than other types of messages.

Chapter 5 demonstrates how credit claiming messages cause this larger increase in support. We present the results of a series of experiments that show constituents are more responsive to the action that legislators report and the type of expenditure they claim and less responsive to the amount of money legislators claim credit for securing. Constituents allocate nearly identical credit for securing an expenditure during the appropriations process and merely requesting an expenditure. This support occurs even though constituents believe that money that has already been secured is more likely to reach the district. Constituents are responsive to the type of expenditure legislators claim credit for securing, but are generally unresponsive even to large increases in the amount of money allocated to a project. In an experiment conducted over several days, we show that increasing the number of credit claiming messages legislators send has a much larger effect on constituent credit allocation than increasing the amount of money legislators claim credit for securing. We then provide evidence that the processes documented in our experiments occur with actual representatives. Using legislators' actual credit claiming rates, we show that legislators with higher rates of credit claiming are evaluated as more effective at delivering money to the district.

Legislators, therefore, have reason to value the opportunity to claim credit for spending, even if they are unable to influence the disbursement of funds. In Chapter 6 we show how legislators—with the help of a subtle linguistic deception and strategic bureaucrats—claim credit for grants that the representative had only an indirect role in securing. Bureaucrats create credit claiming opportunities to cultivate support for their program, particularly when the bureaucrats are otherwise unable to manipulate grant decisions. Legislators take advantage of the opportunity to announce the expenditure, while never explicitly taking credit. We use an experiment to show this linguistic deception is effective, leading constituents to believe that legislators who only "announce" a grant are responsible for securing it. Once we reveal that legislators are only implying they deserve credit, however, legislators' credit is decimated. The credit claiming opportunities are also effective for bureaucrats because members of Congress take advantage of the opportunities to defend the agency when their budget is threatened.

Legislators use rhetoric to ensure they receive credit from constituents for spending and that constituents evaluate the expenditures positively. This leaves legislators open to attacks from opponents that they are fiscally irresponsible—an attack that has become increasingly common. After Barack Obama's election, Republican activists mobilized to oppose the Obama administration's policies and perceived government overreach—creating the Tea Party movement. As we show in Chapter 7, the emergence of the Tea Party movement corresponds with a spike in antispending rhetoric among congressional Republicans, who criticized particularistic projects that other legislators use to cultivate a personal vote. We use two experiments to show how this criticism undermines credit for spending, causing constituents to be much less supportive of expenditures in the district. And we show that the effect of the criticism extends beyond the experiment. Once budget criticism is introduced, it causes constituents to evaluate legislators who claim credit at high rates more negatively.

In Chapter 8 we conclude, examining the implications of our argument for representation. The credit claiming, credit allocation process we characterize enables accountability, but it also forces us to reconsider our priorities in representation and how we might privilege transparent communication at the expense of efficient policy outcomes, and vice versa. If we prioritize truthful and transparent discussion, then the credit claiming, credit allocation process is problematic. We also suggest some reforms in reporting and congressional credit claiming that could make the process more transparent and limit legislators' ability to engage in systematic deception. But if we prioritize the consequences of the credit claiming, then the process we describe may work well, by incentivizing legislators to work throughout the appropriations process and ensuring legislators support efficient expenditures. We also explain how our work could be extended, and highlight yet-to-be-answered questions about how legislators build support.

Cumulatively, our evidence demonstrates how legislators claim credit for spending and how constituents respond to those messages in controlled experiments. The use of experiments ensures that our results are internally valid. Throughout the book we also attempt to demonstrate that our results are externally valid—that our text and experimental evidence capture how constituent credit allocation actually occurs. We demonstrate external validity using a variety of evidence. We use survey evidence to link legislators' actual credit claiming rates with constituent credit allocation. This reveals a persistent relationship between legislators' credit claiming rates and constituents' evaluations of their representatives. We also provide evidence about how constituents encounter legislators' messages—both press releases in local newspapers and representatives' posts on social media sites. And finally, we use case studies to illuminate how legislators think they are affecting constituents' beliefs. The evidence we present suggests that the type of process we document in this book occurs broadly. Like other studies in observational social science, we are unable to definitively and conclusively demonstrate the external validity of our findings. But we provide evidence for their external validity and explain why our results are important on their own.

In this book we document how legislators use credit claiming to ensure they receive credit from constituents. Of course, we do not view this as the only way spending may develop support in the district, because some constituents are particularly motivated to track spending decisions. For example, owners of construction companies are likely to track additional highway expenditures, and local elected officials may have more intimate knowledge of local budgets, so they may be more responsive to the size of the grants. Our focus, however, is on the audience for legislators' credit claiming messages—that is, how legislators use credit claiming statements to cultivate broader support with their reelection constituency.[36]

1.3 CONCLUSION

The credit claiming, credit allocation process that we describe is at the heart of American political representation. It also reveals the dynamic way in which representation often occurs in a democracy.[37] When legislators engage in this credit claiming, they act as entrepreneurs. They anticipate how constituents will react and attempt to tailor their message to create support. Legislators make the case as to why they are responsible for government actions and why constituents should

[36] Fenno (1978).
[37] Arnold (1992); Mansbridge (2003); Ashworth (2012).

reward the legislator for those actions. Constituents, in turn, evaluate and respond to the messages.

The credit claiming, credit allocation process ensures that constituents exercise control over their legislator's actions, though this is not the reactive control common in quantitative models of ideological political representation.[38] Throughout this book, then, we examine the implications of legislators' entrepreneurial activities for representation and legislators' personal vote. Legislators' marketing efforts enable them to influence the terms of evaluation and to receive credit for activities that constituents might otherwise never associate with a representative. They also create new possibilities for institutional design and risks when politicians criticize spending as wasteful. We begin this examination in the next chapter, where we explain when and how legislators engage in credit claiming and how constituents respond to legislators' credit claiming efforts.

[38] Miller and Stokes (1963).

CHAPTER 2

Solving the Representative's Problem and Creating the Representative's Opportunity

WHEN AT HOME IN THEIR DISTRICT, LEGISLATORS OFTEN USE their public appearances to announce new grants, or to celebrate the completion of spending projects. Consider, for example, Pete Visclosky (D-IN)—a long time Democratic incumbent from northwest Indiana. On November 11, 2011 Visclosky was in Gary, Indiana for a ribbon cutting ceremony for a bike trail along Lake Michigan's southern shore. At the ceremony, Visclosky praised the trail as "a wise investment of our tax dollars—improving the quality of life and the health of everyone who lives in our communities," an investment made possible with the help of an earmark inserted in a 2004 Appropriations bill. His appearance at the ribbon cutting is indicative of how Visclosky spends his time in the district. A few months prior to the ribbon cutting ceremony in Gary, Visclosky broke ground at another bike trail, further south in his district in the small town of Schererville.[1] The funding for this project was allocated in a 2007 grant which, as Visclosky explained, was "for park expansion and improvements."[2] Even sewer projects—with the Army Corps of Engineers deciding on the funding—are celebrated with an appearance from Visclosky. At one groundbreaking in the blue collar town of Whiting, Visclosky explained that "the installation of these sewer improvements will create good-paying jobs for Northwest Indiana."[3]

Pete Visclosky's appearances in his district are part of an effort to receive credit for federal projects. Visclosky uses his public appearances to draw attention to the expenditures, to explain that he is at least partly responsible for delivering the money to the district, and that the projects are useful to local communities. The complicated federal expenditure process makes it necessary for Visclosky to engage in credit claiming to ensure constituents allocate credit for district spending. Sometimes

[1] Rico (2011).
[2] Visclosky (2007).
[3] Laverty (2012).

there are long delays from allocation of funds to actual expenditure. For example, Visclosky had to wait seven years—and several elections—to cut the ribbon for the bike trail in Gary and four years to break ground on the bike trail in Schererville. In other instances federal expenditures are coupled with local expenditures, obscuring the federal government's role in directing money to the district. For example, the Army Corps of Engineers provided primary funding for the sewer in Whiting, but it was also partially funded by the city.

The complicated expenditure process makes it hard for legislators to track spending, let alone for constituents to tally expenditures in the district.[4] The structure of representation exacerbates the problem. Constituents lack the incentive to track the complicated expenditures. A large literature in political science has documented how constituents have little incentive to acquire new information on their own.[5] And even if constituents did happen to acquire information on local spending, it is unclear how they would evaluate that information. This is hardly a critique of the American public's democratic competence. Rather, it is a recognition that to understand how spending will affect a local community often requires technocratic knowledge that no one would expect constituents to hold.

Visclosky uses his public appearances to overcome what we call the *representative's problem* in American democracy. The perquisites of office give incumbents resources to build an incumbency advantage, but incumbents have to use the resources to gain the attention of largely inattentive constituents. Visclosky's appearances in the district demonstrate how legislators solve this problem: rather than rely on constituents to learn on their own about what their legislator does while in office, representatives show they are responsible for spending that occurs in the district. To receive credit for directing funds to the district, legislators use credit claiming statements to create the impression of influence over expenditures among constituents—to cultivate a reputation as effective at delivering money to the district. Constituents, in turn, respond to the messages—legislators' messages affect constituents' long-term evaluations of their member of Congress.

The credit claiming, credit allocation process that we document often turns the representative's problem into the representative's opportunity. It enables legislators to claim credit broadly—ensuring legislators can argue they are responsible for much more than spending as it occurs in the district. Representatives use statements to claim credit for expenditures that are still far removed from the district, expenditures that have only a

---

[4] Lee (2003*b*).
[5] Downs (1957).

chance of actually occurring, and even for expenditures a representative has merely requested be allocated to the district. And legislators are able to receive credit for a wide array of expenditures—much more than just earmarked money in appropriations bills. Legislators are able to imply they are responsible for money they had only an indirect role in securing, even if legislators had little direct influence over those expenditures.

Legislators' credit claiming messages are effective—constituents allocate credit in response to legislators' credit claiming messages. But constituents tend to focus on the actions that legislators report and the recipients of the expenditure, rather than the amount of money that legislators report securing. This occurs because constituents often lack the context to assess how levels of spending will affect local interests and needs. Even if constituents had the context, however, there are psychological mechanisms that make it hard for constituents to reward legislators for the amount secured. Constituents tend to evaluate credit claiming messages rapidly, making it hard for them to identify and evaluate numerical information. In contrast, constituents are well equipped to assess a legislator's action on an expenditure, the recipient, and the reported benefits.

In this chapter we introduce our argument about how legislators claim credit for federal projects and how, in turn, constituents allocate credit. We provide a mechanism to explain how federal expenditures in the district lead to legislator support, complimenting existing studies on federal expenditures.[6] We also explain how actions that could potentially lead to expenditures can cultivate support for legislators. This implies that spending can have a loose relationship with legislators' electoral support and still be an important component of the personal vote. Expenditures and credit claiming together lead to increased support, but spending alone is unlikely to be noticed and unlikely to lead to increased support. This is because constituents, on their own, are unlikely to reward legislators for federal expenditures. We begin this chapter by explaining why it is so hard for constituents to learn about spending.

2.1 THE REPRESENTATIVE'S PROBLEM

Legislators' primary goal is to be reelected—Mayhew (1974) famously characterized representatives as "single-minded seekers of reelection." Of course legislators also have other goals—they want to influence policy, be powerful in Congress, obtain a higher office, or even secure personal

[6] Levitt and Snyder (1997); Strömberg (2004); Chen and Malhotra (2007); Shepsle et al. (2009).

wealth. But reelection is the primary goal, a necessary condition to achieve many of legislators' other broader goals. Political scientists often argue that legislators perform actions in Congress to bolster support with constituents to pursue reelection. And legislators have a wide array of tools to cultivate support. They may cast votes that align with district opinion,[7] perform constituency service,[8] or invest in work in Congress that advocates district interest.[9]

The problem for legislators is that constituents, on their own, are unlikely to learn about many of these activities. Legislators may faithfully work to build constituent support, but constituents may fail to reward legislators simply because they never have the chance to learn about the work. This problem arises as a natural and intended consequence of the structure of political representation in republican governments.[10] Constituents delegate authority to elected officials, who use the authority to govern. This enables constituents to attend to other tasks, but it limits their ability to track what their many elected officials do while in office.

The representative's problem—that work done in Congress to build support may go unnoticed—is also a problem for constituents.[11] A common assumption in models of representation is that constituents want legislators who are accountable to constituents—representatives who take actions that align with constituents' interests and exert effort to enact policies constituents prefer.[12] The risk for constituents is that they may select a legislator who has priorities or positions that are misaligned with the district, legislators who exert little effort while in office,[13] or representatives who pander to secure reelection.[14]

The representative's problem is particularly pressing in federal spending. Both politicians and political scientists recognize the electoral value of delivering pork to the district,[15] but spending is also one of the most difficult activities for constituents to track. The complicated and decentralized way federal disbursements occurs makes tabulating total district expenditures difficult for members of Congress, let alone constituents. Frances Lee argues that this is difficult for House members

---

[7] Miller and Stokes (1963); Achen (1978); Canes-Wrone, Brady, and Cogan (2002).

[8] Cain, Ferejohn, and Fiorina (1987).

[9] Hall (1996).

[10] Madison (1787).

[11] Ashworth (2012).

[12] Ashworth and Bueno de Mesquita (2006); Daley and Snowberg (2011); Ashworth (2012).

[13] Ashworth (2005).

[14] Canes-Wrone, Herron, and Shotts (2001).

[15] Weingast, Shepsle, and Johnsen (1981); Stein and Bickers (1994); Levitt and Snyder (1997).

"[b]ecause House districts are not administrative units in the federal system, systematic data on the amount of money they receive in federal grants is difficult to obtain."[16] It is also difficult for House members to tabulate expenditures in any year, because there can be a lengthy delay between when funds are earmarked or a grant allocated and an actual expenditure is made in the district. Further, the amount set aside in an expenditure process nearly always differs from the amount actually spent. When accumulated over several spending bills, this difference can be substantial. For example, in August 2012 the Obama administration announced a plan to spend $470 million in funds earmarked in transportation bills passed from 2003 to 2006 that had not yet been spent—either because projects were completed under the allocated budget or because delays had caused long planned projects to not yet begin.

Even if constituents could tabulate the exact amount of particularistic spending in a district in a particular year, constituents may still struggle to recognize whether expenditures made in the district originated with the federal government.[17] Suzanne Mettler characterizes a wide array of federal programs as creating a "subterranean state": government spending that is not obviously connected with the government.[18] This obscures the federal government's role in expenditures, making it less likely constituents—on their own—will connect projects in the district with expenditures in Washington. For example, firefighters hired with federal grants are indistinguishable from other firefighters hired with funds from a municipal budget, and educational equipment purchased with educational grants are difficult to distinguish from other equipment in schools.

The complicated coordination between federal, state, and local officials to disburse funds makes it even more difficult for constituents to identify federal spending and attribute it to members of Congress. Consider, for example, the allocation of highway funds. The money used to build and repair roads comes from many sources and with differing levels of coordination across levels of government. The bulk of highway funds are allocated through a formula process, which provides local and state officials substantial control over how the funds are spent. Members of Congress approve formulas for states to build highways based on the needs of the state and the amount paid in highway related taxes.[19] Once the money has been allocated to a state, state and local officials decide where to direct the funding and how to pay for the

---

[16] Lee (2003*b*), 715.
[17] Mettler (2011).
[18] Mettler (2011).
[19] Martin (2012).

matching expenditures.[20] But other ways of allocating money afford state officials less direct control. Legislators, at least prior to reforms to the process in the 112th Congress, would include funding for specific highway projects in appropriations bills. Certainly local official and state officials help identify areas of need for such projects, but members of Congress are given the most control over where the the earmarked money is directed. Other expenditures can occur entirely through executive discretion. The Department of Transportation can use its discretion to target projects.[21] With highway spending alone, there is substantial variation in who is responsible for securing money and directing where it is spent. Across other programs there is even more variation—and more ambiguity—about who deserves credit for spending that occurs in the district. Some programs we describe later in the book (see Chapter 6) allocate expenditures through a competitive process with little legislator involvement. Other expenditures, including Army Corps of Engineers projects, more directly involve legislators.[22]

And even if constituents were able to tabulate expenditures and attribute responsibility to legislators appropriately, they might still struggle to allocate credit. Constituents generally lack the context necessary to assess the size of expenditures. After all, we would not expect many residents in a town to know how much money is necessary for a local fire department to buy new gear, for a local police station to purchase bulletproof vests, or to repave local highways. Constituents also lack the incentive to think carefully about the expenditures—resulting in psychological processes that make incorporating information about the size of expenditures in evaluations difficult.

Constituents, then, are unable to account for spending on their own in the district. This creates a problem for legislators, who would use expenditures in the district to cultivate a personal vote and to grow an incumbency advantage. We now explain how legislators turn this problem into an opportunity, to receive credit for much more than spending that occurs in the district.

2.2 THE REPRESENTATIVE'S OPPORTUNITY: THE CREDIT CLAIMING, CREDIT ALLOCATION PROCESS

Legislators use credit claiming statements to shape constituents' impressions of their representative's influence over federal expenditures. As

---

[20] Shirley (2011).
[21] Shirley (2011); Kriner and Reeves (2012).
[22] Ferejohn (1974); Arnold (1992).

David Mayhew (1974) first defined, credit claiming is "acting so as to *generate a belief* in a relevant political actor...that one is personally responsible for causing the government...to do something that the actor considers desirable."[23] Credit claiming statements help constituents complete the difficult task of learning about expenditures in the district and attributing responsibility. Of course, helping constituents learn about the expenditure benefits the legislator.

An example credit claiming statement, from Hal Rogers (R-KY), illuminates how. In the summer of 2009, Rogers released a press release that began:

> U.S. Congressman Harold "Hal" Rogers (KY-05) announced today that the House of Representatives has approved $5 million to continue retrofitting U.S. Army helicopters with leak proof transmission fluid drip pans for the HH-60 Blackhawk Helicopter that are produced by workers at Phoenix Products in McKee. Rogers secured this funding in H.R. 3326, the Department of Defense Appropriations Bill, which passed the House of Representatives on July 30, 2009 and is awaiting further action by the Senate.[24]

Rogers provides information about the expenditure, ensuring constituents do not have to acquire information themselves. He also tries to "generate a belief" that he is responsible for securing the expenditure, informing constituents that he "secured this funding" in a Defense Appropriations Bill. And Rogers makes clear that constituents should consider this expenditure desirable. Later in the press release Rogers explains that "[t]he drip pans...have a strong reputation for quality and durability which is essential to keeping this Army air workhorse maintenance free and ensuring these aircraft are safe in the skies over Afghanistan."[25]

Legislators use credit claiming statements to associate themselves with spending in the district and to ensure they receive credit for expenditures. We now explain when and how legislators engage in credit claiming and how, in turn, constituents allocate credit.

2.2.1 Credit Claiming: How Legislators Create an Impression of Influence

Legislators use public statements to explain how they represent their constituents while in office, defining to constituents the type of

---

[23] Mayhew (1974), 52–53 (emphasis added).

[24] Rogers (2009c).

[25] Rogers (2009c). Of course, credit claiming can go well beyond public statements. Many members of Congress regularly attend ground breaking ceremonies, ribbon cutting events, or make public appearances to appear responsible for money spent in the district. In each instance, legislators are ensuring constituents associate projects with the representative.

representation their legislator provides them.[26] While communication is often conceptualized as cheap talk, legislators are constrained in how many public statements they can make effectively. Part of the constraint comes from limited staff resources. Communications staff are experts at composing messages, but still require time to write effective messages. The constraints also come from the audience. Newspaper editors have only limited space available for congressional news and cap the number of stories they will publish from any one legislator. Even more direct communication has limits. Franking rules limit the number of newsletters legislators can send during a term. And constituents' attention limits the number of stories that can be included in e-newsletters. Legislators, therefore, have only a limited number of opportunities to make an impression with constituents.

The limited number of possible messages forces legislators to face trade-offs when deciding what to say to constituents. When legislators decide what to say and emphasize, they anticipate how constituents will react. Recent theoretical and empirical work describes a trade-off between emphasizing work done to deliver money to the district—claiming credit for expenditures that occur in the district—and broader national policies—articulating positions on salient policy debates.[27] When legislators articulate credit claiming positions they portray themselves as nonpartisan advocates for their district. This provides legislators an opportunity to cultivate valence, or a personal vote—support that is not based on the representative's ideological position nor their partisan affiliation.[28] When credit claiming for district spending, however, legislators forgo the chance to portray themselves as effective representatives on broader national policy debates. Instead of credit claiming, legislators may articulate positions on proposed policy changes. This ensures legislators can remind their constituents about their representative's partisan affiliation and clarifies the legislator's positions on major national political events.

Previous work on congressional communication demonstrates the prominence of the credit claiming, position taking trade-off in Senators' presentational styles—how they define the type of representation they provide constituents. Using a text as data method that discovers presentational style categories and a new collection of Senate press releases, Grimmer (2013) shows that senators' presentational styles lie on a credit claiming, position taking spectrum. At one end of the spectrum are

[26] Grimmer (2013).

[27] Groseclose (2001); Ashworth and Bueno de Mesquita (2006); Dropp and Peskowitz (2012); Wichowsky (2012); Grimmer (2013).

[28] Fiorina (1977); Cain, Ferejohn, and Fiorina (1987); Stein and Bickers (1994).

Position Takers—senators who engage in the most prominent national policy debate, but tend to avoid engaging in credit claiming. At the other extreme of the spectrum are Appropriators: senators who engage in credit claiming for state spending and rarely take positions on prominent policy debates. Between the two extremes are legislators who blend the two styles—striking a balance between engaging in broad national policy debates and claiming credit for local spending.

When deciding how to present their work to constituents, legislators must decide how to balance credit claiming and position taking. And because legislators' primary motivation is reelection, we expect that who legislators represent will influence their rate of credit claiming—legislators will engage in credit claiming when the relative electoral return is high.[29] The district's demographic characteristics will affect the return on credit claiming messages. Low income districts are particularly reliant on federal spending. Constituents who live in low income districts rely on basic services provided through block grants that fund basic public services like bus-lines, subsidized housing, or rural development grants. The popularity of the programs within the district creates incentives for legislators to clarify to their constituents that their representative is responsible for providing the funding for the vital services. In higher income districts, however, voters have a less clear relationship with much of the spending.[30] The result is that the district demand for particularistic spending decreases with income. Similarly, legislators who represent districts with lower education have an incentive to engage in credit claiming. Lower education constituents tend to be less attentive to salient partisan and ideological debates, making claiming credit for spending more valuable.[31] Other demographic characteristics—such as the type of jobs residents hold—create demand for spending. For example, districts with a large concentration of union workers have constituents who are better equipped to recognize a personal value in credit claiming messages. Union construction workers recognize that highway funds create jobs and public sector employees often depend on grant spending for hiring and equipment purchases.

The partisan composition of a district is likely to have an even more potent effect on the relative electoral return of credit claiming.[32] Marginal legislators—those representing a district with a large share of opposing partisans—have greater incentive to engage in credit claiming than more aligned representatives—those who represent districts with

---

[29] Ashworth and Bueno de Mesquita (2006).
[30] Mettler (2011).
[31] Campbell et al. (1960); Lauderdale (2013).
[32] Grimmer (2013).

a large share of copartisans. For marginal legislators to win a general election, they have to obtain the support of independents and even moderate members of the other party, while maintaining the support of their own partisan base. This makes articulating positions risky for marginal legislators. Clarifying positions in line with their party risks alienating members of the other party, while emphasizing positions that align with the other party risks alienating their copartisans. Stephanie Herseth-Sandlin faced this problem in her 2010 reelection campaign. Facing a conservative electorate, Herseth-Sandlin cast a vote against the Affordable Care Act, and regularly referenced her vote against the healthcare reform on the campaign trail. The opposition to the reform blocked a potential attack from her opponent. But it also demobilized her partisan base and nearly prompted a primary challenge from a liberal South Dakota doctor.

Credit claiming gives marginal legislators the opportunity to claim credit without the risk of alienating an important component of the electorate. By announcing new projects, marginal legislators portray themselves as effective advocates to the district. This allows the marginal legislators to cultivate support, without alienating their heterogenous reelection constituency.

Aligned legislators face different electoral risks. Because of the composition of their districts, more aligned legislators face both primary and general electorates with a larger share of like minded copartisans.[33] The risk for aligned legislators, then, is not that articulating positions will alienate supporters. The risk for the more aligned legislators is that they will face an opponent in a primary election that is more ideologically extreme or more appealing to copartisan constituents. For aligned legislators, then, credit claiming is less appealing, because it does not help them to clarify their ideological positions to the base, nor demonstrate their partisan work in the institution. To be clear, claiming credit for spending will still help ideologically extreme and aligned legislators to cultivate a personal vote. But, credit claiming is relatively less effective for aligned legislators than marginal legislators.

How legislators present their work to constituents will also be correlated with how legislators work in Washington.[34] This correlation may arise because constituent demand also affects legislators' work in Washington, or because constituents select a particular kind of legislator in elections.[35] For example, legislators value a seat on the Appropriations committee because it enables them to be more closely associated with

[33] Brady, Han, and Pope (2007).
[34] Grimmer (2013).
[35] Fenno (1978); Hall (1996).

spending in the district. Similarly, marginal legislators tend to be more moderate than legislators well aligned with their district.[36] And as a result we expect that legislators credit claiming propensity will be systematically related to their ideology—even if this relationship may not be causal. Legislators' work in Washington may correlate with their credit claiming propensity because they have broad policy goals or plan to pursue higher office. In both cases, legislators will engage in broader national debates at the expense of claiming credit for local projects.

Given a rate of credit claiming, we expect that legislators will be able to claim credit for a wide array of expenditures and much more than actual spending in the district. Indeed, Mayhew (1974) suggests this in the original definition of credit claiming, where he asserted that legislators need only "generate a belief" they are responsible for the government action. We expect that legislators can claim credit for projects they could have plausibly influenced—even if the actual influence is only indirect. This includes expenditures long before they reach district. Even before expenditures occur, legislators are able to explain how they used their influence to insert expenditures in spending bills, or how legislators will use their influence to request spending. Both contribute to a reputation— or impression—of influence over expenditure processes in Washington. Claiming credit throughout the process also means that legislators can claim credit many times for the same expenditures. Legislators can announce that they secured money in Washington, they can attend ground breaking ceremonies as expenditures begin, and even claim credit for projects at ribbon cutting ceremonies when a project is completed.

Not only can legislators claim credit for expenditures throughout the process, they can cultivate support with projects they had only an indirect role in securing. Bureaucrats at spending programs insulated from political influence use credit claiming opportunities to cultivate congressional support. Legislators take advantage of the opportunities, using carefully constructed language to imply that they deserve credit for the spending. Credit claiming ensures that legislators have a broad set of plausible expenditures they can use to cultivate support—even when legislators have exerted little effort in delivering the project.

Legislators are able to claim credit broadly, for a wide array of expenditures. Representatives focus, however, on claiming credit for projects that are likely to yield the largest increase in support among their constituents. Legislators could claim credit for more controversial funding projects—such as art projects in conservative districts or gun ranges in liberal enclaves. But claiming credit for funding controversial

---

[36] McCarty, Poole, and Rosenthal (2009).

projects undermines the usefulness of engaging in credit claiming—legislators pay an opportunity cost in electoral support when they do not announce the most popular programs. More attractive to legislators, then, are expenditures that elicit a positive response from constituents-such as firefighters, police officers, roads, national parks, homeland security, and local education. That legislators anticipate constituent reaction to credit claiming about spending facilitates representation on expenditures. Legislators, then, are motivated to claim credit for expenditures to cultivate electoral support. And therefore legislators have incentive to maintain spending programs that are popular with constituents.

Legislators act like entrepreneurs when engaging in credit claiming, anticipating how constituents will respond when deciding how to present their work to constituents. Legislators vary their credit claiming rates in response to the relative return on credit claiming. And they vary the content of the credit claiming messages in response to include actions that are likely to be popular and recipients likely to cultivate support. We now turn to constituents, explaining how they are likely to respond to legislators' credit claiming messages.

2.2.2 Credit Allocation: How Constituents Respond to Legislators' Credit Claiming Messages

Legislators act as entrepreneurs when engaging in credit claiming—anticipating rewards from constituents and rarely responding to explicit constituent demand. Legislators must be entrepreneurial because constituents tend to hold only vague and sometimes inconsistent preferences on government spending.[37] This occurs because constituents have little reason to think hard about how they government should spend money. And expansive government spending makes it nearly impossible for even the most informed constituents to hold strong preferences on how the government should allocate funds across projects.

Even though constituents lack detailed preferences on how the government should spend money, they can still react to legislators' credit claiming efforts. But the lack of information and the limited incentives to think carefully about the credit claiming efforts causes constituents to avoid some kinds of information. This is especially true of quantitative information, like the size of expenditures that legislators are claiming credit for securing. Constituents are unlikely to know much about local budgets, so it is hard for them to know how grants to local programs will

[37] Hansen (1998).

affect local services. Even if constituents had information about local budgets, they might still find it hard to identify the amount of money legislators claim credit for securing and to evaluate how this affects local budgets. The result is that large increases in the dollar amounts allocated to the district may have a similar effect on support for legislators.

Voters not only lack information about expenditures, they also lack incentives to think deeply and carefully about what legislators are saying in their credit claiming statements. This causes particular psychological processes to operate that makes responsiveness to the amount of money legislators secure even more unlikely. When thinking quickly, it is difficult for our brains to identify and reason about quantitative information.[38] Previous studies, for example, have shown that it is difficult to rapidly evaluate large numbers and to quickly convey the differences in their magnitude.[39] This is particularly true for dollar figures. We have intuitive experience with small figures, but larger expenditure figures are difficult for constituents to evaluate and to consider their relative size.

In place of the quantitative information, constituents use qualitative information—evaluating the actions that legislators report performing, the recipient of the spending, and the reported benefits. Constituents have the context to react to qualitative information in credit claiming statements. Consider the following simple thought experiment. Suppose you learn that your local fire department will receive $10,000. Now, suppose that you never read the first statement, and you find out that the local fire department will receive $30,000. Without being able to compare the two grant sizes, would you expect that you are more excited about the $30,000, rather than the $10,000? Yet, it is likely that all of us would be happy that our local fire department is receiving additional funding—even though we are unable to differentiate based on the size of the expenditure.

Cognitive processes accentuate the attention to qualitative information, making it more likely that constituents will evaluate the actions reported and the recipient of the expenditure, rather than the amount secured. Without substantial cognitive effort, constituents can quickly evaluate who is making a claim, what they are claiming, and the benefits of the claim. The result is that constituents are able to make a quick assessment about whether or not they think the expenditure will be beneficial for the district. Legislators provide information to make it more likely that constituents will view the expenditure positively. As the example from Hal Rogers showed earlier in the chapter, legislators use

[38] Ariely (2000); Conlisk (1996); Kahneman (2003).
[39] Hatano and Osawa (1983).

credit claiming statements to explain why allocations are beneficial for the district.

The result of the lack of information and cognitive process is that constituents reward legislators for their broad credit claiming activities. Rather than just allocating credit for actual money spent in the district or actual new projects created, we expect that constituents will allocate credit for legislators requesting money, even if the likelihood of the money reaching the district is low or very uncertain. Taken even further, we expect that constituents will reward legislators for merely stating their intention to request spending for the district. Because the action is what is being evaluated, constituents are merely responsive to the report that their legislator is working for the district.

Constituents' focus on actions and their limited attention to money creates incentives for legislators to regularly claim credit for small expenditures, rather than occasionally claiming credit for larger projects. Numerous actions will be easy for constituents to recall, cultivating an impression that the legislators are influential over a diverse area of projects.[40] In contrast, it is hard for constituents to tally the amount of expenditures across several messages.[41] The credit claiming process amplifies the value of actions for legislators—even if those expenditures have not reached the district yet—and dampens the importance of expenditure size to cultivate support.

Constituents' lack of information about how federal expenditures occur and rapid evaluation of credit claiming statements creates the opportunity for legislators to receive credit for expenditures—even when representatives never *literally* claim credit for the expenditure. Our intuitive brains seek coherence in short statements and establishing a causal sequence is essential for making a statement coherent.[42] The result is that when reading our brains tend to infer causality—even when no causal statement is explicitly established. The linguist Paul Grice (1989) calls this inference an "implicature"—because we tend to reach conclusions in language that are only implied in a statement, even if never literally stated.[43]

Consider a press release from Frank LoBiondo who "*announced* that the Forest Grove Volunteer Fire Company will receive $108,063 in federal funding from the Assistance to Firefighters Grant (AFG) Program."[44] Note the verb leaves ambiguous LoBiondo's role in securing

[40] Loewenstein and Prelec (1993).
[41] Stein and Bickers (1994).
[42] Kahneman (2011); Hassin, Bargh, and Uleman (2002).
[43] Grice (1989).
[44] LoBiondo (2012) (emphasis added).

the expenditure. If we read this sentence quickly, however, we may fail to notice the subtle verb usage. Instead, when reading quickly voters will form a spontaneous causal inference—attributing the funding to LoBiondo.[45]

The statement from LoBiondo makes an implication that causes the formation of a spontaneous causal inference. The result is a subtle deception—perpetrated merely with the verb "announce"—that enables legislators to claim credibly that they never lied about their role in securing the expenditure. The ability to engage in this deception is of substantial value to the legislator, allowing her to receive credit for an expenditure the representative may have had only an indirect role in securing. This subtle deception broadens what legislators can claim credit for delivering to the district. Not only will legislators claim credit for spending that is earmarked in an Appropriations bill. Legislators will also claim credit for expenditures and programs allocated through bureau-cratic agencies, perhaps even through competitive processes. Indeed, the value of announcements implies that legislators are able to receive credit for expenditures any time they can merely imply they are responsible for an expenditure.

Constituents respond to legislators' credit claiming efforts, seizing on information about the actions that legislators report, rather than the amount secured. The rhetoric around spending also determines when constituents' budget preferences affect the credit they allocate legislators' for particularistic spending. This is because constituents hold seemingly contradictory preferences. Constituents commonly prefer higher levels of spending in popular programs, while also expressing a preference for overall budget reduction.[46] For example, a Pew Research poll conducted in January 2012 found that 69% of Americans have a preference for reducing the budget. And yet, another poll conducted shortly after in February 2012 found that in almost every potential area of cuts, the public preferred increases in expenditures. So constituents may reward legislators for expenditures in the district, even if constituents—such as conservative constituents—have a strong preference to reduce the federal budgets.

Constituent budget preferences will only affect credit, however, when they are made salient with budget criticism. When opponents—either challengers in an election or other critics—explain how expenditures affect the budget deficit or the federal debt, they remind constituents of a preference for budget reduction. The result is that legislators will be penalized for their association with "wasteful" spending in Washington.

---

[45] Kahneman (2011); Hassin, Bargh, and Uleman (2002).
[46] Hansen (1998).

When legislators engage in credit claiming they solve the representative's problem—drawing constituents' attention towards expenditures in the district. And constituents are responsive to the credit claiming messages—using the information legislators provide to infer legislators' ability to influence expenditures in the district. But the process implies that legislators are able to receive credit for much more than expenditures as they occur in the district or grants as they are created. This creates an opportunity for legislators to cultivate a personal vote using an even broader set of activities.

2.2.3 Spending, Lying, and the Media

It may be tempting to conclude from our argument that the actual spending matters little—after all, legislators are able to claim credit for projects they had little role in securing or expenditures that may have only a slim chance of reaching the district in the far future. But actual spending is essential for legislators to create an impression of influence. Because members of Congress are often able to exert influence over how spending occurs, it is *plausible* that legislators are influencing spending to reach the district. As Mayhew (1974) observed, this plausibility is essential for legislators to claim credit for performing actions in the district.

A second reason that actual spending matters is that legislators have a strong aversion to explicitly lying about their accomplishments to constituents. This aversion is because legislators—and their staff—expect disaster if caught in an outright lie.[47] Legislators know that if caught lying they risk undermining the benefit of credit claiming. Being caught in a lie provides ammunition to potential opponents and undermines valence characteristics at the heart of the personal vote.

Legislators are not the only ones who can influence constituents' impressions about who is responsible for spending. Political opponents may try to undermine legislators' credit claiming efforts. Part of the undermining effort may occur when constituents accuse legislators of being spendthrifts. But we might expect that opponents would try to clarify that legislators had only a limited role in securing some expenditures. The timing of congressional elections makes this sort of attack unlikely. During most of a legislator's time in office they do not have an obvious opponent who could criticize a credit claiming statement. And even if there is an opponent who wants to criticize an expenditure, the careful language dampens the force of a potential attack.

---

[47] Arnold (1992).

After all, when claiming credit for competitive grants, legislators only imply they deserve credit for the spending and never literally lie about their role in delivering the funds. This makes a pithy, accurate, and effective attack difficult to mount.

The media may also provide another check on legislators' credit claiming efforts. We might expect that reporters would limit legislators' ability to claim credit for expenditures or would better clarify legislators' role in securing expenditures. But shrunken budgets have limited newspapers' capacity for original Washington reporting.[48] The result is that newspapers are increasingly reliant upon legislators for content about what is happening in Washington.[49] Far from a check on legislators, then, newspapers are now a tool that helps legislators amplify their message and reach more constituents. And legislators' other credit claiming mediums operate outside of newspapers or other media—such as newsletters.

2.3 CONCLUSION

Legislators use credit claiming messages to ensure constituents allocate credit for expenditures that occur in the district. The credit claiming, credit allocation process solves a problem for representatives—ensuring they receive credit for actions popular with constituents. It also creates opportunities for representatives. It enables legislators to vary their association with spending and to claim credit for more than disbursements as they occur in the district. And it affects how constituents allocate credit for expenditures—causing constituents to focus on the actions that legislators report, rather than the total amount spent.

Throughout the book we present evidence for how this process occurs and show how this process matters for representation and policy—how it affects the relationship between legislators and constituents and the way the federal government disburses funds. We begin in the next chapter, where we use a new collection of House press releases to characterize when and how legislators claim credit for spending.

[48] Vinson (2002).
[49] Grimmer (2013).

CHAPTER 3

How Legislators Create an Impression of Influence

A LONG TIME DEMOCRATIC MEMBER OF CONGRESS, BART STUPAK HAS strong incentives to cultivate an impression of influence over spending. This is partly because of his district's demographics. As industry has fled northern Michigan, Stupak's working class district has become increasingly reliant on federal investments to sustain the few jobs that remain. It is also because Stupak represents a swing district: in 2000 and 2004 it voted for George W. Bush, but in 2008 the district narrowly swung to Barack Obama. To win reelection Stupak needs a personal vote—that is, support not based on partisan affiliation or ideological positions—to win over both political independents and moderate Republicans.

Stupak creates an impression of influence, in part, by making regular appearances at new federal projects in the district. For example, he was on Mackinac Island on May 31, 2008 to participate in a groundbreaking ceremony for a new hospital. At the ceremony, Stupak praised the federal investment in the hospital asserting that it was "a vast improvement on the old facility."[1] Stupak's office also regularly issued press releases claiming credit for federal projects in the district. One press release "announced that the U.S. Department of Agriculture's (USDA) Rural Development fund has approved a loan of $440,000 to Calumet Township for improvements to the Township's wastewater system."[2] In a different press release Stupak "announced [that] Northern Michigan University in Marquette has received $673,462 for the university's Electrical Power Technician job training program."[3] And in another he "announced three grants totaling $80,000 for the cities of Beaverton and Gladwin to purchase vehicles for public safety."[4] In still another statement Stupak asserted that he "was able to secure $3.4 million for a wide variety of vital projects for northern Michigan communities and

---

[1] Polk (2008).
[2] Stupak (2007).
[3] Stupak (2010*c*).
[4] Stupak (2010*b*).

facilities" in an Appropriations bill.[5] His office's credit claiming efforts translated into local news coverage. One story broadcasted that Stupak announced "$750,000 grant...award to Central Michigan University."[6] Another story explained how "the city of Gladwin has received two grants totaling $65,000 to assist local businesses" and included a quote from Stupak who explained that "we must do everything we can to help create and save jobs in our communities."[7]

Stupak uses the press releases to cultivate an impression among constituents that he is influential in delivering money to the district. And the hope is that this impression of influence will lead to electoral support. In this chapter, we demonstrate that Stupak's strategic response to his district reflects a broader pattern in who claims credit for spending and what projects they claim credit for obtaining. Legislators' incentives to cultivate an impression of influence vary across districts and, therefore, so too does their credit claiming behavior. The incentive to credit claim can arise from district demographics—such as median income or level of education—and from the partisan composition of the district.

We also demonstrate what legislators claim credit for securing. Legislators do claim credit for spending that actually occurs in the district and cut ribbons at new facilities. But they also claim credit for action taken throughout the appropriations process that are far removed from actual expenditures—including requesting that expenditures be included in spending bills. Legislators also claim credit broadly. Not only do they tout earmarks secured during the appropriations process, they also claim credit for grants allocated by executive agencies, where legislators have only indirect influence. And we show that legislators tend to announce relatively small grants. In some instances legislators announce expenditures that are as small as $1,000. More typical expenditures are only slightly larger, with the usual expenditure announced providing only pennies per capita in the district.

The evidence in this chapter shows why communication is essential for understanding how representation occurs around spending and why actual spending and projects in a district provide only an incomplete picture of how legislators use particularistic projects to cultivate a personal vote. This picture is incomplete, in part, because legislators differ in how closely they strive to be associated with spending.[8] Some legislators work hard to be closely associated with projects. Other legislators avoid an association with spending projects and instead focus

[5] Stupak (2005).
[6] Jankoviak (2009).
[7] Staff (2010a).
[8] Stein and Bickers (1994).

on policy work. It is also incomplete because legislators claim credit for projects long before they reach the district and even when the chance of the spending actually occurring in the district is small. As a result, the credit that legislators receive does not necessarily have a strong relationship to the actual levels of spending or the actual number of new projects. And as we show throughout the book, a strong relationship between money and credit is not necessary for more effective representation.

To demonstrate how legislators use the spending process to create an impression of influence we analyze a new and large collection of House press releases–every press release, from each House office, from 2005 to 2010. This collection is comprised of nearly 170,000 press releases. To analyze the abundance of text, we make use of statistical tools applied to text, which facilitate efficient analysis of extremely large text collections.[9] Applying these tools, we measure how often legislators claim credit for spending and what legislators claim credit for delivering to the district. With the measures of legislators' credit claiming behavior in hand, we provide comprehensive evidence of how legislators create an impression of influence.

Before examining evidence of legislators' credit claiming, however, we want to emphasize that this chapter is not intended to demonstrate the causal effect of various district characteristics on legislators' rhetorical choices. Like many other studies of how legislators engage constituents (see our discussion in Chapter 4), we lack a strong identification strategy to examine how district characteristics alter legislators' strategies.[10] Measuring causal effects is all the more challenging because we analyze several facets of district demand each of which are intertwined, with some features being causal consequences of others. Rather than provide causal estimates of the effect of district characteristics or institutional activities on credit claiming frequency, we instead document the systematic relationship between characteristics of districts and legislators' strategies. While the simple comparisons that we make in this chapter are insufficient to establish the causal effect of district characteristics on legislators' strategies, they are sufficient to establish an important descriptive fact: legislators who represent different types of districts adopt different types of strategies.[11] And building on this descriptive fact in subsequent chapters, we use a series of experiments to demonstrate the causal effect of legislators' credit claiming statements on constituent credit allocation and the personal vote.

[9] Grimmer and Stewart (2013).
[10] Caughey and Sekhon (2012); Sekhon and Titiunik (2012).
[11] Grimmer (2013).

3.1 MEASURING LEGISLATORS' CREDIT CLAIMING PROPENSITY

To measure how legislators cultivate an impression of influence we use an original collection of congressional press releases. Press releases may seem an odd choice for analyzing congressional communication, but there is growing evidence that press releases provide a reliable source for studying how members of Congress communicate with constituents. Using a collection of Senate press releases, Grimmer[12] shows that press releases broadly reflect senators' priorities in Washington and that the content of press releases are likely to reach constituents. Press releases commonly affect the content of newspaper stories and are sometimes run verbatim in local papers.

Press releases are also a medium in which legislators regularly claim credit for spending. Press releases can be issued on any day and on any topic and are thus particularly useful for legislators who may want to announce a new grant or expenditure. Floor speeches are less useful for studying credit claiming because legislators rarely claim credit for money on the House or Senate floor.[13] Newsletters are another potentially useful source for studying how members of Congress claim credit for spending.[14] The prominence of franked mail makes it a potentially useful place for legislators to cultivate support with constituents, but only a few newsletters are sent each year so they are unable to reflect legislators' broader credit claiming efforts.[15]

One of the virtues of press releases is that they are plentiful and therefore likely to capture how members of Congress cultivate a relationship with constituents. But this virtue is also a problem, because the abundance of text makes analyzing the corpus of press releases costly. The vast number of these press releases render an individual analysis and classification of each item practically impossible. Simply reading and attaching a label to each press release would be an immense task. Even at the extremely fast rate of one press release read every two minutes, classifying all the documents three times would require over 16,800 hours of a coder's labor.

The usual alternatives are not ideal for studying how members of Congress cultivate support. Scholars of congressional communication commonly analyze only a small sample of legislators,[16] but the small samples often make it difficult to detect relationships that are present

[12] Grimmer (2013).
[13] Grimmer (2013).
[14] Lipinski (2004).
[15] Lipinski (2004).
[16] Schiller (2000); Lipinski (2004); Sulkin (2005); Sellers (2010).

among all members of Congress. Further, the specific samples usually include only behavior from a particular year[17] or particular set of policy debates.[18] The small samples provide valuable insights from the time periods studied, but are inappropriate for reaching more general conclusions.

Rather than rely on only a sub-sample of press releases, we analyze the entire collection of press releases using computational methods that ease the cost of analysis.[19] We make use of supervised learning methods to efficiently classify the content of our press releases.[20] Supervised learning methods begin like traditional manual content analysis. The first step is to manually classify a sample of the press releases. But then the sample of press releases are used to train—or supervise—statistical algorithms that classify the remaining documents. The end product is a set of labeled documents that, if the classification is performed accurately, allow us to analyze the entire collection of press releases as if they were hand labeled.

To classify the press releases we began with a four part coding scheme, developed from the classic typology of congressional action advanced in Mayhew[21] and then refined with our team of three coders. To refine our scheme we made two pilot attempts at coding documents. We used an existing coding scheme, assigned our coders to classify a set of documents, and then met with the coders to diagnose ambiguity and to clarify disagreements. After two rounds, agreement improved substantially and we settled on our final coding scheme. All the press releases that we use to train our models were labeled *after* we settled on a coding scheme, ensuring we are not artificially inflating our agreement rates.

The first category in our coding scheme—the target category—is for *credit claiming* press releases. Building on the definition of credit claiming advanced in Mayhew,[22] we define a credit claiming press release as one that explicitly announces an expenditure targeted to the district. Credit claiming includes tax expenditures—that is, tax breaks that are targeted at particular districts. Because we are interested in *particularistic* expenditures, we exclude expenditures that are national in scope, such as a legislator discussing spending on a war. The focus on district categories ensures that our study of legislators' credit claiming aligns with the type of district-level spending that comprises a large literature on how legislators use spending to cultivate support.[23]

---

[17] Lipinski (2004); Sulkin (2005).

[18] Sellers (2010).

[19] Grimmer and Stewart (2013).

[20] Hillard, Purpura, and Wilkerson (2008); Hopkins and King (2010).

[21] Mayhew (1974).

[22] Mayhew (1974).

[23] Ferejohn (1974); Weingast, Shepsle, and Johnsen (1981); Levitt and Snyder (1997);

The second category describes *egregious-earmark* press releases. These press releases discuss earmarks and particularistic spending, but criticize such legislation rather than claim credit for it. Disaggregating this category in our coding protocol helps ensure that our classifier distinguishes these linguistically similar press releases. The vast majority of the egregious-earmark press releases come from Jeff Flake (R-AZ), a conservative legislator known for his opposition to government spending projects. In a similar style to William Proxmire's Golden Fleece awards, Flake used creative messages to highlight spending he viewed as inappropriate. One press release criticized spending aimed at addressing abandoned mines. In it, Flake stated that "With this earmark, taxpayers are quite literally getting the shaft."[24]

The remaining categories describe other types of messages that have little relationship with spending. Our third category comprises *advertising* press releases and press releases that honor the achievements of local constituents (see Chapter 4). Press releases in this category commonly include those announcing winners of congressional art contests or announcing nominations for the service academies. The fourth category are *position taking* press releases. This category includes press releases in which a legislator touts a position on a prominent policy debate, claims credit for passing legislation that does not fall into the previous categories, or explicitly attacks the other party.

With this coding scheme, we asked our team of three coders to classify 800 sampled press releases—a number that we chose to balance the accuracy of our statistical models against the cost of hand coding documents.[25] Our coders displayed extremely high accuracy. Across all documents, at least one pair of coders agreed on 98% of documents and all three coders agreed 68% of the time. Agreement is even higher if we focus on just the credit claiming press releases—with all three coders agreeing 87% on whether a press release claims credit for an expenditure or not. Across categories we have an extremely high level of agreement, with a Krippendorff's Alpha of 0.66.

A further indication of our coders' reliability is that words that we expect to be associated with credit claiming messages are much more likely to occur in press releases that our coders labeled as credit claiming. The words that best distinguish credit claiming documents are: `funding`, `million`, `announces`, `grant`, `funds`, `department`, `project`, `secured`. As we will see below, each of these words is regularly used when legislators

---

Strömberg (2004); Chen and Malhotra (2007); Berry, Burden, and Howell (2010*b*); Kriner and Reeves (2012).

[24] Flake (2008).

[25] Hopkins and King (2010); Jurafsky and Martin (2008).

cultivate an impression of influence over spending that occurs in the district.[26]

Because we primarily focus on understanding credit claiming behavior, we use the hand labels to identify whether each press release claims credit or not. To train the statistical models, we first need to reconcile the three labels from our hand coders. Given the extremely high agreement, we used a voting procedure to determine each document's label and the modal code for each document is the final label.

With an accurate sample of hand-labeled documents, we are ready to train statistical models to classify all the remaining press releases. To classify all of the nearly 170,000 press releases from this relatively small sample of hand-coded documents we use an ensemble classifier, which combines a collection of prediction methods to predict whether each document is claiming credit. Ensemble methods are increasingly used in machine learning tasks.[27] This is because ensemble classifiers usually improve accuracy, while also making predictions more stable. Ensemble classifiers also facilitate learning about more complicated functional forms than any one of the constituent methods of the ensemble. We include five methods in our ensemble: a support vector machine (SVM), LASSO,[28] elastic-net,[29] random forests, and Kernal Regularized Least Squares (KRLS).[30] Our ensemble of classifiers weights methods according to their predictive accuracy, which we assess using a cross-validation procedure.[31] The ensemble method attached weight to three of the constituent methods: 61% of the weight was given to random forest, 23% to elastic net, and 16% to SVM. (For full details on processing the texts, training the ensemble, and measuring its accuracy see the Appendix.)

This ensemble method is accurate and is able to achieve very reliable, individually coded documents.[32] We assess the performance of our ensemble method by replicating our classification task using *cross-validation*.[33] We create our entire ensemble for a subset of hand-coded

---

[26] To identify the words that are more likely to occur in press releases labeled credit claiming we use the *mutual information* between words in a document and their label. See Manning et al. (2008). Heuristically, mutual information measures how well a single word separates credit claiming press releases from other press releases—higher mutual information indicates that a word better separates categories than a word with lower mutual information.

[27] Dieterich (2000); Hillard, Purpura, and Wilkerson (2008).

[28] Hastie, Tibshirani, and Friedman (2001).

[29] Hastie, Tibshirani, and Friedman (2001).

[30] Hainmueller and Hazlett (2014).

[31] van der Laan, Polley, and Hubbard (2007).

[32] Hillard, Purpura, and Wilkerson (2008); Hopkins and King (2010).

[33] Hastie, Tibshirani, and Friedman (2001).

documents and then use the ensemble to classify the held-out, hand-coded documents. This method allows us to test the performance of our model against the "gold standard" of hand-labeled documents. It also demonstrates that the ensemble method is able to accurately replicate hand coding: 90% of our out-of-sample classifications agreed with the hand coders. Given that a document is credit claiming, we identified it at a high rate (67%) and given that we made a prediction that a document was credit claiming, it was very likely to actually be credit claiming (85%).[34]

Given this high accuracy rate, we trained our ensemble of classifiers on the full sample of hand coded press releases and applied it to our collection of 169,779 press releases. The product is that each press release is labeled as credit claiming or not. This reveals a relatively high rate of overall credit claiming—20.3% of all the press releases—over 34,000 press releases—are labeled as credit claiming press releases. This is in line with prior estimates of credit claiming in work on Senate press releases over a similar time period.[35]

The labeled documents are useful on their own, but our primary interest is in assessing legislators' credit claiming rate. We characterize the legislators' credit claiming rate with the proportion of press releases each legislator, in each year, allocated to credit claiming.[36] The simplest estimate of this proportion would just count the total number of a legislator's press releases that are credit claiming in a year and then divide by the total number of press releases from that year. But some House members issue only a few press releases in a year, causing the estimated proportion to be highly variable.[37] We introduce a small amount of smoothing—determined in a multilevel model—to obtain a less variable estimate of legislators' propensity to credit claiming (and to decrease the mean square error of our estimate of the credit claiming rate).[38] The smoothed estimates still provide accurate assessments of the

[34] These two measures are often known as *recall* and *precision*, respectively. To make the binary classification we had to determine a cutoff in the probability of being a credit claiming document. We did this to maximize an out-of-sample of measureof our performance—setting the threshold at 0.46. We have performed a wide array of robustness checks on the classification algorithm and our measures. Indeed, we replicate all the findings in this chapter without performing the binary classification, instead using the ensemble-weighted probability a press release is a credit claiming document.

[35] Grimmer (2013).

[36] Grimmer (2010).

[37] Gelman and Hill (2007).

[38] Gelman and Hill (2007). The smoothing was quite mild—the primary effect being to ensure that legislators who issued only a few press releases were not incorrectly labeled as sending press releases only from one category. Again, rerunning our analyses without smoothing yields the same results, though the estimates are more variable.

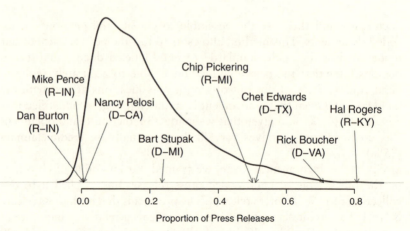

FIGURE 3.1. Substantial Variation in Credit Claiming Propensity.
This figure shows the substantial variability in credit claiming propensity across House members, as measured in the proportion of press releases that claim credit for spending.

proportion of press releases legislators dedicate to credit claiming. But (heuristically), they also ensure that we provide accurate predictions of future performance, not extreme predictions based on too few documents analyzed.

After smoothing, we now have a measure of the proportion of press releases from each representative in each year that claim credit for expenditures in the district.

3.2 STRATEGIC CREDIT CLAIMING RATES

Using our measures of credit claiming, we characterize how often legislators claim credit for expenditures. Figure 3.1 summarizes the distribution of credit claiming propensities in the House of Representatives from 2005 to 2010. The density plot shows the substantial variation in how often legislators use credit claiming in their press releases and provides further face validity to our measures of credit claiming propensity. At one end of the extreme is Dan Burton (R-IN), who allocated only 0.5% of his press releases to credit claiming in 2008. Burton had strong electoral incentives to avoid credit claiming. He is a prominent conservative Republican who represents a heavily Republican district in central Indiana. In 2008, Burton faced a difficult challenge from John McGoff. McGoff alleged that Burton failed to fight against earmarks and pork, and that Burton's actions "are not the actions of a fiscally conservative congressman who cares about personal responsibility."[39] Mike Pence (R-IN) and Nancy Pelosi (D-CA) also allocated a similarly small share of their press releases to credit claiming, reflecting their pursuit of higher office and Washington activities. Pence (R-IN), who was chairman of the Republican Conference, worked to cultivate a reputation as a staunch fiscal conservative who supported earmark reform and successfully ran for governor of Indiana in 2012. Pelosi (D-CA) was minority leader in 2005 and 2006 and Speaker from 2007 to 2010, leading her to focus her attention on policy, with less space allocated to claiming credit for money spent in her district.

Moving along the distribution, we find legislators who allocate a larger share of their press releases to credit claiming. Bart Stupak, for example, allocates about a quarter of his press releases to credit claiming. More marginal Democrats—such as Chet Edwards (D-TX) and Rick Boucher (D-VA)—allocate an even larger share of their press releases to credit claiming statements. More marginal Republicans—such as Frank LoBiondo (R-NJ)—also allocate a larger share of their press releases to credit claiming in order to cultivate support with independents and even some Democrats.

And at the opposite extreme from Dan Burton is Hal Rogers (R-KY), who used 80.7% of his press releases in 2008 to claim credit for spending. Rogers, who has served on the Appropriations committee for nearly 30 years, was described in a Washington Times profile as using "his seat on the Appropriations Committee to protect one of his district's most important economic engines."[40] Rogers represents one of the poorest districts in the country, a rural district in Eastern Kentucky with few industries. Many of the industries that are in his district rely on federal contracts to stay open. And Rogers is not particularly ideological. He once remarked to his colleagues that "we can't afford a luxury like ideology." Perhaps it is not surprising that a *Lexington Herald-Leader* profile of Rogers proclaims that he is the "prince of pork."[41] Between the extreme examples of Dan Burton and Hal Rogers, representatives adopt distinctive strategies for associating themselves with spending in the district. We now examine how characteristics of the district—and legislators' experience in Washington—covary with where legislators fall on this distribution.

The variation in legislators' credit claiming propensity is strategic and determined in part by a consideration of how legislators can cultivate

[39] Munsey (2008).
[40] Staff (2012).
[41] Cheves (2005).

support among constituents.[42] The decision calculus is straightforward: legislators tend to use credit claiming more often when it is valuable to them electorally and when alternative strategies are likely to be less effective. District demand for spending partially determines the value of claiming credit: when there is a greater need for spending there is likely a greater return on credit claiming efforts. Median district income will partially affect this perceived demand. Residents of low-income districts, like Stupak's Michigan district or Hal Rogers' Kentucky district, are more reliant on federal spending to build new infrastructure, to continue providing public services, and to create jobs.

The top plot in Figure 3.2 shows that legislators from low-income districts tend to claim credit more often than their colleagues who represent wealthier districts. In Figure 3.2 we plot the proportion of legislators' press releases allocated to credit claiming against median district income. We summarize the relationship with a simple nonparametric regression,[43] with cross-validation determining the amount of smoothing. The thick line in the top plot of Figure 3.2 summarizes the relationship between proportion of press releases allocated to credit claiming and median district income, while the gray band is a 95 percent confidence envelope.

This plot shows that representatives of the poorest districts consistently make the case that they exercise influence over the Appropriations process and deliver money to the district. And the expected proportion of press releases allocated to credit claiming decreases as the median district income increases, with the relationship relatively flat for higher levels of income. The nonparametric regression clearly shows that representatives of the poorest districts claim credit at a higher rate than other legislators. A simple parametric comparison provides a clear sense of the magnitude of this difference. Legislators who represent districts in the lowest quartile of income—districts with median incomes below $39,000— claim credit for spending in 4.6 percentage points more of their press releases than other representatives (95 percent confidence interval, [0.02, 0.07]) and 6.5 percentage points more than the representatives in the richest districts (95 percent confidence intervals, [0.04, 0.09]).

The bottom plot in Figure 3.2 shows a similar relationship with district education. Higher levels of education are obviously correlated with income and may also indicate that residents have different, more ideological, priorities. The horizontal axis has our measure of district education—the proportion of district constituents over 25 who hold a Bachelor's degree—and we place legislators' credit claiming rate on the

[42] Mayhew (1974); Stein and Bickers (1997).
[43] Cleveland (1979).

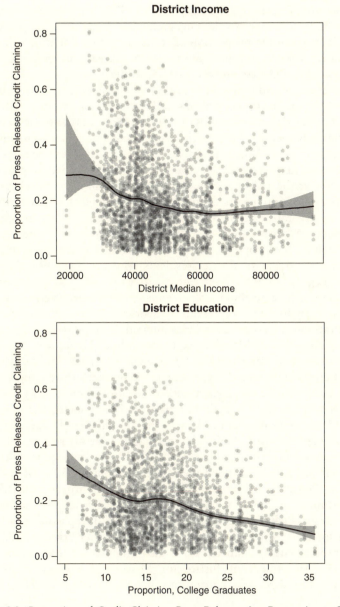

FIGURE 3.2. Proportion of Credit Claiming Press Releases Are Responsive to District Characteristics.

This figure shows that the representatives of the poorest districts tend to claim credit for federal projects at a higher rate than representatives of richer districts and that representatives of districts with a lower percentage of college graduates tend to engage in credit claiming at a higher rate than representatives of districts with a higher percentage of college graduates.

vertical axis. Legislators' who represent well-educated districts allocate substantially less space to claiming credit for money. A seven percentage point increase in the proportion of residents with a Bachelor's degree is associated with a 4.5 percentage point decrease in credit claiming (95 percent confidence interval, [−0.05, −0.04]).

The types of industries in a district and residents' occupations will also affect legislators' perceptions of how spending is rewarded in the district.[44] The density of unions in a district is one of the strongest indicators that a district is filled with the types of constituents who will reward federal spending.[45] Union members recognize that government spending can lead to new construction, or provide much-needed resources for education or the public sector. Representatives in districts where there are more unions do tend to claim credit for spending at a higher rate than other representatives, though the differences are more subtle than income differences. We can summarize this relationship with a simple linear regression of the proportion of press releases that are credit claiming against the percent of district residents who are members of a labor union. Legislators who represent a district at the 75th percentile of unionization allocate about 2.5 percentage points more to credit claiming than a legislator who represents a district at the 25th percentile of unionization (95 percent confidence interval, [0.01, 0.04]).

Chip Pickering (R-MS), located to the right of Figure 3.1, exemplifies a legislator who represents a lower-income district and has a high rate of credit claiming. He represented Mississippi's third congressional district, a working class district with a median income of only $34,750, in a state that has a weak tax base and few social services. This makes Pickering's district particularly reliant on federal expenditures to provide basic services. And Pickering makes clear his role in delivering money to the district. From 2005 to 2008, the four years Pickering is in our sample, he claimed credit for spending in 50% of his press releases. Pickering announced a variety of expenditures in his district supporting basic public services, including education, fire, and police. For example, Pickering announced a "$2,468,070 Department of Justice Grant for Mississippi State University for computer crime training and law enforcement assistance."[46] He also announced "five grants from the U.S. Department of Justice for Mississippi law enforcement"[47] and "Homeland Security Operations and Safety Grant of $75,391 for

---

[44] Adler and Lapinski (1997).
[45] Adler and Lapinski (1997).
[46] Pickering (2006a).
[47] Pickering (2006b).

the Forest Fire Department."[48] He also claimed credit for money to fund local infrastructure. This infrastructure spending included funding secured in a supplemental appropriation for highway spending, including "$25 million in funding for projects in Mississippi's Third District", which included $10 million to "widen MS Hwy 19 between Philadelphia and Collinsville."[49]

A contrast to Chip Pickering is Tom Price, a prominent conservative Republican from Georgia. Price represents one of the most affluent, educated, and Republican districts in the country. The median income in his district is over $78,000 and has the highest percentage of constituents with a college degree. And Republican presidential candidates enjoy substantial support in his district, reflecting the district's deeply Republican and conservative constituency. In 2004, for example, John Kerry received only 29.5% of the vote. Barack Obama fared only slightly better in 2008, receiving only 35% of the vote. Because Price can win reelection by focusing on wealthy, well educated copartisans, he has little reason to base his appeals to constituents on his ability to deliver money to the district. And Price rarely claims credit for spending—allocating only about 3% of his press releases to credit claiming from 2005 to 2010. Rather than make the case that he deserves credit for spending, Price presents himself as an ideological and partisan legislator. He attacks Obama administration policies and articulates conservative positions in salient policy disputes. Both types of messages are more likely to appeal to the affluent and educated Republicans in his district.

Slowly changing district demographics—such as income and union concentration—are one type of district characteristic that covaries with legislators' credit claiming priorities. But legislators also consider the political consequences of their credit claiming statements. They decide how to balance appeals to copartisans and the cultivation of a personal vote with opposing partisans and independents. The tension between the personal and partisan vote became particularly strong for Republicans after Barack Obama was elected president. As we show in Chapter 7, Republicans became increasingly critical of stimulus spending after Obama's election. The objection to spending was reenforced by Tea Party activists, who articulated boisterous objections to particularistic spending in the districts.[50] The combination of opposition to Obama's expenditure policies and pressure from the partisan base made claiming credit for expenditures less valuable for Republicans. The result is a substantial decrease in the Republican credit claiming rate.

---

[48] Pickering (2007).
[49] Pickering (2005).
[50] Skocpol and Williamson (2011).

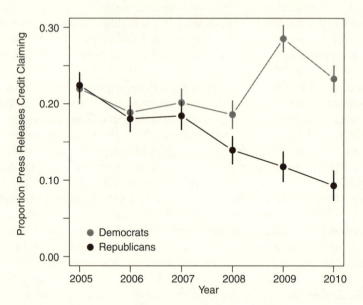

Claiming Credit for Particularistic Spending

FIGURE 3.3. The Decline of Republican Credit Claiming.
This figure shows the decline in Republican credit claiming after Obama's election. The figure presents the proportion of credit claiming from Republicans (black) and Democrats (grey) over the 6 years of press releases included in this study. The points are the average for each year and the thick lines are 95 percent confidence intervals. While the two parties claimed credit at about the same rate in 2005, by 2010 Democrats claimed credit for spending over two and a half times as much as Republicans claimed credit for spending.

Figure 3.3 shows the proportion of press releases from each party that claimed credit for spending from 2005 to 2010. In 2005, Republicans and Democrats allocated nearly the same share of their press releases to claiming credit—Republicans claimed credit for spending in 0.5 percentage points *more* of their press releases than Democrats, but the difference is indistinguishable from zero (95 percent confidence interval, [−2.2, 3.1]). This nearly identical credit claiming behavior persisted in 2007—the year that the Republicans lost their majority in the House. Beginning in 2008, however, a small difference emerged between the parties. That year, Democrats claimed credit for spending in 18.6% of their press releases, while Republicans claimed credit in only 13.9% of their press releases—a 4.5 percentage point difference (95 percent confidence interval, [2.2, 7.1]).

This initial decline corresponds with a surge in conservative attention to the earmarking process. This occurred, in part, because in the 2008 presidential race John McCain took his anti-pork barrel rhetoric to a broader audience. John McCain regularly attacked Barack Obama as a big spender, using Obama's earmarks while in the Senate as evidence. In the first presidential debate between the general election candidates, McCain argued that Obama was not credible on spending reform because "he has asked for $932 million of earmark pork-barrel spending, nearly a million dollars for every day that he's been in the United States Senate." At the third debate, McCain became more specific, criticizing Obama for "including $3 million for an overhead projector in a planetarium in his hometown." McCain's criticism raised the salience of growing Republican discontent with the earmarking process and prominently labeled as wasteful some of the projects legislators use to cultivate a personal vote.

After the 2008 election, as anger about stimulus spending rose, the Republican credit claiming rate dropped further. In 2009, Republicans claimed credit for spending in only 11.7% of their press releases— a decline from the 2008 Republican credit claiming rate of 13.9%, and substantially less than Democrats. Democrats claimed credit for spending in over 28.5% of their press releases—with the stimulus bolstering their credit claiming opportunities. The decline in Republican credit claiming is even more pronounced in 2010—when the Tea Party movement had emerged as a force in American politics (see Chapter 7). That year Republicans claimed credit for spending in only 9.3% of their press releases. In just five years, then, Republicans reduced their credit claiming propensity 13.1 percentage points (95 percent confidence interval, [−15.7, −10.6]), with many Republicans nearly abandoning credit claiming for spending all together. The result is that Republicans were much less likely to cultivate support using credit claiming messages.

The Republican decline in credit claiming propensity occurred both because of who lost in the 2008 congressional elections and how the remaining Republicans altered their credit claiming rates. Republicans who focused on credit claiming were routed in the 2008 election—in part because they represent marginal districts that were most likely to swing towards Obama. Republicans who left Congress—either because they lost reelection, retired, or sought a higher office—claimed credit for spending in 18.2% of their press releases in 2008, while the Republicans who returned to Washington claimed credit for spending in 12.8% of their press releases. This 5.4 percentage point difference explains in part why the Republican caucus that arrived after Obama's reelection was so opposed to spending: they relied upon it less to cultivate support with constituents (95 percent confidence interval, [−0.09, −0.01]).[51]

---

[51] This systematic elimination of credit claimers occurs only once in our data set—among Republicans after the 2008 election. There was no difference between Republicans who

The elimination of the Republican credit claimers changed the composition of the Republican caucus, eliminating those Republicans who relied most on credit claiming to cultivate electoral support. Selection, however, is only part of the reason that there is such a dramatic drop in credit claiming among Republicans. The remaining Republicans altered their credit claiming behavior in response to pressure from party activists, with the largest changes occurring among those Republicans who were likely to feel the strongest pressure from conservative activists. Republicans from the most conservative districts—those where McCain performed best—had the largest declines in their credit claiming frequency. To demonstrate this responsiveness to activists, we regressed the proportion of credit claiming press releases for the remaining Republicans in 2009 against the proportion of their press releases that were credit claiming in 2008, and the proportion of district voters who supported McCain. This regression shows that a 10 percentage point increase in support for McCain in a district is associated with a 1.6 percentage point decrease in credit claiming focus (95 percent confidence interval, [−3.2, −0.00]). The relationship is robust. If we measure the change in credit claiming as a difference or include a variety of potentially confounding variables we still find that Republicans from districts where McCain performed well—districts that served as the base for Tea Party movement—had sharper declines in their credit claiming propensity.[52]

While Republicans were systematically avoiding credit claiming, Democrats embraced it. The American Recovery and Reinvestment Act provided ample credit claiming opportunities for Democrats, resulting in a substantial boost in Democrats' propensity to claim credit for spending. In 2009 Democrats increased their credit claiming rate 9.9 percentage points (95 percent confidence interval, [0.07, 0.13]). This increase was

---

returned and left Washington after the 2006 election, when Republicans lost their majority. The Republicans who returned to Washington after the 2006 claimed credit for spending in 0.3 percentage points more of their press releases, a difference we cannot distinguish from zero (95 percent confidence interval, [−0.04, 0.05]). There was also no systematic differences in credit claiming behavior between the Democrats who returned to Washington and those who left after the 2008 election. Those who won claimed credit in 0.4 percentage points fewer of their press releases, a difference indistinguishable from zero (95 percent confidence interval, [−0.07, 0.06]).

[52] The decrease in credit claiming propensity among Republicans in Republican districts is particular to 2009 and 2010. After the 2006 election—when Republicans lost their majority in the House—there was no systematic relationship between district vote share and change in credit claiming behavior. A 10 percentage point shift in a pro-Republican direction after that election is associated with only a 0.5 percentage point increase in credit claiming frequency, an increase that is indistinguishable from zero (95 percent confidence interval, [−0.02, 0.03]).

nearly universal among Democrats, with new representatives claiming credit at nearly the same rate as the returning incumbents. Though the increase was largest among the misaligned representatives—that is, those with the greatest incentive to bolster their credit claiming rates to cultivate constituent support. The Republican party's response to the anti-spending mobilization of their base and the Democrats' response to the increased stimulus spending show the power of short-term political forces to shape the propensity to claim credit for spending. And yet, the characteristics of a district still create incentives that are associated with differential rates of credit claiming in the district. Legislators who are misaligned with their districts still have incentive to engage in credit claiming more often than legislators who are well aligned with their constituency. Though the relationship will depend upon the relative return on credit claiming and the costs to touting particularistic spending.

Stephanie Herseth-Sandlin (D-SD)—whom we profiled in Chapter 1— is an example of a marginal representative who attempts to generate support from independents and opposing partisans with credit claiming statements. Herseth-Sandlin represented South Dakota in the House from 2004 to 2010—a state that the Republican presidential candidate carries regularly. To cultivate support with constituents, Herseth-Sandlin regularly claimed credit for spending in the state in addition to touting her blue-dog Democrat stances, such as voting against the Affordable Care Act. Her highest rate of credit claiming occurring in 2009, when she claimed credit for spending in 42.5% of her press releases. This contrasts sharply with Cynthia Lummis (R-WY). Lummis is an aligned representative: a Republican representing Wyoming, a deep red, conservative state. Lummis almost never claims credit for spending that occurs in Wyoming—allocating only about 2.8% of her press releases to credit claiming.

Figure 3.4 shows that Herseth-Sandlin and Lummis exemplify a broader pattern in how legislators' credit claiming strategies relate to the partisan composition of their district. Marginal Democrats and Republicans claim credit for spending more often than their well-aligned colleagues. Consider the bottom row of Figure 3.4, which shows how Democratic representatives' credit claiming propensity varies across different districts. Each panel plots representatives' credit claiming propensity against the two-party vote share for the Democratic presidential candidate from 2005 (left-hand plot) to 2010 (right-hand plot). In each year, the more marginal Democrats are more likely to claim credit for spending than their more aligned colleagues. Overall, a shift from a district that supported the Democratic presidential candidate with 69% of the vote (the 75th percentile of districts with a Democratic representative) to a district that supported the Democratic presidential candidate

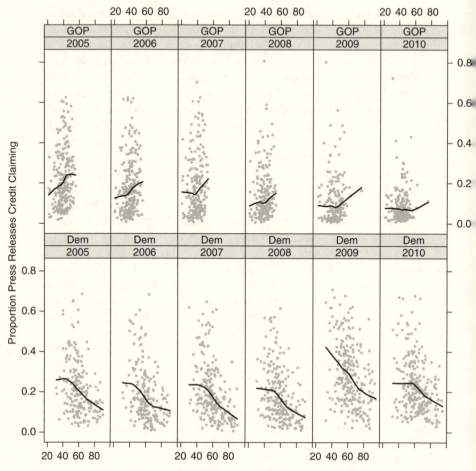

FIGURE 3.4. Proportion of Credit Claiming Press Releases Are Correlated with Partisan Composition.
This figure shows the relationship between the partisan composition of a district and representatives' propensity to credit claim. Representatives with the strongest incentive to cultivate a personal vote—Republicans in Democratic districts and Democrats in Republican districts—have the highest rate of credit claiming. Legislators who are well aligned with their district—Democrats in Democratic districts and Republicans from Republican districts—claim credit much less often.

with 52% of the vote (25th percentile of districts with a Democratic representive) is associated with a 5.1 percentage point increase in credit claiming propensity (95 percent confidence interval, [0.03, 0.07]). This relationship is strongest in 2009—when the stimulus spending provided ample opportunity for marginal Democrats to claim credit for spending. That year the same shift in support is associated with a 6.1 percentage point increase in credit claiming (95 percent confidence interval, [0.03, 0.09]).

The top row of Figure 3.4 shows how marginal Republicans strategically responded to the decreased value of credit claiming—evidence of how representatives trade off pressure from the base and the need to cultivate a personal vote with constituents. From 2005 to 2007 there is a strong relationship between the composition of a district and Republicans' credit claiming propensities. In those years, a shift from a district that supported the Democratic presidential candidate with 35% of the vote (75th percentile of Republican districts) to a district that supported the Democratic presidential candidate with 44% of the vote (25th percentile of Republican districts) is associated with a 2.9 percentage point increase in the credit claiming rate (95 percent confidence interval, [0.01, 0.05]). But, as congressional Republicans made increasingly strong objections to particularistic spending, the relationship between district partisanship and credit claiming rate weakened. In 2010 the same shift in alignment is associated with a decrease in credit claiming propensity of 0.2 percentage points, a much smaller change in behavior (95 percent confidence interval, [−.017, 0.012]).

Legislators' credit claiming rates reflect both district characteristics and short-term political forces. The significance of these short-term forces, though, will be on the margin, causing legislators to deviate from their previous strategies. Because the short-term forces affect styles on the margin and because district characteristics tend to change gradually, legislators who remain in Congress adopt a relatively stable credit claiming rate. Indeed, legislators' credit claiming rate in a previous year is an excellent predictor of the credit claiming rate in the subsequent year. This stability is reflected in the correlation between the two years' credit claiming propensity—a strong 0.71. Even when there are shifts in the credit claiming propensity, there is still a strong relationship between legislators' credit claiming propensity from year to year. For example, in 2009 the Democratic credit claiming rate surged, and yet the correlation between Democrats' credit claiming propensity in 2008 and 2009 remains a high 0.72.

Legislators adopt relatively stable styles that reflect the characteristics of their constituency—taking both demographic and partisan factors into consideration. Legislators' credit claiming propensities also reflect their work in Washington. One reason for this reflection is that constituents also affect work in Washington, inducing a correlation. Consider Figure 3.5, which shows the relationship between the proportion of credit claiming press releases against legislators' DW-Nominate scores.

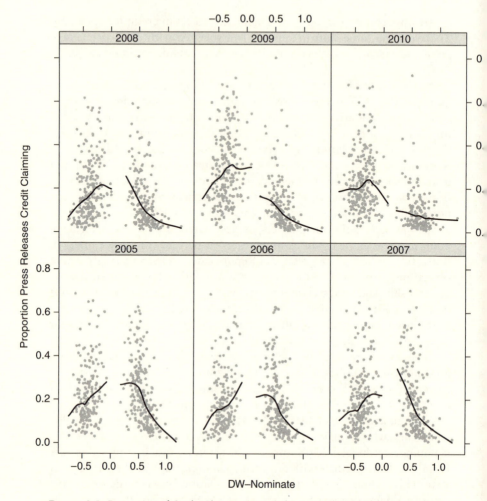

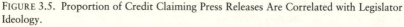

FIGURE 3.5. Proportion of Credit Claiming Press Releases Are Correlated with Legislator Ideology.
This figure shows that ideological moderates are the most likely to engage in credit claiming.

DW-Nominate scores are a well validated measure of legislator ideology, based on voting coalitions that occur in Congress.[53] The lines in each cell summarize the relationship between credit claiming rate and ideology for Democrats (left-hand line) and Republicans (right-hand line).

Figure 3.5 shows that moderate legislators, for most of the years presented here, are much more likely to claim credit for spending.

[53] Poole and Rosenthal (1997).

Consider, for example, 2006—the bottom, center cell in Figure 3.5. That year moderate Democrats claimed credit for spending in 23% of their press releases, while liberal Democrats only claimed for spending in 16% of their press releases—a substantial and significant difference in credit claiming strategy (7.1 percentage point difference, 95 percent confidence interval, [2.4, 11.7]). The relationship between ideology and credit claiming was even stronger for Republicans in 2005 and 2006. Moderate Republicans in 2005 allocated 16.6 percentage points more of their press releases to credit claiming than the most conservative Republicans (95 percent confidence interval, [0.12, 0.20]).

Figure 3.5 also shows how the decline in the value of credit claiming dampened the incentive for moderate Republicans to engage in credit claiming. In 2010—the top-right cell in Figure 3.5—there is a weaker relationship between credit claiming propensity and ideology for Republicans. In 2010, moderate Republicans had a 7.6-percentage point higher rate of claiming credit than moderate Republicans (95 percent confidence interval, [0.03, 0.12]), but in 2005 moderate Republicans had a 16.5-percentage point higher credit claiming rate.

The relationship between ideology and credit claiming is partially due to responsiveness to district preference. But the relationship also reflect legislators' personal policy preferences. For example, libertarian crusader Ron Paul (R-TX) has one of the lowest credit claiming rates; he is estimated to claim credit for spending in only about 3% of his press releases from 2005–2010. Paul's aversion to credit claiming is one component of his much broader set of objections to government spending. During Paul's time in Congress he built a national base of support with a libertarian message that called for massive cuts from the federal government. Both for his own personal beliefs and to remain a consistent spokesman for his agenda, Paul had to avoid claiming credit for spending. Pete Stark (D-CA), a California liberal, had a similar aversion to credit claiming. Stark has bolstered his national profile by opposing expenditures he views as unnecessarily helping businesses—including farm subsidies and government bailouts of financial institutions.

Another reason that moderates may credit claim more often is that they may be in the best position to extract earmarks for their votes in Congress. As Diana Evans explains, earmarks have been an important tool that party leaders use to push legislation through Congress.[54] To use earmarks, party leaders set up a market in which legislators can trade their votes for the opportunity to earmark funds in an appropriations bill. Moderates are likely to have an advantage in this market, because these legislators are cheaper to purchase than more ideologically extreme

[54] Evans (2004).

members of their coalition. This market behavior certainly could explain some of the differences in legislators' credit claiming. But, as we show in the next section, legislators claim credit for a wide array of expenditures and legislators who want to claim credit for spending certainly have the opportunity to claim credit for this spending; they are not limited to earmarked funds in the district.

Legislators' roll call voting history—one facet of their work in Washington—is systematically related to their credit claiming propensity. Away from the floor, we should expect other facets of what representatives do in Washington to be systematically related to their propensity for credit claiming. Consider members of the Appropriations Committee. They tend to use the Committee to direct funds to the district, and thereby, to bolster support among constituents.[55] If representatives are using their position on Appropriations to bolster the impression of their influence, then we should expect members of the Committee to claim credit for spending at a higher rate than other representatives.

Press releases provide evidence for this expectation: members of Appropriations claim credit for spending at a higher rate than other representatives. Members of the Appropriations committee allocate 8.3 percentage points more of their press releases to credit claiming than other representatives (95 percent confidence interval, [0.06, 0.10]). No representative makes better use of their position on Appropriations than Hal Rogers. Rogers' credit claiming statements covered a wide array of expenditures. Their subject matter includes small grants, such as when he "announced that the U.S. Department of Agriculture and Rural Development (USDA-RD) program has approved a $41,523 grant for the Leslie County Sheriff's Department,"[56] and larger expenditures, such as when he explained how an Appropriations bill that recently passed committee "included $9.5 million for flood control and flood damage reduction activities."[57]

This section shows the systematic relationship between legislators' strategic incentives and their credit claiming propensity. Legislators who represent different types of districts adopt different credit claiming rates. The result of this process is that legislators will be differentially associated with spending in the district and will differentially cultivate an impression of influence over expenditures.

[55] Fenno (1973); Deering and Smith (1997).
[56] Rogers (2009*a*).
[57] Rogers (2009*b*).

3.3 What Legislators Claim Credit for Securing

So far we have shown that credit claiming rates matter because legislators have differential incentives to claim credit for spending that occurs in the district. As a result, legislators will have differential association with spending in their district. A second reason that credit claiming matters is that it expands the set of activities legislators can claim credit for performing. In this section we show that legislators regularly claim credit for expenditures that are still far from the district or allocated primarily through executive agencies. One approach to demonstrating what legislators claim credit for would be to develop a more complex coding scheme, have our coders reclassify documents, and then refit our supervised learning method to the collection of press releases. This method, however, is difficult to implement. More nuanced coding schemes pose a challenge for even experienced coders. They (the coders) tend to struggle to remember the rules, confuse terms, or overuse particular categories. It is also difficult to identify the categories of expenditures beforehand, as there are many and diverse ways that the government potentially can spend money.

Rather than define the categories beforehand, we use a statistical method that discovers a set of *topics*[58] and estimates how documents are divided across those topics. The particular model that we apply—Latent Dirichlet Allocation (LDA)—defines a topic to be a set of words that tend to occur together across documents. For example, words like highway, road, transportation, and bridge are likely to co-occur as members of Congress claim credit for highway expenditures. Unlike our supervised methods that require us to specify topics beforehand, LDA is an unsupervised method—that is, LDA discovers the topics that occur in documents. Given a set of topics, LDA then estimates the proportion of these topics that occur in each document. LDA allows us to identify simultaneously what legislators claim credit for securing and how often legislators discuss those particular topics.

We applied LDA to the credit claiming press releases that we identified in the previous section.[59] We set the number of topics at 25—a number that we arrived at using a substantive search from five to fifty topics. Following Quinn et al., we look for substantive topics that are not about particular subgroups, such as states.[60] On the one hand, if we had too few topics, the result was a merging of distinct spending topics— such as farming and highway expenditures. On the other hand, too

---

[58] Blei, Ng, and Jordan (2003); Quinn et al. (2010); Grimmer (2010).

[59] We estimated the model in MALLET.

[60] Quinn et al. (2010).

many topics produced too many location-specific areas. Twenty-five topics represented an excellent middle ground between the two extremes, capturing distinct topic areas without too many area specific topics.

Table 3.1 presents the estimated topics and their frequency in representatives' credit claiming messages. The first column provides a short, one-word summary for each of the estimated topics. To obtain this summary, we read a random sample of about 10–15 press releases that have a large share of their content allocated to the topic.[61] The second column contains words that occur with a high frequency under each topic. The third column measures the proportion of documents that are allocated to each of the topics.

The topics in Table 3.1 reveal the diverse types of spending, which legislators claim credit for directing to their district. Detailed exploration shows the many stages in the appropriations process where legislators announce expenditures. This is evident in the most prevalent topic: *Requested appropriations*. These are expenditures that representatives have inserted into spending bills, but have yet to be allocated to the district. For example, in one press release Dave Camp (R-MI) "announced today that he was able to secure $2.5 million for widening M-72 from US-31 easterly 7.2 miles to Old M-72."[62] Later in this press release, Camp explains that the funding actually has "two more hurdles to clear to make sure the money is in the bill when it hits the President's desk: a vote in the Senate and a conference committee."[63] In a similar message, Mike Ross (D-AR) issued a press release stating that he "has successfully secured $5,122,000 for Millwood Lake in the Fiscal Year 2010 House Energy & Water Appropriations Bill. The bill passed the full U.S. House of Representatives July 16" and that he would "continue fighting for these important infrastructure dollars as they move through the appropriations process. Upon passage of the Energy & Water Appropriations Bill in the Senate, the measure will then go to a Conference Committee."[64] And Doc Hastings (R-WA) stated he "boosted federal funding for work on the Odessa Subaquifer for next year. This year Hastings has added $1 million, which when combined with the funding in the President's budget request, totals $1.185 million for Fiscal Year 2008" even though the funding had "been approved by the full House Appropriations Committee"—with a final passage vote in the House still needed.[65]

---

[61] Quinn et al. (2010).
[62] Camp (2005).
[63] Camp (2005).
[64] Ross (2009*a*).
[65] Hastings (2007).

TABLE 3.1
Credit Claiming Topics.

Labels	Key Words	Proportion
Requested appropriations	bill, funding, house, million, appropriations	0.08
Fire department grants	fire, grant, department, program, firefighters	0.08
Stimulus	recovery, funding, jobs, information, act,	0.06
Bureaucratic compliance	state, federal, congress, states, secretary	0.06
Transportation	transportation, project, airport, transit, million	0.06
Local education	education, school, students, program, college	0.05
Grants	rep, grant, news, county, release	0.05
Economic development	development, economic, business, jobs, county grants	0.05
Water projects	water, project, river, projects, corps	0.04
Justice grants	enforcement, law, police, program, justice	0.04
Rural grants	rural, agriculture, usda, development, county	0.04
HUD/Block grants	housing, program, grants, home, families	0.03
Tax credits	tax, act, small, credit, bill	0.03
Health care	health, care, services, veterans, medical	0.03
Disaster declarations	disaster, assistance, fema, federal, emergency	0.03
Winter heating	liheap, rep, maine, funding, funds	0.03
National parks	national, park, jersey, land, area	0.03
Defense construction	military, defense, million, air, army	0.03
University research	research, university, technology, center, science	0.03
New York projects	york, rep, hinchey, ny, federal	0.03
Energy projects	energy, renewable, efficiency, oil, fuel	0.02
Ribbon cutting/Assistance	county, florida, rep, office, north	0.02
Arkansas projects	arkansas, connecticut, state, washington, rep	0.02
Local disaster declarations	rep, san, california, county, maryland	0.02
Homeland security	security, homeland, border, million, emergency	0.02

This table shows what legislators discuss in their credit claiming statements.

The prevalence of claiming credit for requests demonstrates that representatives believe they are able to use a broad set of actions to create an impression of influence over federal expenditures. Not only are legislators able to claim credit for spending once it has been finally approved, or when the expenditure actually occurs in the district, they also claim credit for inserting an expenditure into a bill. They even claim credit for merely requesting an expenditure for the district. Rather than claiming credit for actual spending, then, legislators claim credit for actions that they perform in Washington. Even if those actions only may lead to spending in the district at some future date.

The second most prevalent topic in credit claiming press releases covers *fire department* grants. Although legislators use these grants to create an impression that they influenced executive-branch spending in their district, they have only an indirect role in the fire department program. The fire department grants for which legislators claim credit are small, executive-branch expenditures made to local fire departments through the Assistant to Firefighter Grant Program (AFGP)—a FEMA-administered competitive grant program (see Chapter 6). Such credit claiming occurs regularly, even though the grants are relatively small. For example, Brian Higgins (D-NY) used a press release to "announce Walden Fire District will receive $75,259 in federal funding through the Assistance to Firefighters Grants Program (AFGP) for fiscal year 2005."[66] In another press release, Mike Rogers (R-AL), "congratulated the men and women of the Mount Olive Volunteer Fire Department and County Line Volunteer Fire Department today for receiving grants from the U.S. Department of Homeland Security." The press release went on to explain that "the Mount Olive Volunteer Fire Department should receive $26,125 in funding and the County Line Volunteer Fire Department should receive $16,957 in funding to help purchase operations and safety equipment."[67] Even smaller expenditures receive Rogers's attention: in one press release he "congratulated the men and women of the Daviston Volunteer Fire Department today for receiving a $9,975 grant from the U.S. Department of Homeland Security."[68] Even Appropriations cardinals claim credit for fire grants. David Obey—while chair of the Appropriations committee in 2007—issued a press release in which he "applauded the release of a $94,196 federal fire grant to the Antigo Fire Department."[69] Legislators' credit claiming over bureaucrats' funding decisions are not limited to fire grants. Table 3.1 shows that representatives take advantage of a wide array of expenditures allocated through grants. These grants include economic development grants for towns, Department of Justice grants for police, grants for rural economic development, and urban block grants to help cities function.

Legislators also claim credit for ensuring that wayward bureaucracies deliver necessary funds or encouraging congressional commissions to reconsider decisions to move funds away from the district.[70] For example, Tom Udall (D-NM) issued a press release to say that he and other members of the New Mexico delegation met "with members of the Base Realignment and Closure (BRAC) Commission." During this meeting, Udall says, they "tackled the flawed reasoning behind the

[66] Higgins (2006).
[67] Rogers (2008b).
[68] Rogers (2007).
[69] Obey (2007).
[70] Cain, Ferejohn, and Fiorina (1987).

Pentagon's decision to target Cannon Air Force Base for closure and expressed appreciation that the commission seems receptive to additional information that might save the base."[71] The credit claiming press releases can defend other military jobs. Maurice Hinchey (D-NY) stated that "in an effort to save local jobs, Congressman Maurice Hinchey (D-NY), a member of the House Appropriations Subcommittee on Defense, today formally announced that he will soon introduce a measure in Congress that would block a recent Pentagon decision to privatize hundreds of inherently government jobs at West Point."[72]

3.4 The Amount Legislators Claim to Have Delivered

Legislators tend to claim credit for relatively small amounts of money. Examples are numerous in our collection of press releases. Henry Cuellar (D-TX) issued a press release in which he "announced $26,000 in funds for the City of Lourdanton Police Department...The funds are part of an earmark to an appropriations bill that Rep. Cuellar helped to secure."[73] With only slightly larger expenditures, Frank LoBiondo (R-NJ) "announced that $30,400 in federal funding has been awarded to Clayton Volunteer Ambulance Inc. from the Assistance to Firefighters Grant Program (AFG),"[74] Gwen Moore (D-WI) "announced that the city of West Allis will today receive the first $100,000 of $576,200 in Energy Efficiency and Conservation Block Grants (EECBG) that it has been obligated under the Recovery Act,"[75] Mike McIntyre (D-NC) "announced today that the Public Schools of Robeson County will receive $1,212,750.77 to help with Internet infrastructure,"[76] and Mike Rogers (R-MI) "congratulated the Knightens Crossroad Volunteer Fire Department today for receiving a $115,200 grant."[77]

The examples are useful for illuminating the size of the expenditures in credit claiming statements, but are not systematic evidence of the dollar amounts legislators claim credit for delivering to the district. The best systematic evidence would provide the dollar amounts discussed in all of our credit claiming press releases. Extracting this information by hand—or with the types of natural language processing commonly

[71] Udall (2005).
[72] Hinchey (2009).
[73] Cuellar (2005).
[74] LoBiondo (2006b).
[75] Moore (2009).
[76] McIntyre (2006).
[77] Rogers (2005).

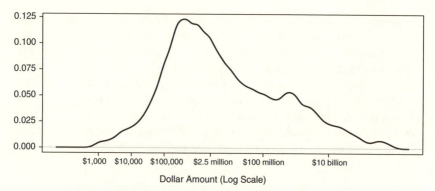

FIGURE 3.6. Legislators Regularly Claim Credit for Small Expenditures.
This figure shows the distribution of dollar figures discussed in credit claiming press releases. Legislators regularly discuss very small amounts and the majority of figures discussed are only a small amount—less than $2.5 million.

used in political science—is an exceedingly difficult task.[78] Variations in how units are reported (for instance, 1 million dollars or $1 million) and variations in notation ($1,100,000 or $1.1 million) make manual extraction nearly impossible. Even with a small sample of press releases, it would be difficult to extract the dollar amount claimed, requiring a very careful and close reading of the entire press release. Identifying the amount discussed across all press releases would be essentially infeasible, requiring an army of coders and substantial time.

Rather than extract the information by hand, we use computational tools. Specifically, we use the *Named Entity Recognizer* (NER) in the Stanford CoreNLP Library,[79] to extract the amount of money that legislators claim credit for securing in their credit claiming press releases.[80] Figure 3.6 presents all the dollar figures discussed in credit claiming press releases. The horizontal axis is the dollar amount claimed on a log-scale, though we provide labels in actual dollar amounts to ease interpretation. Figure 3.6 reveals several instances of legislators claiming credit for very small amounts of money—some as little as $1,000. For example, Eddie Bernice-Johnson (D-TX) "announced that the National Endowment for

---

[78] Grimmer and Stewart (2013).

[79] Finkel, Grenager, and Manning (2005).

[80] The named entity extraction classifies the types of objects—entities—that occur in sentences. We use the software to identify dollar figures that are discussed in press releases. To do this, the model exploits the structure of sentences to identify entities in sentences and uses the same sentence structure to determine if the entity is a dollar amount. Applying this algorithm produces our ideal data set: a collection of all the money (with appropriate units) discussed in each press release. We then restrict our attention to the credit claiming press releases to identify what legislators claim credit for securing.

the Humanities has made a grant to the Old Red Museum of Dallas County History & Culture. The museum will use the $1,000 grant to support its Transportation Fair, 'Stagecoaches to Segways: Celebrating Transportation of Dallas County's Past, Present and Future'"[81] and Jim McDermott (D-WA) "presented a check for $1,000 to the Lifelong AIDS Alliance at the beginning of the 21st AIDS Walk over the weekend in Seattle."[82] This was not an isolated incident—legislators from all parts of the country and both parties claimed credit for small amounts of money. Doc Hastings (R-WA) issued a press release to announce that the "Chelan County Fire District #3 will receive $13,737 from the Assistance to Firefighters Grant program."[83] Bart Stupak "announced Alcona, Iosco, Menominee, Montmorency, Ontonagon and Oscoda Counties have received grants totaling $65,250 to provide shelter, food and support services to assist individuals in northern Michigan currently facing economic crisis." This announcement included a $7,950 grant for Alcona County.[84] Representatives and senators will even issue joint press releases to claim credit for small expenditures. One press release declared that "Mike Ross [D-AR] along with U.S. Senators Blanche Lincoln [D-AR] and Mark Pryor [D-AR] today announced that Nevada County will receive a $17,000 Rural Development grant from the Department of Agriculture to help repair three malfunctioning tornado sirens."[85]

Discussions of small amounts of money—like the examples provided—occur regularly in credit claiming press releases. 19.0% of credit claiming press releases reference an expenditure of $50,000 or less, and 24.1% of credit claiming press releases contain a dollar amount that is $100,000 or less. Overall, legislators claim credit for—at most— about $0.16 per resident. Larger dollar amounts are discussed, but even these figures are still relatively small. For example, in another joint press release "Sen. Edward M. Kennedy [D-MA], Sen. John F. Kerry [D-MA], and Rep. John W. Olver [D-MA] announced today that the U.S. House of Representatives has approved the Interior Appropriations conference report containing $650,000 in funding for land acquisition in the Silvio O. Conte National Fish and Wildlife Refuge."[86] Other announcements list relatively small expenditures. Bud Cramer (D-AL) issued a press release stating that "North Alabama will receive funding for the following projects: $10 million for the Patton Island Bridge

---

[81] Johnson (2008).
[82] McDermott (2007).
[83] Hastings (2008).
[84] Stupak (2010*a*).
[85] Ross (2009*b*).
[86] Olver (2005).

Corridor, $3 million for the Huntsville Southern Bypass, $1 million for the Interchange at I-65 and Limestone County Road 24, $1 million for the Jackson County Industrial Park Access Road."[87] And Hal Rogers (R-KY)—a powerful member of the Appropriations committee—often claims credit for securing relatively small amounts for targeted programs in his district, like the drug treatment program Operation UNITE. In a press release Rogers "announced today that $1.15 million for Operation UNITE was approved by a key congressional subcommittee."[88]

The dollar amounts claimed in these press releases are indicative of the types of expenditures that legislators discuss with constituents. Across all credit claiming press releases, the median expenditure discussed is $2.85 million. This amount, though, is an overestimate of what legislators claim credit for securing. In many press releases legislators will discuss the cost of the entire bill—the whole of which they cannot plausibly claim to have enacted[89]—and then describe the amount allocated to the district. To account for this, we can take the median of the amounts discussed in each press release—which is more likely to reflect the amount claimed. The median of the median amount claimed in each press release is $1.7 million—only about $2.86 per resident in the district.

3.5 CONCLUSION

The evidence of this chapter shows why legislators' impression of influence over expenditures matters for understanding how legislators receive credit for particularistic spending in the district. Representatives differ in the extent to which they associate themselves with spending in the district. Some legislators have a strong incentive to pursue a personal vote—their reelection coalitions depend on winning the support of independents and even some opposing partisans. Other legislators, however, have a strong incentive to appeal to their copartisans, so they allocate a smaller share of their press releases to credit claiming. If representatives regularly attach themselves to spending in the district, then we expect (and we show in subsequent chapters) that representatives will be perceived as more efficacious at delivering money to the district. Legislators who do not engage in this credit claiming will not have the same association and will not receive the same benefit. Spending alone can help legislators cultivate a personal vote, but claiming credit makes

---

[87] Cramer (2005).
[88] Rogers (2008a).
[89] Mayhew (1974).

it more likely that constituents will reward legislators for expenditures in the district.

We also show that the opportunity to claim credit extends far beyond money actually being spent in the district and for projects of many different sizes. Legislators claim credit for appropriations as they move through Congress. Even when money is far from being spent in the district or will not be spent for some time, legislators are able to claim credit for the spending. And legislators need not have a direct role in securing the money. Legislators are able to create an impression of influence across a variety of actions and the opportunities are expansive and regularly occurring. Further, the opportunities are only loosely constrained by the size of the expenditure or project.

When legislators engage in the types of credit claiming that we describe in this chapter, they shape their relationship with constituents.[90] Credit claiming efforts are one example of how legislators attempt to dictate the terms of evaluation to constituents. When legislators regularly claim credit for money spent in the district, they invite constituents to perform evaluations based on the extent and type of federal projects in the district, but when legislators avoid discussing spending, they encourage more ideological and partisan evaluations. This shift in evaluation may help explain the incumbency advantage and explain how legislators attempt to cultivate leeway.[91] It also has broad, though ambivalent, normative implications—a point we address in this book's conclusion.

[90] Grimmer (2013).
[91] Fenno (1978).

CHAPTER 4

Creating an Impression, Not Just Increasing Name Recognition

THE PREVIOUS CHAPTER DEMONSTRATES HOW OFTEN LEGISLATORS use credit claiming statements to cultivate support and what legislators claim credit for delivering to (or requesting for) the district. This strategic credit claiming, we argue, helps legislators cultivate an impression of influence over expenditures and, in turn, build a personal vote with constituents. Before providing direct evidence of how constituents allocate credit in response to legislators' credit claiming messages, we consider a simpler explanation for why legislators claim credit: to increase name recognition.

Cain, Ferejohn, and Fiorina first demonstrated that incumbents have a substantial advantage in name recognition, an advantage that grew at the same time as the incumbency advantage.[1] To increase this recognition, they argue, legislators work outside of Congress and engage constituents in the district. Constituency service is part of this engagement: members of Congress use their staff to help constituents navigate the complicated federal bureaucracy.[2] Legislators also maintain prominent district offices,[3] make regular appearances in the district,[4] send newsletters to constituents,[5] and use nonpolitical *advertising* statements to bolster their name recognition.[6]

There are also psychological mechanisms to explain why name recognition will cultivate support among constituents. A large psychological literature documents how "mere exposure" to an entity causes people to evaluate it more positively.[7] When applied to name recognition, this research implies that constituents who repeatedly see their representa-

---

[1] Cain, Ferejohn, and Fiorina (1987).
[2] Cain, Ferejohn, and Fiorina (1987).
[3] Fiorina (1981); Rivers and Fiorina (1989).
[4] Fenno (1978).
[5] Lipinski (2004).
[6] Mayhew (1974).
[7] Zajonc (2001).

tive's name are more likely to have positive feelings toward toward the legislators and, in turn, to support the representative on Election Day.

A reasonable explanation for why legislators engage in credit claiming, then, is that they are merely trying to bolster their recognition among constituents. This certainly is true—credit claiming provides legislators the opportunity to disseminate their name to constituents. But we show in this chapter that credit claiming does much more than just increase name recognition and that mere exposure alone fails to explain how credit claiming bolsters support. We use an experiment to show that credit claiming also helps legislators cultivate an impression of influence over federal spending. The result is that credit claiming statements cause a larger increase in support for legislators than other nonpartisan statements and that alternative explanations are unable to account for this finding. Our experiment is subtle, limiting the chance that experimental demand, participants attempting to fulfill researchers expectations, explains our results. And we show in Chapter 5 that constituents, on their own, are unlikely to raise concerns about the cost of a project.

In addition to showing that credit claiming does more than increase name recognition, this chapter introduces our methodology for assessing how legislators cultivate support with credit claiming messages. While the mode of delivery and format of the messages varies, we use randomized experiments embedded in a survey to examine how individual credit claiming messages affect constituent credit allocation.[8] Experiments are useful for assessing the effects of credit claiming messages because they allow us to control who sees the messages. This control eliminates the possibility of confounding factors that bias estimates of messages' effects. Experiments also enable us to have precise control over the content of the messages. This gives us the granular information necessary to test subtle hypotheses about how constituents respond to legislators' credit claiming messages. As we explain in this chapter, we design our experiments to correspond as much as possible with how legislators actually engage in credit claiming. Of course, demonstrating conclusively the external validity of our studies is close to impossible, but we couple our experiments with observational evidence that corroborates our experimental findings.

Before explaining why experimental analyses of legislators' credit claiming messages are useful, we first explain why we expect credit claiming statements to have distinct and additional effects over other nonpartisan types of speech.

---

[8] Sniderman and Grob (1996).

4.1 WHY CREDIT CLAIMING DIFFERS FROM OTHER NONPARTISAN MESSAGES

Political scientists have shown the power of name recognition to win elections. Cain, Ferejohn, and Fiorina argue that the rise in the incumbency advantage was to a large extent due to an increase in legislators' name recognition.[9] They show—and a wide array of subsequent scholarship confirms—that the public readily identifies their member of Congress, an advantage when voters are deciding who to support in the voting booth. Politicians and political consultants recognize the value of name recognition—early decisions about whether to enter a race are often based on a candidate's name recognition.

Legislators strategically use the tools of their office to bolster their name recognition among constituents.[10] In this chapter we focus on one tool for increasing name recognition: *advertising* messages. Mayhew (1974) defines advertising "as any effort to disseminate one's name among constituents in such a fashion as to create a favorable image but in messages that have little or no issue content."[11] Opportunities for legislators to engage in advertising are bountiful. For example, each year Congress holds an art contest, with a potential winner from each district. The art contest provides numerous opportunities for legislators to advertise. At the start of the contest, members of Congress announce that they are accepting submissions. For example, Todd Rokita (R-IN) issued a press release in which he advertised that "Representative Todd Rokita has announced that his office will be accepting entries for the annual Congressional Art Competition starting today."[12] Legislators, such as Rokita, also take the opportunity to announce the winner. Two months after announcing the contest, Rokita issued a press release announcing that "[e]arlier today, U.S. Rep. Todd Rokita met in Washington with 4th District Congressional Art Competition winner Annie Hegarty, a junior at Jefferson High School in Lafayette."[13] Legislators take advantage of many other opportunities to increase name recognition. This includes announcing residents appointed to military academies, congratulating local sports teams on championships, commemorating national holidays, or discussing symbolic ceremonies of personal interest to constituents.

Credit claiming statements do increase legislators' name recognition— reminding constituents of their representative and increasing the chance

[9] Cain, Ferejohn, and Fiorina (1987).
[10] Cain, Ferejohn, and Fiorina (1987).
[11] Mayhew (1974), 49
[12] Rokita (2012*a*).
[13] Rokita (2012*b*).

that constituents will feel more familiar and supportive. But credit claiming messages also show how legislators work in Washington to improve life in the district. Legislators inform constituents about actions that are performed and tangible benefits that will be delivered to the district—presumably because the legislator acted in Congress. And when composing the messages, legislators and their staff make this information easy to access, ensuring that even inattentive constituents will recognize the distinct content in the credit claiming statement.[14]

Credit claiming is effective at creating an impression of influence over federal disbursements because constituents can easily identify the distinct content of the messages. This implies that credit claiming statements cause constituents to perceive their member of Congress as more effective at delivering money to the district. And because constituents value representatives who are effective at delivering particularistic resources to the district,[15] credit claiming statements provide a bigger overall increase in support than advertising messages. Put simply: constituents reward legislators who appear effective at delivering for the district and credit claiming press releases provide legislators the opportunity to explain how and what they deliver.

Credit claiming messages should bolster support among constituents more than advertising messages suggests a simple goal for this chapter: to test whether credit claiming press releases actually do provide a larger increase in support for legislators than simple advertising messages. To make this determination, we use an experiment that varies the content of messages in order to identify their effect. This test is part of our more general strategy in this book—we use experiments to identify the effect of legislators' credit claiming messages on constituents.

4.2 Why We Use Experiments to Evaluate the Effects of Credit Claiming

When previous scholars assessed the consequences of legislators' direct engagement with constituents, they have tended to use observational designs.[16] Scholars examine the relationship between legislators' actual actions and constituents' actual votes or expressed support.[17] To infer the causal effect of the actions, studies use information about legislators

---

[14] Hassin, Bargh, and Uleman (2002).

[15] Cain, Ferejohn, and Fiorina (1987).

[16] Fenno (1978); Fiorina (1981); Cain, Ferejohn, and Fiorina (1987); Lipinski (2004); Grimmer (2013).

[17] Holland (1986); Dunning (2012).

and constituents and then a statistical model to limit the influence of confounding factors.

Observational studies are essential for understanding representation. They provide detailed information about what legislators do to cultivate support and provide raw correlations that reveal how legislators' strategies covary with the characteristics of the district and length of time in office. But establishing a causal relationship from legislators' credit claiming strategies from observational data is difficult.[18] This is due, in part, to the strategic nature of how legislators use the tools of office. For example, in Chapter 3 we demonstrated that more marginal representatives tend to claim credit more often than legislators who are more aligned with their districts. More marginal representatives also tend to face stronger competition in general elections.[19] This difference could cause a perverse pattern to occur in observational data: credit claiming statements may appear to have a small or null effect because the legislators using the statements the most are also the legislators facing the toughest reelection campaigns.[20] This potential for a perverse pattern is a more general problem when studying how legislators cultivate constituent support. Morris Fiorina argues that legislators' campaign and legislative efforts are responsive to the characteristics of the district. Strategic efforts lead to similarly perverse correlations, with increases in legislative effort appearing to decrease support.[21] As Fiorina writes, the negative correlation between effort and vote share occurs because, "'good,' attentive, hard-working incumbents can 'work' a marginal seat until it appears safe, *for them.*"[22] For example, campaign spending is negatively correlated with vote share, because incumbents spend more money when they are facing tough electoral competition.[23] And engaging with constituents in the district—with visits, increased staff expenditures, or more district offices—is unrelated to a legislator's electoral support.[24]

Observational data is also too coarse to test specific hypotheses about how the content of credit claiming messages affects constituent credit allocation. Previous observational studies of the effects of legislators' statements have only aggregated measures of the content of legislators' statements and occasional measures of constituents support.[25] This

---

[18] Caughey and Sekhon (2012); Sekhon and Titiunik (2012).

[19] Brady, Han, and Pope (2007).

[20] See, for example, Bickers et al. (2007).

[21] Fiorina (1981).

[22] Fiorina (1981), 545 (emphasis in original).

[23] Jacobson (1978); Gerber (1998); Erikson and Palfrey (2000).

[24] Fiorina (1981).

[25] Lipinski (2004); Bickers et al. (2007); Grimmer (2013).

coarseness makes evaluating our more subtle hypotheses about how constituents evaluate the content of *individual messages* impossible. To perform our tests, we need specific control over the content of messages and we need to assess how constituents respond to the content of those specific messages.

We address the problems of strategic legislators and coarse data with a series of credit claiming experiments. Using credit claiming messages from actual legislators as a template, we create a series of fictitious credit claiming messages. We intentionally crafted the messages to strongly resemble legislators' actual credit claiming statements. In this way, our experimental prompts use the same language and are about similar kinds of expenditures discussed in actual credit claiming statements. With the templates as a device to deliver our interventions, we then randomly assign participants to read distinct content, which constitutes our interventions. The randomization ensures that our experiments are internally valid—it will identify the causal effect of our intervention for the population included in our study.

Where possible, we designed our experiments to push beyond internal validity. In our experimental designs, we also strive for ecological validity. When designing our experimental protocol, we attempt to replicate how legislators actually claim credit for spending in the district. To bolster ecological validity—the extent to which our interventions explicitly replicate credit claiming messages that legislators actually send—most of our experiments send fictitious credit claiming messages ostensibly from our participants' actual members of Congress. (We are sure to debrief our participants at the end of the intervention.) We accomplish this by using information we collect about each participant's location. We also provide additional contextual information about the participant's congressional district and state.

We also designed several of our studies to diminish the possibility of demand effects.[26] That is, we constructed experiments to diminish the possibility that our design might unintentionally inform participants about our goal, leading participants to try and conform with that goal. In some of our experiments—such as the experiment in this chapter— our participants never knew that they were in an experiment until after the study was over. (Again, we thoroughly debriefed participants after completing our study.) In other studies we designed our treatments and questions to minimize the chance that our participants could infer our goal. Some of our designs are subtle, making it difficult for participant demand to explain our results. In other designs where the risk of participant demand is more real, we ask questions about

[26] Orne (1969).

overall evaluations first, ensuring constituents would not conclude we are conducting a study of how government spending builds support for legislators.

We also made concerted efforts to increase the external validity of our experimental results. Many of our experiments are administered on samples that are representative of the US population. Most of our studies are conducted as experiments embedded in nationally representative surveys.[27] And even when we deviate from nationally representative samples, we suspect our results still provide accurate assessments of how constituents respond to credit claiming statements. To conduct more complicated experimental designs—such as the experiment we present in this chapter—we use a less representative sample collected using Amazon.com's Mechanical Turk service. While Mechanical Turk samples have a different composition than nationally representative samples, respondents replicate results from classic experiments and are more representative than typical experimental pools, such as college students.[28]

And our results are stable. To show this stability, we replicate our experimental results in multiple experiments. We show that our findings occur in distinct populations and, where possible, through related but distinct interventions. The replication of our results compliments the recent movement to prevent fishing in the analysis of experiments—that is, the deceptive practice of analyzing many dependent variables in order to find a statistically significant result.[29] A community of scholars have proposed publicizing an analysis plan before receiving the data. This ties scholars' hands, limiting the potential to find ephemeral results through fishing. Our use of replication has a similar effect, but suggests our results are even more stable than if we had proposed a pre-analysis plan. Not only do our results emerge organically in the context of our experiments, they are found in new survey populations and with related, though distinct, interventions.

Of course, a threat to our findings is that the types of experimental interventions that we deliver to our participants may only rarely occur in actual politics or are much stronger than constituents actually encounter. Demonstrating conclusively that this risk is not manifested in our study is essentially impossible—indeed, it plagues nearly every experimental study. That said, when analyzing our experiments, we also introduce observational evidence that raises our confidence that our experimental results are realistic. Using the observational evidence, either we

---

[27] Sniderman and Grob (1996); Gaines, Kuklinski, and Quirk (2007).

[28] Berinsky, Huber, and Lenz (2012).

[29] Humphreys, Sanchez de la Sierra, and van der Windt (2013).

explain how constituents tend to encounter messages, or we abandon experimental control and assess the relationship between legislators' actual credit claiming rates and constituent evaluations. The observational data provide further evidence for the validity of our experiments.

We use experiments because they provide powerful tools for understanding how legislators' messages matter for representation around spending. With this motivation, we present our first experiment in the next section. Using an experiment embedded in an online social media website, we show that credit claiming messages do more than just bolster name recognition.

4.3 STUDY 1: ISOLATING THE EFFECTS OF CREDIT CLAIMING STATEMENTS

To isolate the distinct effects of credit claiming, we conducted an experiment in a setting where constituents could plausibly encounter legislator messages: Facebook, a popular social media website.[30] Before analyzing that experiment however, we examine how legislators engage with their constituents on Facebook. Specifically, we selected a three-month period and gathered data on how often legislators posted to their accounts and how many times those posts actually appeared in Facebook users' news feeds. News feeds provide information automatically upon logging into Facebook. Legislators post regularly on Facebook and have fairly large followings. The median House member has 3908 fans—Facebook account holders who have liked their page and can automatically receive the content that legislators publish. Over a three-month period, the average legislator posted 103 messages to her page and the median representative posts about 79 messages to her page.

And these messages appear to be regularly consumed. Figure 4.1 shows the number of Facebook users who saw each post by the representative's political party. Because the histograms have a long right-hand tail we took a logarithm of this total, but we have exponentiated the horizontal axis to aid in interpretation. The median post receives 616 total views, the third quartile of posts receives 1368 views, while some posts reach upwards of 200,000 viewers. And each representative publishes many such posts, upwards of 100 on average. Further, the

[30] Our experiment in this chapter and the experiments in this book were conducted as independent researchers at Stanford University, in compliance with all necessary legal and ethical research guidelines. Study participants were hired through Amazon.com's Mechanical Turk. All of our experimental protocols were approved by the Stanford Institutional Review Board (IRB).

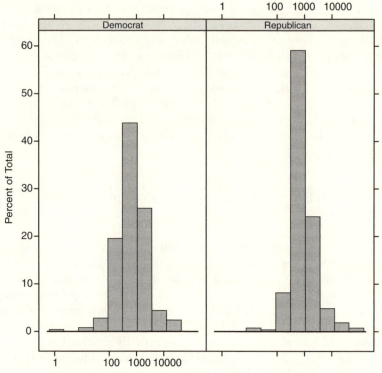

FIGURE 4.1. The Reach of Congressional Facebook Posts.
This figure shows the distribution of the average number of views of each member's posts on Facebook, which appeared in the participants' Newsfeed.

Facebook posts are just one component of legislators' broader media strategies, which include many other forms of media—newsletters sent directly to constituents.

To conduct our experiment, we created a proprietary application for Facebook called the *US Congressional Connection*. The use of Facebook and the proprietary application allows us to minimize the chance of demand effects. Our participants did not know they were involved in an experiment—instead, they were told that they were assisting a group of Stanford researchers who wanted to evaluate a new Facebook application that was designed to connect constituents with their representative in Congress. Our experiment also involved real members of Congress in that our application sent messages ostensibly from *actual* members of Congress (though we created the content) to our participants' Facebook accounts. (We thoroughly debriefed our respondents after our experiment was conducted, ensuring no mistaken impressions remain).

Implementing this design using standard experimental tools is difficult and, perhaps, impossible. Among these standard tools, survey experiments have become popular because they can credibly claim to measure a treatment effect on a representative sample. However, survey experiments are unable to accommodate our multiday experiments, nor can they deliver multiple treatments in isolation from data collection. We will present results from a series of experiments embedded in surveys to understand the effect of credit claiming messages on constituents, but when our focus in on conducting experiments in plausible contexts, survey experiments are less useful.

Another popular alternative experimental population, convenience samples of college students, are also unattractive for our experiment. College students tend to concentrate in only a few congressional districts (even at universities that draw applications nationally) and constitute the subset of the population that is probably least interested in particularistic spending in their home districts.

As we describe in the previous section, as an alternative we use Amazon's Mechanical Turk service to recruit participants for our experiment. Berinsky, Huber, and Lenz show that this service provides a sample more representative than most in-person convenience samples and that experimental participants who use Mechanical Turk replicate experimental benchmarks.[31] Indeed, our sample (used in this chapter) replicates this finding: our sample of respondents is more diverse than a typical sample of college students, though it is not representative of the United States as a whole. Further, the correlations in our sample closely follow correlations in benchmark survey data: Democrats, Republicans, liberals, and conservatives in our sample respond like Democrats, Republicans, liberals, and conservatives in other studies. The high quality of our Mechanical Turk-recruited participants is an oft-replicated finding. Validation studies conducted in other fields demonstrate the effectiveness of Mechanical Turk.[32] These studies show that Mechanical Turk and traditional laboratory subjects are nearly indistinguishable—both in replicating recent experiments[33] and in reproducing the results of classic experiments.[34] To increase the internal validity of our study, we used a series of questions that assess whether the subjects were engaged with our pretest and posttest battery of questions.

---

[31] Berinsky, Huber, and Lenz (2012).
[32] Buhrmester, Kwang, and Gosling (2011); Sprouse (2011).
[33] Sprouse (2011).
[34] Buhrmester, Kwang, and Gosling (2011).

While recruiting experiment participants through Mechanical Turk may seem novel, it provides several advantages over survey or lab experiments.[35] As mentioned before, it makes it possible for us to use a social media website, a setting where legislators actually conduct credit claiming efforts. Our measurement strategy also separates exposure to a treatment and the measurement of its effect. All of our post-experiment surveys are conducted on the day after the treatment is completed. Together, recruiting participants through Mechanical Turk provides a powerful tool for isolating the distinct effects of credit claiming messages.

Using Mechanical Turk, we recruited 462 participants to participate in our study. After completing a preliminary survey and providing a nine-digit zip code (we assisted participants in obtaining this), we directed participants to install our Facebook application.[36] Upon installation of the application, participants were randomly assigned to one of three treatment conditions. In our *control* condition no messages were sent to the participant. Maintaining the true control condition ensures that we have a credible baseline to compare the effects of repeated exposure to information. In our credit claiming condition subjects were sent credit claiming messages from their representative. The amount, content, and subject of each credit claiming message vary over each day and are representative of the types of projects legislators claim credit for obtaining and the amount secured. And in our advertising condition subjects were sent messages with minimal political consequence, but that advertised the legislator's name. Again, the content of the messages reflects the type of messages that legislators commonly send constituents. This condition is analogous to a placebo-control group in that it allows us to disentangle the effect of credit claiming from the effect of merely contacting constituents and informing them about their representative.

Table 4.1 contains two example posts, as they appear on our server and before they were rendered and sent to our subjects. After identifying the subject's legislator, we fill in the information in Table 4.1 with the legislator's information—creating the impression of a press release from the subject's representative. For example, at each instance of |lastName in Table 4.1 we placed the legislator's last name and at each instance of |party we place the legislator's party. To ensure that our messages closely approximated the actual statements legislators would issue, we based all our manipulations on actual press releases.

---

[35] It is also very common in other fields—including Communication, Psychology, Economics, and Linguistics.

[36] Nine-digit zip codes are necessary to avoid ambiguities about representatives whose districts overlap in five-digit zip codes.

TABLE 4.1
Example Templates for Facebook Posts.

Credit Claiming	Advertising
Headline: Local Fire Departments to Receive Over $68,000 for Operations and Firefighter Safety	**Headline:** Rep. |lastName: Local Student Wins Art Contest
Short description: A total of $68,763 in grants for operations and safety programs were awarded to local fire departments from the Department of Homeland Security, Rep. |lastName announced.	**Short description:** Rep. |firstName |lastName, |party-|state, announced that 17-year-old Sara Fischer won first place in the annual congressional district art competition.
Full text: A total of $68,763 in grants for operations and safety programs was awarded to local fire departments from the Department of Homeland Security, Rep. |NAME announced.	**Full text:**
|firstName|lastName (|party-|state) announced the grants today. Specifically, the grant will be used to improve training, equipment, and make modifications to fire stations and facilities in local fire departments.	Rep. |firstName |lastName, (|party-|state), announced that 17-year-old Sara Fischer won first place in the annual congressional district art competition.
"This is great news for our local community," said Representative |lastName. "With these funds, our local fire departments will continue to train and operate with the latest in firefighter technology."	Sara's winning art, "Medals," was created using colored pencils. |lastName said Sara's artwork will be displayed in the U.S. Capitol with other winning entries from districts nationwide.
	Sara is a senior in high school, and will study art and political science at The George Washington University in Washington, D.C., beginning this fall.
	"Sara is a very talented young person," |lastName said. "The congressional art competition is vigorous, and Sara should be very proud of her talents and efforts."
	Each year, |lastName hosts the competition for all local high school students and enlists the help of local art leaders to serve as judges for the special event.
	More than 20 students participated in this year's art competition.

Key

\|lastName: The representative's last name
\|firstName: The representative's first name
\|party: The representative's party
\|state: The representative's state

For five consecutive days participants received different messages from our application that corresponded to their assigned treatment. These messages displayed in the participant's news feed. Our story appeared naturally in the news feed, which also contains information about the participant's "friends" and displays content these friends recommend. The news feed also displays "subscribed" content, often from media outlets and public officials. The left-hand image in Figure 4.2 provides an example of one post from our manipulation as it appeared in a subject's news feed. The headlines and short descriptions of each message were chosen so that they contained the desired treatment: our subjects received the treatment without any additional action. If subjects did click on the provided link they received the entire statement. The right-hand image in in Figure 4.2 provides an example of an actual statement on Facebook from Anna Eshoo (D-CA). The striking similarity between our manipulation and actual content illustrates our experiment's ecological validity. After five days, participants were asked to complete a post-study survey, in which we asked a battery of questions designed to assess the effects of our interventions.[37] Participants answered representative identification questions first, then questions about attitudes towards the representative, and finally questions about the performance of the representative. All questions were randomized within the three blocks.[38]

Table 4.2 summarizes the results across the experimental conditions (rows) and for four dependent variables (columns). In the first column, we provide a manipulation check: demonstrating that participants assigned to the advertising (top row) and credit claiming (middle row) conditions were significantly more likely to select their legislator in a multiple-choice quiz than participants assigned to the control condition (bottom line). When compared to the control group, participants assigned to receive advertising press releases were 29 percentage points more likely to select the correct representative (95% confidence interval, [0.20, 0.39]), while participants assigned to receive credit claiming messages were 32 percentage points more likely to identify the correct legislator (95% confidence interval, [0.22, 0.41]). As the prior literature predicts, either type of message bolsters legislators' name recognition among constituents.[39]

---

[37] The five days of messages represent a strong treatment, though a treatment useful for examining differences in response to legislators' messages. An important variation on our experiment would be to examine how longer delays between treatments and how longer delays in collecting participants' responses affect our results. Alternatively, we could conduct an analogous experiment before an election and record actual voting behavior.

[38] This study was conducted in the summer of 2011 on the pre-Timeline version of Facebook.

[39] Cain, Ferejohn, and Fiorina (1987).

A total of $68,763 in grants for operations and safety programs were awarded to local fire departments from the Department of Homeland Security, Rep. Eshoo announced.

Local Fire Departments to Receive Over $68,000 for Operations and Firefighter Safety

A new press release from Representative Eshoo

 via US Congressional Connection

 Congresswoman Anna Eshoo
December 10, 2009

Rep. Eshoo Secures $2.8 Million in Funding for the 14th Congressional District
December 10, 2009

Washington, D.C. – Rep. Anna G. Eshoo (D – Palo Alto) voted today for H.R. 3288, the Consolidated Appropriations Act of 2010, legislation which contains $2.8 million in funding for critical undertakings in the 14th Congr...

FIGURE 4.2. Example Message from Our Facebook Application, Compared to Actual Credit Claiming on Facebook.
This figure compares a message from our application that is ostensibly from Anna Eshoo (D-CA) (left-hand picture) to an actual credit claiming message from Anna Eshoo (right-hand picture). The strong resemblance is evidence of the ecological validity of our treatments. "How Words and Money Cultivate a Personal Vote: The Effect of Legislator Credit Claiming on Constituent Credit Allocation," by Justin Grimmer, Solomon Messing, and Sean J. Westwood, *American Political Science Review*, Volume 106, Issue 04 (November 2012), pp. 703–719. Copyright © 2012 American Political Science Association. Reprinted with the permission of Cambridge University Press.

TABLE 4.2
The Effect of Credit Claiming and Advertising on Constituents.

Condition	Identify Name	Money Delivering	Passing District Legislation	Legislator Feeling Thermometer
Advertising	0.87	3.99	3.96	50.32
	[0.81, 0.93]	[3.77, 4.21]	[3.73, 4.19]	[46.22, 54.43]
Credit Claiming	0.90	4.49	4.51	56.01
	[0.83, 0.96]	[4.26, 4.71]	[4.27, 4.74]	[51.75, 60.27]
Control	0.58	3.68	3.72	45.16
	[0.51, 0.64]	[3.46, 3.91]	[3.49, 3.96]	[40.97, 49.35]

This table shows that credit claiming messages are more effective at cultivating support than advertising messages. Each row contains the conditions: the top row is the advertising condition, the middle row is the credit claiming condition, and the bottom row is the control condition. The columns contain the outcome variables. Each entry is the corresponding condition's average for the dependent variable, with a 95 percent confidence interval below this average. The first column contains a manipulation check, demonstrating that our study increases name recognition, evidence that subjects received our treatments. The second and third columns demonstrate that claiming credit increased the impression that legislators were effective at delivering money to the district and passing legislation beneficial for the district. The fourth column shows that credit claiming messages cultivated more support for the legislator.

Both credit claiming and advertising messages increased a legislator's name recognition. But credit claiming messages also cultivated an impression of influence, leading constituents to believe that their legislator is more effective at delivering money to the district and passing beneficial legislation. The second column shows that subjects in the credit claiming condition rated their legislator as more effective at delivering federal money to the district. Subjects were asked to rate how effective their representative has been at "bringing federal money to your community" on a seven-point scale. Credit claiming statements cause legislators to receive an increase in their perceived effectiveness of delivering money to the district. Subjects in the credit claiming condition rated their representative 0.80 units higher than subjects' evaluations in the control condition (95% confidence interval, [0.48, 1.12]) and 0.49 units more effective than participants assigned to the advertising condition (95% confidence interval, [0.16, 0.82]).[40] The third column shows that subjects in the credit claiming position also rated their legislator as more effective at "passing legislation that helps your community" on the same seven

[40] Participants assigned to the advertising condition also rated their legislators slightly more effective at delivering money than participants assigned to the control condition. This small increase is consistent with studies demonstrating that merely exposing participants to information about an individual can raise familiarity and cause increases in evaluations in unrelated areas. See Zajonc (2001).

point scale. Subjects assigned to the credit claiming condition rated their representative 0.78 units more effective than the control condition (95% confidence interval, [0.46, 1.11]) and 0.55 units more effective than those assigned to the advertising condition (95% confidence interval, [0.21,0.88]).

Credit claiming messages cause an increase in perceived effectiveness, causing legislators to be more positively evaluated. The fourth column in Table 4.2 shows that credit claiming messages are more effective at cultivating support than advertising messages. Following a wide array of studies (for example, Stein and Bickers 1994), we measure the effect of our experiment on constituent evaluations using a 100-point feeling thermometer: a score of "0" is the lowest possible score and a score of "100" is the highest possible rating. Subjects assigned to the credit claiming condition had an increase in average feeling thermometer rating of 10.85 points over the control condition (95% confidence interval, [4.87, 16.83]) and an increase in average feeling thermometer rating of 5.69 points over the advertising condition (95% confidence interval, [−0.27, 11.65]).

This is a substantial increase in favorability—nearly as large as the increase in favorability associated with having a copartisan representative. Among our control group, copartisans rated their representative 13.56 units higher than respondents without a copartisan representative. Credit claiming messages increased the average rating of representatives 10.85 units over the control group—an effect 80% the size of the copartisan difference—and 5.69 units over the advertising group, an effect 42% of the size of the copartisan difference.

4.4 THE DISTINCT EFFECTS OF CREDIT CLAIMING

In this brief chapter we accomplish two objectives. We provide our first evidence of how legislators' credit claiming affects constituent credit allocation. Using an experiment administered in a setting where legislators communicate with constituents, we show that credit claiming messages do more than just bolster name recognition. Claiming credit for spending also cultivates an impression of influence over the expenditure process. After reading credit claiming messages, voters perceive their representative as more attentive to the district and more effective at delivering money to the district. The result is that credit claiming messages cause a larger increase in support than other nonpolitical messages.

We also introduce our strategy for measuring the effect of credit claiming statements. Throughout this book, we use experiments to assess how constituents evaluate the content of legislators' credit claiming messages and how this rhetoric subsequently affects support for the incumbent. The experiments also provide us with the precise control over message content, control that is essential for testing subtle theories of how constituents allocate credit. Our experiments also provide the ability to measure constituent response, giving us the granular information necessary to test theories of how voters evaluate subtle differences in credit claiming statements. And by randomizing the type of messages constituents receive,these experiments allows us to avoid the problems that plague observational studies of how legislators engage constituents to cultivate constituent support.[41]

Credit claiming messages have an effect distinct from advertising messages. But the experiment in this chapter reveals only that there is a difference, it does not reveal how constituents respond to the content of credit claiming messages. In the next chapter, we use a series of experiments to identify how voters allocate credit. The experiments reveal a surprising pattern in how constituents allocate credit: voters evaluate the action legislators report, rather than the amount claimed.

[41] Fiorina (1981).

CHAPTER 5

Cultivating an Impression of Influence with Actions and Small Expenditures

THE PREVIOUS CHAPTER SHOWS THAT WHEN LEGISLATORS CLAIM credit for spending they do more than simply bolster their name recognition. They cause constituents to perceive their representative as effective at delivering money to the district and this perception subsequently causes an increase in overall evaluations of the legislator. This result shows that credit claiming is an effective and distinct strategy for building support with constituents.

This chapter uses a series of experiments and observational data to examine how constituents allocate credit in response to legislators' credit claiming messages and to show how this response affects accountability. As we argued in Chapter 2, constituents tend to evaluate messages from political officials quickly, with limited cognitive effort, and often without broader context about the expenditure. The rapid evaluation of content causes constituents to reward legislators for more than just spending as it occurs in the district. Constituents reward legislators for claiming credit for spending and make only slight distinctions between money that has already been secured, money that will definitely be spent in the distant future, and spending that has only a small probability of reaching the district.

Even when constituents rapidly evaluate legislators' credit claiming statements, some information is easy for them to use. We show that constituents are responsive to the type of expenditure that legislators claim credit for securing and who announces the expenditure. Constituents, however, are less responsive to the amount of money secured. Across several experiments we show that legislators' credit has only a loose relationship with the amount of money legislators claim credit for. Legislators receive credit for spending even if they claim credit for relatively small amounts and even if they are ambiguous about the amount delivered to the district.

While responding little to increases in money, constituents have a sustained and large response to increases in the number of credit claiming messages legislators articulate. Increasing the number of credit claiming messages causes constituents to perceive their legislator as more effective at delivering money to the district and causes them to increase their overall evaluation of their representative's performance. The result is that frequent credit claiming for smaller amounts of money is more effective at cultivating support than claiming credit for one, much larger, expenditure. This is not because participants view larger expenditures as wasteful—large increases in the size of expenditures have little effect on perceptions of a program's wastefulness. And the results are not due to experimental demand—as in Chapter 4, we use subtle designs that minimize the chance demand explains our results. Rather, we show that constituents lack the information and context to evaluate the size of expenditures, but are well equipped to evaluate legislators' actions.

Our evidence enables us to characterize how legislators claim credit for spending and how constituents respond to those credit claiming efforts. The experimental variation provides internal validity, ensuring that we can isolate the causal effects of our interventions. And our analysis of legislative statements shows that legislators regularly communicate credit claiming messages. But we have yet to demonstrate that legislators' statements actually reach constituents and affect political representation. To show that our characterization of the credit claiming, credit allocation process matters for representation, we use additional survey evidence to show that there is a relationship between legislators' credit claiming rates and constituents' evaluations of their representative. Using this observational data, we show that legislators who claim credit at higher rates are viewed as more effective at delivering money to the district and are evaluated more highly overall. This effect is particularly strong among constituents who identify with the opposite party of the representative— evidence that credit claiming cultivates a personal vote that sustains support for representatives.

One of the primary ways representation occurs around spending, then, is through legislators' statements and constituents' evaluations of those statements. As we describe in the conclusion to the chapter, this communication creates new complications for accountability on spending, creating potential pitfalls and new possibilities. Perhaps the potential pitfalls of the rhetoric of representation are easiest to identify and most familiar to political scientists. By rewarding legislators throughout the appropriations process, there is a risk that legislators will fail to deliver appropriations to the district. And when legislators fail to include information about expenditures, constituents may fail to incentivize legislators to provide adequate spending levels in the district. But there may be positive consequences of this process. By rewarding legislators throughout the appropriations process, constituents may actually increase the effort legislators exert to deliver money to the district.

And by recognizing their limited information about expenditures, constituents may ensure that their preferred projects are funded in the district and that legislators avoid engaging in wasteful spending.

This chapter presents extensive evidence characterizing how representation occurs around spending, including a series of experiments and observational data. We turn now to our first experiment, which shows that legislators receive nearly equal credit for requesting and securing spending, and that constituents appear not to consider information about spending when evaluating legislators' credit claiming efforts.

5.1 STUDY 1: EVALUATING THE MERE REPORT OF AN ACTION, NOT MONEY DELIVERED

Our first experiment tests two observable implications of constituents evaluating the report of an action in a credit claiming statement, rather than the actual delivery of money to the district. First, if constituents evaluate legislators' actions alone, then legislators will be able to cultivate support for more than simply securing money for the district. The appropriations process contains many points where legislators perform actions that are necessary for securing funds and could lead to money being spent in the district, even if those actions do not directly result in spending in the district. For example, prior to the 112th Congress, representatives could request that funds be earmarked for particular projects. Even with the ban on earmarks, legislators could submit letters of support or make phone calls to encourage bureaucrats to allocate grants to particular groups. If constituents allocate credit based on their evaluation of performed actions, then we expect that claiming credit for such requests will cultivate support–and perhaps as much support as actually securing the money for the district. Second, if constituents evaluate the report of the action, then explicitly stating the dollar amount should have little affect on how constituents allocate credit.

We test the observable implications with a survey experiment. We use a sample of 2,020 respondents from the Survey Sampling International (SSI) panel, census matched to be representative of the United States. For all respondents not assigned to the control condition, we randomly selected one of the respondent's two senators for our experiment. We then told the participants that we "found the most recent newspaper article covering" the randomly selected senator.

Our experiment simultaneously varied the *action* that the senator claimed credit for performing and whether the article mentioned an explicit *amount* of funds that would be secured for the project. The three action conditions vary the work that a legislator performed in procuring spending for the district. In the first action condition, the respondent's senator announced that she *secured* funds for a "local road project" and that the money *will* be spent in the district. This unambiguously informs constituents that the money has been secured and will be delivered to the district. But if constituents evaluate the mere report of actions that could lead to expenditures, we expect that representatives will be able to cultivate support by claiming credit for actions that occur before the district actually receives funding. In the second action condition, the senator claims credit for *requesting* funds, while explaining how the funds *would be* spent if delivered to the district, leaving more uncertainty about whether the district will actually receive the money. Claiming credit for merely requesting money leaves ambiguity about whether the district will receive the money. But we expect that legislators will be able to receive credit for actions that leave even greater uncertainty about the amount of money to be delivered to the district and when the money will actually be allocated. If credit is allocated in response to a rapid evaluation of a message, then legislators should be able to receive credit for merely expressing their intent to request funding for the district. We test this hypothesis in the third action condition. Respondents in this condition read a news story in which their senator announces that she *will request* money for the district, again reporting how the money would be spent if secured.

We crossed the three action conditions with two *money* conditions that vary the specificity that legislators use when describing the funding for the project. In the first money condition, the exact dollar amount of funding for the project was provided—$84 million. We set the amount of money extremely high, to bias our study against our hypotheses that the money will matter little. In the second money condition, we suppressed the dollar amount, instead indicating that legislators secured/sought undefined *support* for the district.

In the control condition—in which we simply ask respondents about their senator—our design constitutes a $3 \times 2 + 1$ experimental design (providing 7 conditions in total). We provide the complete intervention in Table 5.1. The content in the parentheses corresponds to the action condition with the order given by (secured/request/will request) and the content in brackets is selected based on the money condition [money/support]. The article is customized for each respondent. After assigning a respondent to a condition and selecting a senator we replace each instance of |senatorName with the senator's name, |senatorParty with the senator's party, and |state with the state. After presenting the intervention to constituents, we asked constituents for overall evaluations of their senator (and other political officials), evaluations of the senator's ability to benefit the district in particular areas, and evaluations of the

TABLE 5.1
Article Content across Conditions.

Headline: Senator |senatorName (secured/requested/will request) [$84 million/support] for local projects

Body: |senatorName (|senatorParty – |State) (secured/requested/will request) [$84 Million/support] for local road projects through the Department of Transportation Federal Highway Administration. Senator |senatorName said "I (am pleased to bring home/ am happy to make this request for/will submit a request for) [$84 Million/support] from the Federal Highway Administration. It is critical that we maintain our infrastructure to ensure that our roads are safe for travelers and the efficient flow of commerce." This funding (will/would/would) repave local roads.

Key
|senatorName: Senator's name
|senatorParty: Senator's party
|state: Senator's state

Treatments
Actions: (Secured/Requested/Will Request)
Money: [Money/Support]

---

program. We randomized the order of our questions in each of the three blocks containing dependent variables in this study and in the remaining studies in this chapter.

Table 5.2 summarizes the results of our experiment across the seven conditions (rows) and five dependent variables (columns). Each entry provides the average responses of the participants in each condition, with the 95 percent confidence interval for that average. Across conditions and dependent variables, we find that credit claiming messages cultivate the impression of a senator's influence over expenditures and increases overall support. But what legislators claim credit for doing has only a slight influence over how constituents allocate credit. This lack of variation is evident in the constituents' evaluations of their senator's ability to deliver money to the district, measured on a seven-point scale and reported in the first column. The six credit claiming conditions caused constituents to evaluate their senator as 0.27 units more effective at delivering money to the district than constituents in the control condition (95 percent confidence interval, [0.08, 0.45]). Across credit claiming conditions, however, we detect only slight differences in perceived effectiveness: constituents appear to reward legislators similarly for securing, requesting, or stating an intent to request. The largest increase in perceived effectiveness does occur for the condition where the senator *secures money* for the district, with legislators rated

TABLE 5.2

Constituents Respond to the Mere Report of an Action, but Are Unresponsive to the Type of Action.

Condition	Delivering Money	Passing Legislation	Legislator Feeling Thermometer	Approve	Likelihood of Receiving Money
Control	3.89	3.91	45.92	0.37	–
	[3.72, 4.06]	[3.74, 4.09]	[42.58, 49.26]	[0.31, 0.43]	–
Will Request Money	4.08	4.04	51.78	0.46	0.34
	[3.92, 4.25]	[3.87, 4.21]	[48.53, 55.02]	[0.40, 0.51]	[0.28, 0.39]
Will Request Support	4.17	4.13	53.33	0.55	0.34
	[4.01, 4.32]	[3.97, 4.29]	[50.30, 56.36]	[0.49, 0.60]	[0.29, 0.39]
Requested Money	4.11	4.13	49.81	0.48	0.33
	[3.94, 4.28]	[3.96, 4.31]	[46.47, 53.15]	[0.42, 0.54]	[0.28, 0.39]
Requested Support	4.14	4.16	50.04	0.46	0.34
	[3.97, 4.31]	[3.98, 4.34]	[46.65, 53.43]	[0.40, 0.52]	[0.28, 0.40]
Secured Money	4.27	4.15	52.23	0.51	0.50
	[4.10, 4.43]	[3.98, 4.32]	[49.00, 55.46]	[0.45, 0.56]	[0.44, 0.55]
Secured Support	4.16	4.16	50.87	0.44	0.40
	[3.99, 4.32]	[3.99, 4.33]	[47.63, 54.11]	[0.38, 0.50]	[0.35, 0.46]

This table shows how constituents' evaluation of legislators varies across conditions (rows) and dependent variables (columns). For evaluations of the legislator, constituents reward legislators similarly for requesting or securing money. This occurs, even though constituents identify differences in the likelihood their district will receive the money.

as 0.38 units more effective at delivering money to the district than senators in the control condition (95 percent confidence interval, [0.14, 0.62]). Senators assigned to other conditions are rated as 0.24 units more effective than senators in the control condition (95 percent confidence interval, [0.05, 0.43]). The difference is substantively interesting—a 0.14-unit difference (95 percent confidence interval, [−0.04, 0.32])—but we show below that it does not subsequently cause an increase in overall thermometer evaluations.

Aside from the *secured money* condition, we find few differences in how constituents evaluate legislators' effectiveness at delivering funds to the district. Participants assigned to the condition where their senator secured an expenditure (averaging over whether an explicit dollar figure was discussed), increase their average evaluation of effectiveness 0.32 units (95 percent confidence interval, [0.12, 0.53]). This increase is similar to the increase that requesting and stating that the representative will request an expenditure causes (0.24 units, 95 percent confident interval, [0.04, 0.44]; 0.24 units 95 percent confidence interval,

[0.03, 0.45], respectively). And even if we collapse the request and will request conditions together (to increase our statistical power) we still fail to find a meaningful difference with the *securing* condition. Securing an expenditure increases the effectiveness rating only 0.09 units more than requesting—an increase in perceived effectiveness, but an increase we cannot distinguish from zero (95 percent confidence interval, [−0.06, 0.23]).

Explicitly stating the amount of money secured also appears to exert little influence over participants' evaluations. Participants assigned to the money condition increased their evaluation of their senator's ability to deliver money to the district 0.27 units (95 percent confidence interval, [0.07, 0.46])—an increase nearly identical to the 0.27-unit increase among participants assigned to the support condition (95 percent confidence interval, [0.07, 0.46]). The second column of the table presents average evaluations of a legislator's ability to pass legislation beneficial to the district—another question indicative of a senator's impression of influence. Across the conditions—both the action and money conditions—we replicate the same result: constituents increase support in response to credit claiming messages, but the magnitude of this increase depends only slightly upon what legislators claim credit for accomplishing.

The credit claiming messages not only cause an increase in perceived effectiveness, they also cause constituents to be more supportive of their senator overall. The third column presents the average feeling thermometer rating for senators across the conditions. Credit claiming increases overall evaluations: averaged across the six treatment conditions, the credit claiming statements increased the senator's average thermometer score 5.5 points (95 percent confidence interval, [1.92, 9.10]). This increase is substantively large—about 25% of the increase in average thermometer score associated with having a copartisan senator in the control condition. But the size of the increase does not depend on the action reported. Claiming credit for securing either money or support for the district increases the thermometer rating only 0.19 points more than claiming credit for requesting or *intending to request* money or support, an increase in effect size that is neither substantively nor statistically significant (95 percent confidence interval, [−2.61, 2.99]). Explicitly stating the dollar amount secured also does not cause a larger increase in thermometer score. Constituents assigned to the money condition increase their thermometer rating of their senator 0.24 points less than constituents assigned to the support condition. Again this difference is neither substantively nor statistically significant (95 percent confidence interval, [−2.88, 2.40]). This pattern is robust to the overall evaluation used: if we use senator approval as the dependent variable we find that constituents are not responsive to the action reported. In the fourth column we report the average rate that participants in each condition approve of the job that the selected senator is performing in Washington, measured as a dichotomous variable. Aggregated together, the six credit claiming conditions cause an 11.4-percentage point increase in the approval rate over the control condition (95 percent confidence interval, [0.05, 17.71]). No matter how we compare responses across the action treatment conditions, we fail to detect substantively significant differences in how the content of the credit claiming messages affects the boost in approval.

Participants appear to allocate credit in response to the mere report of an action—with the type of action or explicit reference to the amount of money to be delivered causing only slight differences in how constituents evaluate messages and reward legislators. The lack of distinction across conditions is all the more surprising because, when prompted, constituents identify differences in the likelihood that the money will reach the district across conditions. The final column of Table 5.2 shows the proportion of participants in each condition who answered that it was likely that the district would actually receive the money.[1]

The right-most column of Table 5.2 shows that participants in the secured condition thought they were more likely to receive the money. Legislators claiming credit for securing the expenditure caused an 11.3-percentage point increase in the proportion of participants who thought that the money was likely to reach the district (95 percent confidence interval, [0.06, 0.17]). The increase was even larger for participants in the secured condition with the explicit mention of money. Participants in the secured condition and whose story explicitly discussed money were 9 percentage points more likely to identify the expenditure as likely to reach the district than participants in the secured condition but whose story only mentioned support (95 percent confidence interval, [0.02, 0.17]) and a 16-percentage point increase over all other conditions (95 percent confidence interval, [0.10, 0.22]).

The content of the message, therefore, systematically affects the perceived likelihood that money will reach the district. Yet, the differences in perceived likelihood do not extend to the participants' evaluations of their senator. Participants across our treatment conditions increased their overall evaluation of their representative a similar amount, regardless of what actions legislators are claiming credit for performing or how explicit legislators are about the money they have secured. These results

---

[1] This question—which depends on reading a newspaper story about local road projects—would make little sense to our control condition, so we did not pose it to them.

constitute evidence that constituents evaluate and reward legislators for the mere report of an action.

The evidence from this experiment, however, relies partly on our failure to detect substantively important differences across a number of treatment arms. This makes it tempting to offer less theoretically interesting explanations for our findings. One explanation is that our failure to find differences across the different actions or explicit report of money is that the participants in our online study were not engaged with their task: they read the statement as quickly as possible, much faster than actual constituents might when reading a newspaper or other news sources. The results of the experiment, however, suggest this is not the case: participants identified substantial differences across the conditions in the likelihood of the district receiving money.

Another explanation is that we simply lack the power to detect differences across our treatment conditions and that we have artificially advantaged our argument by equating it with a failure to reject null hypotheses. We are sympathetic to this alternative explanation, because it is improbable that any two interventions have exactly the same effect. Yet, our results show that there are generally only slight differences in the credit allocated across conditions—even if we avoid relying on null-hypothesis tests, we would still conclude that there are few meaningful and robust differences across credit claiming conditions.

This first study shows that legislators can cultivate support by claiming credit for securing money or merely requesting spending for the district and the credit allocated does not appear to depend on explicit reference to money. Our second study explicitly examines the role of money in credit allocation. We show that extremely large shifts in the amount of money legislators claim credit for securing have little effect on the credit that constituents allocate to their legislators.

5.2 STUDY 2: THE LIMITED RESPONSIVENESS TO THE AMOUNT CLAIMED

Evaluating the amount of money allocated for a project in a credit claiming message is a difficult task for constituents. The task is difficult, in part, because constituents often evaluate legislators' credit claiming messages quickly. And when we think quickly we often struggle to identify and extract numerical information.[2] But even if constituents were to think carefully about the amount of money for a project in a credit claiming message, they may still struggle to use it to evaluate

---

[2] Hatano and Osawa (1983).

the expenditure. Without additional expertise or information, it is often hard to know how much an expenditure will affect the budget of local organizations or the likely impact on local infrastructure. In the absence of this context, constituents may find it difficult to reward legislators for dollar amounts secured and instead choose to reward legislators simply for the project allocation.[3]

That said, some voters who read quickly and lack context may nonetheless be able to make coarse distinctions between certain kinds of spending. Familiar numerical quantities are often easily evaluated and incorporated in evaluations. For example, Ansolabehere, Meredith, and Snowberg show that survey respondents can accurately recall gas prices and unemployment rates, because respondents are used to seeing these numbers and thinking about their implications for their day-to-day life.[4] Similarly intuitive evaluations are possible when constituents evaluate the funds that legislators use in credit claiming statements. To see how, consider an extreme and fictitious example: a legislator who claims credit for a $5 project in the district. Constituents deal with this small amount of money every day, so without much effort they will recognize this as a small amount of money and that the expenditure is essentially inconsequential. By way of comparison, suppose that the legislator claimed credit for delivering a $1,000,000 grant to the district. Without much effort, and without calculating the actual numerical difference constituents recognize $1,000,000 as a lot of money and certainly recognize that it is much more useful than $5. When dealing with amounts that they can quickly evaluate, constituents may give credit to legislators who claim credit for money being delivered to the district. But constituents will likely struggle to reason intuitively about differences in larger, less familiar, sums of money. As a less extreme example, consider one legislator who claims credit for $10,000,000 delivered to the district and another who claims credit for $1,000,000. Few people regularly deal with exchanges involving $10,000,000 or $1,000,000. Without being able to make the direct comparison, it will require more effort for constituents to conceptualize the difference between the two amounts, making it less likely that one expenditure will be readily identified as substantially larger than another. This is true even though the difference between $10,000,000 and $1,000,000 is much larger— nine times—than the difference between $5 and $1,000,000.[5]

It is also possible for a large range of expenditures that constituents are simply unable to incorporate dollar amounts into their evaluations.

[3] Stein and Bickers (1994).

[4] Ansolabehere, Meredith, and Snowberg (2013).

[5] Tversky and Kahneman (1974); Kahneman (2011).

This may occur because even small amounts of money claimed in press releases—which we document below—are actually much larger than the stark contrast we created in our hypothetical example. This would blunt the potential for familiarity to assist in evaluating credit claiming statements.

To test how constituents respond to the amount of money allocated for an expenditure, we designed a pair of experiments to assess how different amounts of money claimed by representatives affect constituent credit allocation. To focus attention on the credit claiming statement—and not the actual representative—in both experiments we told participants that "we have obtained a very short newspaper story about a representative, whose name we are withholding." The participants were then presented with a newspaper story in which the representative's name was redacted (using a rectangular black box, as is common practice in redactions in government documents). Then using actual credit claiming statements, we created templates for credit claiming statements. In this first iteration of the design, the representative claimed credit for securing a grant to "hire and train" new police officers.

Within the template, we randomly varied the amount of money that legislators claimed credit for securing. To obtain constituents' response over a broad range of potential dollar values, we randomly drew the amount that legislators' claimed credit for securing from a continuous uniform distribution, with a minimum amount claimed of $10,000 and a maximum amount claimed of $10,000,000. We used the uniform distribution to obtain a large spread throughout the interval and to simplify the analysis of the experiment. We provide a summary of our treatment in Table 5.3.

We administered this study using an experiment embedded in an online survey and using the sample of 2,020 respondents from the SSI online panel we used in Section 5.1. Each respondent completed the first study in this chapter and then was given the prompt for this second study. This creates the possibility that the intervention in our first round may affect the treatment in the second round. But analyses show that there is little relationship between the respondent's condition in our first study and how they responded to this study.[6] After providing respondents

---

[6] The random assignment of whether the respondent saw an explicit dollar figure in the first condition is particularly useful, because it allows us to check for anchoring effects (see Tversky and Kahneman (1974)). An anchoring effect would occur if the large amount in the first study created an artificial baseline that our participants used to assess expenditures in this study. We find little evidence that seeing the much larger expenditure in the first experiment affects how constituents allocate credit in this intervention. As this finding implies, we replicate our results if we include respondents' condition in our first experiment.

TABLE 5.3
Measuring Constituent Responsiveness to the Dollar Amount Claimed.

Headline: Representative (redacted): ([D/R]-|state) Secures |amount to Expand Local Police Force

Body: Representative (redacted) ([D/R]-|state) secured |amount today to hire and train new police officers. The money, which is from the Edward Byrne Memorial Justice Assistance Grant (JAG) Program, will help local police departments cope with recent budget cuts. When asked for comment, Representative (redacted) said "It is critical that we bolster our local police departments to maintain the safety of our community. I am pleased to announce |amount for local law enforcement."

Key
|state: representative's state

Treatments
Money:|amount
Party: [D/R]

---

with the newspaper article, we asked the respondents about their overall assessments of the legislator.

Our goal is to estimate a curve that summarizes how varying amounts of money cultivate support for legislators. To estimate this curve, we use a flexible nonparametric regression.[7] The use of the nonparametric regression ensures that we have enough information to discover how constituents allocate credit, without failing to discover systematic differences across the dollar amounts because we lack statistical power. To do this, nonparametric regression borrows information about the responses from constituents who were assigned similar dollar amounts. We determine the amount of smoothing using ten-fold cross-validation, choosing the total smoothing to minimize the mean square error, a measure that balances bias (how much we borrow across amounts claimed) and variance (how much uncertainty we have for our estimates).

Figure 5.1 shows how constituents allocate credit in response to their representative. The plot shows the overall relationship between the feeling thermometer assessment of the redacted legislator (vertical axis) and how many millions of dollars were claimed in the grant announcement (horizontal axis), averaging over whether the representative was identified as a Republican or a Democrat. The black line is the conditional mean, determined using the nonparametric regression and

---

[7] Cleveland (1979).

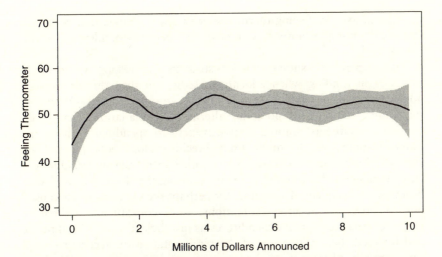

FIGURE 5.1. Massive Increases in Expenditures Cause Only a Small Increase in Support. This figure shows how average feeling thermometer ratings increase in response to the amount of money claimed (in millions of dollars). The expected curve is shown with the dark black line and 95 percent confidence intervals are shown in lighter grey. Participants—particularly opposing partisans—are initially responsive to the amount claimed. But for very large increases, there is little response to the dollar amount claimed.

gray bands are a 95 percent confidence interval, which we determined using bootstrapping.

In this iteration of the experiment it appears that constituents are responsive to the amount claimed, but as we see this response is relatively small and we fail to find this increase in the second iteration of this experiment. The lowest level of support for the legislator, an average thermometer ranking of 43.2, occurs at the smallest amount of money claimed to help hire and train police officers—a mere $10,000, hardly enough to provide partial training for one police officer (95 percent confidence interval for the average, [37.3, 48.6]). As the amount secured increases over this low baseline, participants raise their evaluation of the representative. A local maximum of support occurs around $1.4 million, with the average evaluation rising to 53.7 (95 percent confidence interval, [50.9, 56.5]).

As the funds are increased substantially, however, there is no additional increase in support for the representative. Constituents do not provide additional rewards to legislators for additional money secured. From $1.4 million to $10 million claimed, evaluations are essentially unchanged, even with a large increase in expenditure. This $8.6 million increase between $1.4 million and $10 million causes only a 0.9-point increase in average feeling thermometer rating, a change that is neither statistically nor substantively significant (95 percent confidence interval, [−0.4, 0.6]).

This experiment shows that constituents are responsive to small increases in funding when allocating credit, but then do not provide additional credit for larger increases in the amount secured. Of course, there are a number of potential alternative explanations that could explain constituents' limited responsiveness to spending. Perhaps the limited response was due to the funding recipient, local police. It could be that constituents are more responsive to other spending sources. Our next study eliminates this possibility, demonstrating that local police tend to be a popular recipient of spending. Or perhaps the spending levels caused both positive and negative evaluations. Some constituents might have perceived relatively small expenditures as insufficient to help local police and lowered their evaluation of the representative for securing such a small amount of money. At the other extreme, constituents might have perceived the large expenditures as wasteful, a judgment that might have dampened their support for the representative.

To address these and other potential concerns, we conducted our dose-response study a second time, on a new set of respondents. In this second instance, we again described how a representative secured money, while redacting the legislators' name. But this time we used a template describing how money was secured for a local transportation project, again varying the amount claimed in the press release continuously. To provide the most power to measure constituents' responsiveness, we focused on the dollar range where constituents were the most responsive in the previous experiment: the amount claimed was drawn from a continuous uniform distribution, with a minimum dollar amount of $10,000 and a maximum dollar amount of $2.5 million. And to determine if legislators were being punished for providing too little money or too much money, we compared the effect of the credit claiming message to an *advertising* statement. We replicated a message from Chapter 4, providing information about a fictitious district resident who won an art contest. Table 5.4 summarizes our treatments.

We recruited 1,000 participants using Amazon's Mechanical Turk and randomized the participants to conditions in two stages. In the first stage, we randomly assigned participants to receive either the advertising condition (with a 10% chance) or credit claiming condition (with a 90% chance). If a participant was assigned to the credit claiming condition, we then randomly generated the amount.

In this iteration of the experiment constituents were less responsive to the amount of money legislators' secured—indicative of the limited effect of increasing spending on legislators' impression of influence.

TABLE 5.4
Measuring Constituent Responsiveness to Dollar Amounts and Comparing to Advertising Condition.

Credit Claiming Condition	Advertising Condition
Headline: Representative (redacted) Secures |amount for Local Road Projects.	**Headline:** Representative (redacted) announces Local Wins Congressional Art Contest
Body: Representative (redacted) secured |amount for local road projects through the Department of Transportation Federal Highway Administration. Representative (redacted) said "I am pleased to secure |amount from the Federal Highway Administration. It is critical that we maintain our infrastructure to ensure that our roads are safe for travelers and the efficient flow of commerce." The funding will repave local roads.	**Body:** Rep. (redacted) announced that 17-year old Sara Fischer won 1st place in the annual Congressional district art competition. Sara's winning art, "Medals?" was created using colored pencils. Rep. (redacted) said Sara's artwork will be displayed in the U.S. Capitol with other winning entries from districts nationwide.

Treatments
Type of Message: Credit Claiming (left-column), Advertising (right-column)
Amount: \|amount

Figure 5.2 shows that the participants' evaluations of the representative were not responsive to the dollar amount claimed. As in Figure 5.1, we examine how the representative's feeling thermometer ratings (vertical axis) change as the amount claimed changes (horizontal axis). The thick line is a nonparametric regression line, the gray bands are 95 percent confidence envelopes.

Figure 5.2 shows that constituents are generally unresponsive to the dollar amount claimed in our study. Indeed, increasing the dollar amount claimed appears to *lower* support for the legislator—though the amount lowered is neither substantively nor statistically significant. This shows that participants are generally unresponsive to increases in the dollar amount claimed across the entire range of spending. It would appear that the limited responsiveness detected with the police force manipulation was not an artifact of the type of expenditure. Even when presented with highway expenditures, constituents are generally unresponsive to the dollar amount claimed. In the third and fourth studies in this chapter, we again replicate this result in different contexts: money appears to have little impact on constituent credit allocation.

But constituents are responsive to the credit claiming message. Participants in the credit claiming condition had a substantially higher evaluation of the representative than participants in the advertising

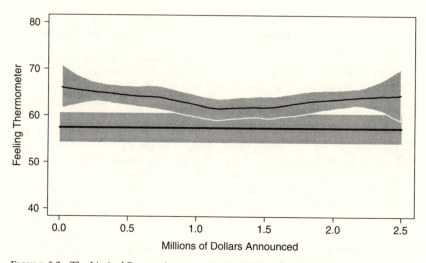

FIGURE 5.2. The Limited Responsiveness to Increases in Dollar Amount.
This figure shows constituents' limited response to increases in the dollar amount claimed. In general, constituents fail to alter their evaluation of the legislator as the amount claimed increases. But, the credit claiming condition does boost support substantially over the advertising condition. Credit claiming messages boost support, but the amount claimed appears to matter little.

condition—replicating our finding from Chapter 4 and providing further evidence of the distinct effects of credit claiming messages on constituents' impression of their legislators' influence. The thick horizontal line in Figure 5.2 is the average feeling thermometer evaluation for participants in the advertising condition, which is below the average feeling thermometer evaluation in the credit claiming condition for the entire range of dollar amounts. Overall, constituents who read the credit claiming message evaluated the representative 6.1 points higher than participants who read the advertising condition (95 percent confidence interval, [2.8, 9.5]). And this difference is just as high for participants who saw only a relatively small amount of money and a large amount of money. Participants who saw a credit claiming message for less than $500,000 rated their representative 7.6 points higher than the advertising message, while participants who saw a credit claiming message for more than $2 million evaluated their representative 5.7 points higher. It does not appear, then, that participants punish representatives for delivering too little money or for being wasteful with large expenditures. Rather, it appears that participants reward legislators for working to deliver money to the district and not conditioning the evaluations on the size of the project.

The lack of responsiveness across the dollar amount secured (and the increase over the advertising condition) provides indirect evidence that constituents do not assess the size or wastefulness of an expenditure. For more direct evidence, we asked participants to evaluate the expenditure and whether it was wasteful or likely to make a difference in the district. And in both cases, it appears that the amount claimed has only a small effect on constituent evaluations. Consider the question about wasteful spending. Overall, relatively few respondents—14.9%— identified the road project as wasteful. And being assigned a press release that claimed credit for more money led to only a small increase in the perceived wastefulness of the spending. Fitting a simple linear regression to the data, a million-dollar increase in amount claimed only caused a 1.9-percentage point increase in perceptions of wastefulness—a small overall increase (95 percent confidence interval, $[-0.01, 0.05]$). Likewise, small expenditures did little to affect perceptions that the spending would accomplish little for the district. Overall, 72.8% of respondents agreed the spending would make a difference in the district. Increasing the amount claimed by a million dollars boosted this perception only 2.6 percentage points—again a relatively small amount (95 percent confidence interval, $[-0.01, 0.07]$).

Our pair of dose-response experiments show that constituents are only weakly responsive to increases in the dollar amount claimed, if at all. This appears to be because constituents reward legislators for expenditure projects, but do not condition the size of the reward on the amount spent in the district. As the next experiment demonstrates, however, other information is much easier for constituents to include in their evaluations of legislators' credit claiming messages.

5.3 STUDY 3: CONSTITUENTS EVALUATE QUALITATIVE INFORMATION, LESS RESPONSIVE TO QUANTITATIVE INFORMATION

Our experiments have varied two salient features of the credit claiming message: the stage in the allocation process and the amount of money allocated for the project. There are many other salient features of legislators' credit claiming messages that vary across the messages that may affect the credit legislators receive. For example, the type of expenditure may affect the credit constituents allocate. This is particularly true because constituents are easily able to identify the type of expenditure and may have sufficient context to know whether they approve or disapprove of the expenditure. Who announces the spending may also affect the credit constituents allocate to legislators. Constituents, for example, may be more willing to internalize messages from copartisan legislators.[8] And legislators often announce spending together, which may affect how constituents allocate credit.[9]

Rather than run several experiments that vary each of the features individually, for this study we designed an experiment that simultaneously varies many features of the message. In doing so, we can isolate the main effects of interest and determine the information constituents use to allocate credit. We also vary legislators' characteristics, to see how who is announcing an expenditure affects how constituents allocate credit. To do this, our design again makes use of a hypothetical legislator whose name has been redacted.

Using the redacted legislator, we varied five pieces of information about the credit claiming message: the recipient of the expenditure, the amount of money secured, the stage in the appropriations process, the legislator's partisanship, and who the legislator announced the expenditure with. Specifically, we used the template in Table 5.5 to construct a message that randomly selects from the following components to construct a coherent credit claiming message:

- Recipient (6): Planned Parenthood, local parks, local gun range, a fire department, a police station, or local roads
- Money (2): $50 Thousand or $20 Million
- Stage (3) : will request, requested, or secured
- Party (2): Democrat, Republican
- Collaboration (3): alone, with a Senate Democrat, with a Senate Republican

We compared the effect of the credit claiming message to a control condition, where the fictitious legislator sends an advertising message— announcing a constituent who won a congressional art contest. We examined the effect of legislators' credit claiming efforts on constituents' propensity to *approve* of the representative's performance in office. Specifically, we ask our participants if they "approve or disapprove" of the way the fictitious representative "is performing (his/her) job in Congress." We use the dichotomous response to examine how the content of a legislator's credit claiming messages affects constituent credit allocation.

To administer the study we recruited 1,074 participants using Amazon.com's Mechanical Turk service, restricting our focus to workers in the United States. After respondents were assigned to a treatment and it was administered, they completed a brief survey that asked respondents

[8] Zaller (1992).
[9] Shepsle et al. (2009); Chen (2010).

TABLE 5.5
Examining the Effects of Credit Claiming Statements on Constituent Credit Allocation.

Advertising Condition

Headline: Representative (redacted) announces annual Congressional district art competition winner
Body: Representative (redacted) announced that 17-year old Sara Fischer won 1st place in the annual Congressional district art competition. Sara's winning art, "Medals" was created using colored pencils. Rep. (redacted) said Sara's artwork will be displayed in the U.S. Capitol with other winning entries from districts nationwide.

Credit Claiming Condition

Headline: Representative (redacted) |stageTitle |moneyTitle |typeTitle
Body: Representative (redacted), |partyMain, |alongMain |stageMain |moneyMain |typeMain.
Rep. (redacted) said "This money |stageQuote typeQuote"

|**stageTitle:**[will request/requested/secured]

|**moneyTitle:**[$50 Thousand/$20 Million]

|**typeTitle** : [to purchase safety equipment for local firefighters/to purchase safety equipment for local police/to repave local roads, to beautify local parks/for medical equipment at the local planned parenthood/to help build a state of the art gun range]
|**partyMain** : [Democrat/Republican]
|**alongMain** : [(No text)/and Senator (redacted), a Democrat/ and Senator (redacted), a Republican]
|**stageMain** : [will request/requested/secured]
|**moneyMain:** [$50 Thousand/ $20 Million]
|**typeMain:** [to purchase safety equipment for local firefighters/to purchase safety equipment for local police/to repave local roads, to beautify local parks/for medical equipment at the local Planned Parenthood/to help build a state of the art gun range]
|**stageQuote** : [would help/would help/will help]
|**typeQuote:** [our brave firefighters stay safe as they protect our businesses and homes/our brave police officers stay safe as they protect our property from criminals/keep our roads in safe and working condition, ensuring that our local economy will continue to grow/create parks that add value to the community and provide our children a safe place to play/provide state of the art care for women in our community"/"provide local residents and local, state, and national law enforcement officials a place to sharpen their skills"]

Summary of Conditions
Recipient: Planned Parenthood, Parks, Gun Range, Fire Department, Police, Roads
Money: $ 50 Thousand, $20 Million
Stage : Will Requested, Requested, Secured
Collaboration: Alone, a Senate Democrat, a Senate Republican
Party: Democrat, Republican

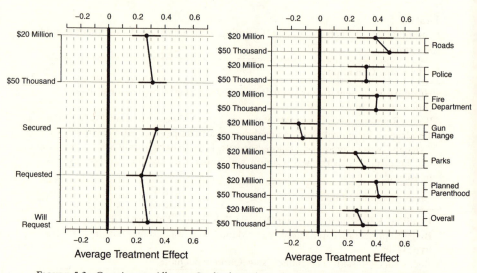

FIGURE 5.3. Constituents Allocate Credit throughout the Appropriations Process and Are Unresponsive to Money.
This figure shows that this study replicates our findings from the previous two studies. Constituents allocate credit for spending throughout the appropriations process and struggle to reward legislators for more money delivered to the district.

about their evaluation of the legislator and then asked about their political preferences. This survey included each respondent's partisan identification and political ideology—which we will use to assess the response to the type of expenditure and who announces the credit claiming activity.

Figure 5.3 shows that this experiment replicates findings from the previous two studies: respondents allocate credit for spending throughout the appropriations process and are largely unresponsive to the amount of money claimed for the project. The left-hand plot shows the marginal effects for the *stage* and *money* conditions: the increase each condition causes over the control condition, averaging over the other conditions. The points are estimates for the marginal effects and the horizontal lines are 95 percent confidence intervals. The lines connecting the points indicate how the effects vary across the conditions.

The bottom three lines show that legislators can claim credit for spending throughout the appropriations process. Stating an intention to request an expenditure increases approval ratings 28.5 percentage points (95 percent confidence interval, [0.18, 0.39]), a slightly larger increase than requesting an expenditure causes (95 percent confidence interval, [0.14, 0.34]). And again, legislators receive a slightly larger increase when they claim credit for securing money for their district—a 34.4-percentage point increase in approval rating (95 percent confidence interval, [0.25, 0.44]).

Constituents also reward legislators similarly for claiming credit for large and small expenditures. Claiming credit for a $50 thousand project causes a 31.4-percentage point increase in approval rating (95 percent confidence interval, [0.22, 0.41]), a slightly larger increase than claiming credit for a $20-million project, which causes a 26.9-percentage point increase in approval ratings (95 percent confidence interval, [0.17, 0.37]). While this finding shows that constituents are unresponsive to the dollar amount claimed, a concern that we raised in the second study is that the effect of money on credit allocation is conditional on the type of project. To test this alternative explanation, the right-hand plot in Figure 5.3 shows the effect of claiming credit for $50 thousand and $20 million (labeled on the left-hand axis) for the six different types of projects and the overall relationship (right-hand axis). While there are differences across the types of projects—a point we explore in a moment—there are few differences in credit allocated for different levels of spending for the same project. It would appear, then, that there is little evidence that constituents are responsive to the dollar amounts claimed.

While constituents have a limited response to money, they are more responsive to information they can easily extract and evaluate from the messages: the recipient of the expenditure and who is claiming credit for the project. To assess how constituents respond to the recipient of the expenditure (or type of expenditure), we condition on political ideology, because we expect liberals and conservatives to have very different reactions to legislators claiming credit for Planned Parenthood and gun range projects. Liberal elites and Democrats tend to vigorously defend Planned Parenthood, providing cues to like-minded citizens that the organization provides valuable services. In contrast, conservatives and Republicans oppose Planned Parenthood, often working to strip the organization of money.[10] Very different cues are available about gun ranges and guns more generally. Many Democrats—particularly liberal-urban Democrats—have argued for increased gun regulation. Republicans and conservatives have argued vigorously for constitutional protection of guns and the party has aligned closely with the NRA to rebut attempts to regulate guns as violations of the Second Amendment.

If constituents use information about the type of expenditure when allocating credit, we expect that the marginal effect of claiming credit for the projects will depend on the respondent's ideology. To test this expectation, we estimate conditional marginal treatment effects for the credit claiming statements, conditional on the

[10] For example, see Kasperowicz 2013.

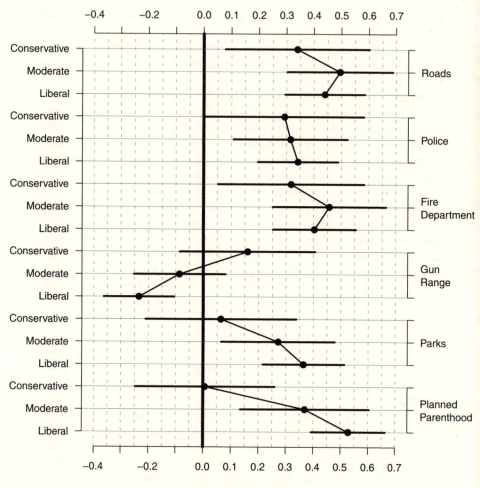

FIGURE 5.4. Constituents Are Responsive to the Type of Project Allocated.
This figure shows that constituents are highly responsive to the type of project legislators claim credit for securing. Liberals reward legislators for claiming credit for projects that help Planned Parenthood, while punishing legislators who claim credit for a gun range. Conservatives, in contrast, are unresponsive to legislators who claim credit for Planned Parenthood, but reward legislators who claim credit for a gun range.

respondent's ideology. Figure 5.4 shows the conditional marginal treatment effect for conservative, moderate, and liberal constituents (left-hand axis) for each of the six types of funding (right-hand axis).

The variation in Figure 5.4 shows constituents are responsive to the type of project in the credit claiming messages. Consider the response to money for Planned Parenthood. Liberals have a strong and positive response to funding for Planned Parenthood: claiming credit for money directed towards Planned Parenthood increases the fictitious legislator's approval rating 52.8 percentage points among liberals (95 percent confidence interval, [0.40, 0.66]). In fact, Planned Parenthood causes the largest increase in approval rating for liberal respondents.

Conservative respondents, however, are essentially unresponsive to a legislator's claiming credit for Planned Parenthood—and much less responsive to spending on Planned Parenthood than liberals. Conservative respondents increase their approval rating of the legislator only 0.5 percentage points over the control condition, an increase that is substantively small and statistically indistinguishable from zero (95 percent confidence interval, [−0.27, 0.28]). Planned Parenthood causes the smallest change in legislator approval rating among conservatives. Given the low approval rate for the representative in the control condition— about 30%—this result is indicative of conservative respondents who are displeased with the representative.

Claiming credit for gun ranges has a strikingly different effect on legislators' approval ratings. Liberal respondents punish legislators: claiming credit for money to be spent on a gun range causes a 23.4-percentage point decrease in legislators' approval rating among liberals (95 percent confidence interval, [−0.35, −0.12]). Conservative constituents, however, reward legislators when they claim credit for spending allocated to gun ranges. Claiming credit for a gun range causes a 16-percentage point increase in approval rating among conservatives (95 percent confidence interval, [−0.15, 0.47]), a significantly more positive response than the moderate or liberal response to the gun range—though we fail to reject the null that the increase in approval among conservative respondents is different than zero.

On other expenditures there is more agreement across ideological types. Liberals, conservatives, and moderates all reward legislators for claiming credit for money directed to fire departments, police departments, and road projects. And moderates and liberals reward legislators for parks in the district.[11]

Constituents also condition on who is announcing an expenditure when deciding how to allocate credit. The legislator's (or legislators') party is one of the strongest pieces of information. A burgeoning literature shows that constituents tend to have an automatic response to

---

[11] There is similar heterogeneity if we condition on partisan identification, instead of ideology. The heterogeneity is even more pronounced in the expected direction if we condition on both ideology and partisanship, which we do using a new model to estimate heterogeneous treatment effects. See Grimmer, Messing, and Westwood (2013).

partisan information, with a more favorable orientation to copartisans and a more negative orientation to opposing partisans.[12] Because we randomly assign our fictitious legislator's party—as well as any collaborator's party—we are able to assess how constituents use party labels in their credit allocation.

Figure 5.5 shows that constituents incorporate information about a legislator's partisanship. The bottom two lines show that partisans are more responsive to credit claiming messages from their copartisans. A credit claiming message from an opposing partisan causes a 22.6-percentage point boost in approval rating (95 percent confidence interval, [0.08, 0.37]), while a credit claiming message from a copartisan causes a 34.2-percentage point increase (95 percent confidence interval, [0.20, 0.48]): an 11.6-percentage point difference in effect. Partisans also rewarded copartisans more when legislators collaborated on announcing a new expenditure. If the representative and senator who announce the grant are from different parties than the respondent, the credit claiming effort causes a 25-percentage point increase in the representative's approval rating (95 percent confidence interval, [0.13, 0.37]). But if the representative and senator are from the same party as the respondent, the credit claiming message causes a 37.1-percentage point increase in the representative's approval rating (95 percent confidence interval, [0.24, 0.50]).[13]

Constituents, then, are responsive to qualitative information about the expenditures that legislators claim credit for securing. Constituents evaluate characteristics of the expenditure—who will receive the money—and characteristics of the legislators who announce the expenditure. This pattern creates incentives for legislators to care more about the type of expenditure they claim credit for securing than the amount secured. The next section provides one more examination of what constituents reward, demonstrating that constituents are responsive to increases in the number of credit claiming messages legislators send.[14]

---

[12] Iyengar and Westwood (2013).

[13] While we avoid focusing on statistical significance and the rather blunt measure of rejecting null hypotheses, we note that both effects of copartisans are not significant if we set a rejection threshold of 0.05. The p-values associated with a null hypothesis test of no difference between the effect sizes is 0.091 and 0.0973 respectively.

[14] One might interpret this result as contradicting our argument as to why marginal legislators allocate more effort to credit claiming. This experimental result, however, does not contradict argument, which is about the relative efficiency of claiming credit for spending or articulating positions. Marginal legislators risk alienating opposing partisans if they articulate positions, while aligned legislators risk not building greater support with copartisans if they focus on credit claiming.

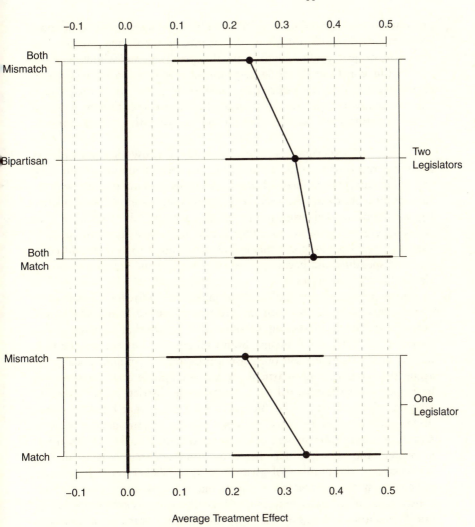

FIGURE 5.5. Constituents Allocate Credit to Opposing Partisans, but Reward Copartisans More.
Partisans differ in the credit they allocate to legislators. Opposing partisans reward legislators for spending, copartisans are more responsive to credit claiming messages.

5.4 STUDY 4: FREQUENT MESSAGES CULTIVATE MORE SUPPORT THAN LARGE EXPENDITURES

Through a series of studies, we have shown how constituents allocate credit in response to legislators' credit claiming messages. We have demonstrated that constituents appear to reward legislators for reporting an action, even if spending is small or unlikely to happen for some time. Constituents do condition their evaluations on qualitative information about the project, evaluating the type of expenditure and who is claiming credit. But constituents are largely unresponsive to where a potential expenditure is in the appropriations process or to the size of the project. This response occurs, we have argued, because constituents tend to seize on information easily available when evaluating credit claiming messages.

In the final experiment of this chapter, we show that constituents are more responsive to increases in the number of messages sent than the dollar amount claimed. Multiple messages provide the opportunity for constituents to update repeatedly their impression of how effective legislators are at delivering money to the district.[15] But we show that claiming credit for more spending across messages does not increase support, both because constituents lack the context to evaluate different levels of spending and because constituents forget the amount of money claimed at different rates.

The expectation that multiple messages will cultivate support with constituents is grounded both in a robust literature in marketing and political science. In marketing, scholars have shown that repeated advertisements are effective at raising brand salience and increasing the likelihood that consumers will purchase a product.[16] In political science,[17] argue that constituents—particularly knowledgeable constituents—will be responsive to the award of a grant in the district, rather than the amount allocated. Stein and Bickers (1994) argue that legislators may prefer several small projects, because the act of announcing may be more important than the size of the expenditure. Yet, the empirical test in Bickers and Stein[18] differs from the argument that constituents are responsive to the number of awards. Instead, Bickers and Stein[19] test the change in the proportion of grants that are new in the district. That constituents are responsive to the increase in this ratio is still interesting, but if constituents struggle to identify the amount awarded for a project, it stands to reason they will also struggle to distinguish new spending from old spending. It remains to be demonstrated that constituents are more responsive to the number of credit claiming statements—even if the statements are not explicitly about a new project—rather than the amount claimed.

---

[15] Lodge, McGraw, and Stroh (1989).

[16] Berlyne (1970); Kirmani (1997); Campbell and Keller (2003).

[17] Stein and Bickers (1994).

[18] Stein and Bickers (1994).

[19] Stein and Bickers (1994).

Using standard experimental tools to test whether constituents are more responsive to the number of messages sent than the amount claimed, though, is difficult. Varying the number of messages sent in a single survey would be challenging to make realistic and to maintain respondents' attention. Delivering several credit claiming messages of standard length in one experiment may cause our respondents to disengage with our survey or begin satisficing, which would make measurement of the effects of multiple messages difficult. And most survey companies prevent researchers like us from contacting respondents on subsequent days, or make the repeated contact in a panel study extremely costly.

Given the limitations of surveys, we conducted this study in a different and perhaps more ecologically valid setting—sending messages by email.[20] Email as a method of delivery has a number of distinct features that complement the strengths of our previous survey experiments. Delivering treatments via email ensured that we could regularly contact our participants without exorbitant costs. Using emails also allowed us to separate the delivery of our treatment from the measurement of the effect. This design enabled us to measure more than ephemeral, short lived effects. Also the delivery of our treatment through emails ensured that our treatments had ecological validity that is difficult to replicate in our survey experiment. Representatives deliver e-newsletters to constituents in this format and the e-newsletters often contain credit claiming statements.

Using emails to deliver the treatment, we exploit an experimental design that allows us to compare the effect of increasing the dollar amount claimed to the effect of increasing the number of credit claiming messages sent. To do this, we use a 2×2 experimental design–which we summarize in Table 5.6. The first condition varies the *number* of messages sent. Subjects assigned to the *five message* condition received emails for five consecutive days, while subjects assigned to the *single message* condition received a single email. The second condition varied the amount claimed across the emails. Subjects assigned to the *large award* condition received emails claiming credit for *one hundred times* the amount of the corresponding *small award* condition with the same frequency. Table 5.7 provides an example of this manipulation, before it was rendered and sent in an email. Again, we use information about the subject's legislator to customize the announcement to create the appearance that it is from the legislator. Depending on the condition, we substitute the dollar amount at each instance of |amount.

We used Amazon.com's Mechanical Turk to recruit a new group of 1,001 participants for the study. To limit demand effects and to enhance

---

[20] Nickerson (2007).

TABLE 5.6
Total Amount Claimed across Experiment Conditions.

	Small Award	Large Award
Single Message	$15,000	$1,500,000
Five Messages	Day 1: $15,000 Day 2: $19,000 Day 3: $85,000 Day 4: $21,000 Day 5: $36,000 Total: $176,000	Day 1: $1,500,000 Day 2: $1,900,000 Day 3: $8,500,000 Day 4: $2,100,000 Day 5: $3,600,000 Total: $17,600,000

TABLE 5.7
Example Credit Claiming Manipulation.

Headline: Representative |lastName (|party, |state-|district) Brings Local Fire Departments |amount for Firefighter Safety

Full text: A total of |amount in grants for operations and safety programs was awarded to local fire departments from the Department of Homeland Security, Rep. |lastName announced.

|firstName |lastName (|party, |state-|district) announced the grants today. Specifically, the grant will be used to improve training, equipment, and make modifications to fire stations and facilities in local fire departments.

"This is great news for our local community," said Representative |lastName. "With these funds, our local fire departments will continue to train and operate with the latest in firefighter technology."

Key

|lastName: The representative's last name
|firstName: The representative's first name
|party: The representative's party
|state: The representative's state
|district: The representative's district
|amount : The dollar amount claimed

the realism of our study, we created a cover story for our Mechanical Turk solicitation. We told the participants that we were researchers at Stanford University working on an application to facilitate connections between legislators and constituents. To ensure comparability across conditions, we followed a similar timeline on the delivery of the pre- and post-treatment surveys. The day after enrolling, subjects began receiving emails with the corresponding treatments. The day after the final email was sent, subjects received an invitation to complete the post-experiment survey. This ensured that our findings would not be the result of effects decaying after subjects participated in our study.

TABLE 5.8
Number of Messages Dominates the Amount Claimed.

Condition	Identify Name	Passing District Legislation
Five Messages $17.6 Million	0.96 [0.92,0.99]	4.86 [4.67,5.06]
Single Message $1.5 Million	0.92 [0.89,0.95]	4.43 [4.25,4.6]
Five Messages $176,000	0.95 [0.91,0.98]	4.72 [4.53,4.92]
Single Message $15,000	0.90 [0.87,0.93]	4.24 [4.06,4.42]

This table shows that subjects received our email messages and that increasing the number of messages bolstered one measure of a legislator's effectiveness more than increasing the amount claimed. The four conditions are placed along the rows and each entry is the corresponding condition's average for the dependent variable, with a 95 percent confidence interval beneath. The first column shows that there is a high level of recognition across our conditions, evidence that subjects received our emails. The second column shows that small award, high frequency subjects evaluated their legislator as more effective at passing legislation for the district, than the large award, low frequency condition.

Given the use of emails to deliver the credit claiming messages, one concern is that our messages would be trapped in email spam filters. The construction of the emails minimized this possibility, but we use a manipulation check to demonstrate that participants received our messages, while also replicating the increase in name recognition for participants in the credit claiming condition that we identified in Chapter 4. The first column in Table 5.8 shows the proportion of subjects in each condition who are able to identify correctly their representative in a multiple choice test. The top entry in each row is the proportion of subjects assigned to each condition who correctly identified their representative and the 95 percent confidence interval is the bottom entry in each row. The first column of Table 5.8 shows that, across the four conditions, there is an extremely high level of recognition. And as expected intuitively, there is a slight increase among the high frequency conditions: 95.2% of the subjects assigned to the high frequency condition could correctly identify their representative, a 4.4-percentage point increase over the low frequency condition (95% confidence interval, [0.01, 0.08]).

Figure 5.6 shows that increasing the number of messages cultivates more support than increasing the amount claimed. Consider the left-hand plot, which shows participants' rating of their representative's effectiveness at delivering money to the district, recorded on the same seven-point scale we use in previous sections. Each dot represents

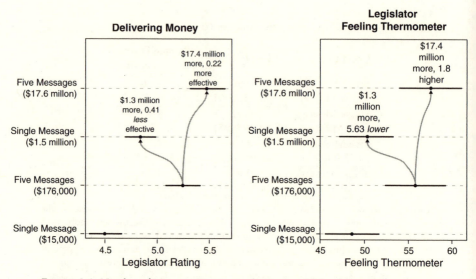

FIGURE 5.6. Number of Messages Dominates the Amount Claimed.
This figure shows that multiple messages cultivate more support than increasing the amount claimed. The left-hand plot presents subjects' evaluations of their legislator's effectiveness at delivering money to the district. The points are the average evaluations and the lines are 95-percent confidence intervals. Even though there is $1.3 million more announced in the large award, single message condition (second line), subjects evaluated their representative as less effective at delivering money than the small award, five message condition (third line). And the large increase in money claimed in the large award, five message condition (top line) does not result in substantially higher evaluations. The right-hand plot shows a similar effect of more messages on feeling thermometer evaluations—that is, the number of messages dominates the amount claimed. "How Words and Money Cultivate a Personal Vote: The Effect of Legislator Credit Claiming on Constituent Credit Allocation," by Justin Grimmer, Solomon Messing, and Sean J. Westwood, *American Political Science Review*, Volume 106, Issue 04 (November 2012), pp. 703–719. Copyright © 2012 American Political Science Association. Reprinted with the permission of Cambridge University Press.

legislators' average effectiveness ratings for each condition and the lines are 95 percent confidence intervals.

The results replicate our findings from our previous studies: small increases in the amount of money claimed do cause an increase in support for representatives. Participants in the single message, large award condition—where $1.5 million was claimed—rated their representative 0.33 units higher than participants in the single message, small award condition (95 percent confidence interval, [0.12, 0.55]).

The increase in support caused by numerous credit claiming messages, however, dwarfs the increase that occurs after claiming credit for more money. Subjects assigned to the small award, five message condition evaluated their representative as 0.41 units more effective at delivering funds than the large award, single message condition (95% confidence interval, [0.18, 0.64]). This result is particularly surprising given the discrepancy in the amount claimed: subjects assigned to the small award, five message condition received messages claiming credit for about *one-tenth* of the funds as subjects in the large award, single message condition. The top estimate shows that subjects assigned to the large award, five message condition had the highest evaluation of their representative's effectiveness, an increase of 0.22 units over the small award, five message condition (95% confidence interval, [−0.01, 0.44]). This increase, however, is small relative to the increase in funds claimed in the large award, five message condition. In this condition, subjects received messages from legislators claiming credit for one hundred times the money as the amount claimed in the small award, five message condition.

This pattern—constituents responding more to the number of actions rather than the amount claimed—was replicated when participants were asked to assess their representative's effectiveness at passing legislation that benefits the district. The right-hand column in Table 5.8 shows that small award, five message subjects evaluated their representative's legislative effectiveness substantially higher than subjects assigned to the large award, low frequency condition (0.30-unit increase, 95% confidence interval, [0.03, 0.56]). And there fails to be a substantial increase in evaluations associated with more money. Subjects assigned to the large award, five message condition evaluated their representative as more effective than the small award, five message subjects–a 0.14-unit increase–though the difference is not statistically significant at standard levels (95% confidence interval, [−0.14, 0.42]).

The increase in perceived effectiveness is coupled with a similar increase in overall support. The right-hand plot in Figure 5.6 shows that increasing the number of credit claiming statements causes large increases in support for the legislator. Each point represents the average feeling thermometer evaluation for the subjects assigned to each of the four conditions and the lines are 95 percent confidence intervals. In both the single- and five-message conditions, we see that the amount of money claimed in the press releases fails to substantially or significantly increase the subjects' evaluations of their legislator—even though the large award conditions contained messages claiming credit for substantially more funds. Subjects assigned to the large award, single message condition had only a 1.6-unit higher evaluation of their representative over the small award, single message condition—a difference that is not significant at standard levels (95% confidence interval, [−2.75, 5.98]). Likewise, subjects in the large award, five message condition evaluated their representative 1.8 units higher than the small award, five message condition, but again the difference is not significant at standard levels (95% confidence interval, [−3.07, 6.70]).

Thus, the money claimed had little effect on the evaluation of legislators, but the number of messages mattered substantially. Subjects assigned to the small award, five message condition evaluated their representative 5.63 units higher than those in the large award, single message condition (95% confidence interval, [1.07, 10.17]). Spreading a relatively small amount of money over several messages is more effective at building support than claiming credit for one large expenditure. To see how much more effective frequent messages are than claiming credit for large amounts of money, we compare how much each dollar claimed increased constituents' evaluations of their legislators, relative to the baseline condition of the small award, low frequency condition. To measure this return, we divided the increase in average feeling thermometer rating by the increase in the amount of funds claimed, measured in units of $10,000. This simple calculation reveals that frequently claiming credit for small amounts of money is a much more efficient way to cultivate support among constituents than increasing the total amount claimed. The return on the large award and five-message condition was an increase in average feeling thermometer ratings of only 0.005 units per $10,000 claimed. The return for the small award, five message condition was much larger. For every $10,000 claimed in the small award, high frequency condition, the average feeling thermometer rating increased 0.45 units—a per-dollar increase in support 90 times bigger than that found for the large award, high frequency condition.

Constituents, then, are much more responsive to the reported actions than the amount claimed. There are at least two salient psychological mechanisms to explain the prominent response to actions. One explanation is that constituents lack the ability to tally expenditures across the messages. As we argue in Chapter 2, numerical information is often much more difficult for constituents to use in intuitive evaluations. This is particularly true over repeated messages, which require constituents not only to identify the amount claimed, but aggregate the amounts claimed over the messages. A second explanation is that constituents are unable to contextualize expenditures. Constituents rarely have the information sufficient to know how different levels of spending will matter for local projects. If this is true, then even if constituents are able to identify differences in the expenditures, we should expect that they will struggle to incorporate those differences into their quickly formed evaluations.

At the end of the post-experiment survey for this study we asked our participants a final question that allowed us to assess the extent to which these two mechanisms induce the lack of response to credit claiming messages. After all other relevant questions were asked and

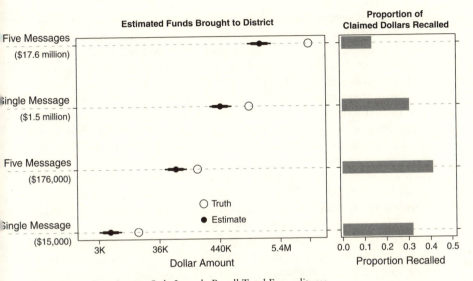

FIGURE 5.7. Constituents Only Loosely Recall Total Expenditures.
This figure shows the average amount of money participants recall their representative as claiming credit for delivering (solid points) and the actual amounts delivered (open points), presented against a log scale. We present the exponentiated axis for ease of interpretation. Experiment participants were able to recover the correct rank order of the amount delivered. But across conditions we see that the participants underestimate the amount delivered to the district. And the errors increase as the amount of money delivered increases, providing one explanation for why constituents fail to be responsive to the increased amount of money delivered.

answered, we asked our participants to recall how much money their representative claimed in the emails they were sent. To make sure that our Mechanical Turk subjects did not cheat, we instructed them not to look at the previous emails and assured them that their compensation would not depend on the answer to this question.

Figure 5.7 shows that both mechanisms help explain why constituents are largely unresponsive to the amount claimed. The left-hand figure presents the average amount reported across the four conditions (the solid black points) and the true amounts claimed (open circles). To compactly display the amounts on a single plot, the horizontal axis is on a logarithmic scale, but we label values on the actual dollar scale for ease of interpretation.

The left-hand plot in Figure 5.7 shows that constituents recall broad differences in how much representatives claim credit for in the emails. When recalling the amount that their representative claimed credit for securing, participant responses correctly ranked the total amounts from the smallest amount claimed (the small award, single message condition) to the largest amount claimed (the large award, five message condition). And the differences across the conditions were often substantial. For example, participants in the large award, five message condition recalled their representative claiming credit for 32 times as much money as participants in the small award, five message condition.

Constituents approximately identify and recall broad differences in how much money legislators deliver to the district. That the differences in expenditure do not subsequently affect differences in evaluations across constituents is evidence that constituents are unable to contextualize the amount claimed and include the differences in their assessments of their representative. Even when constituents are able to approximately recall the information in a credit claiming statement, they struggle to translate the quantitative information about different levels of spending into different levels of support for legislators. This result is consistent with constituents who are not experts on local particularistic projects and therefore are unsure what different levels of spending actually imply for their district. Given this lack of context, it is much easier for constituents to evaluate that a project may potentially come and who receives the money than to reward legislators for the size of the expenditure.

While the left-hand plot in Figure 5.7 shows that participants are able to recall broad differences in the amount legislators claim credit for directing to the district, systematic errors are still made in participants' tallies. In each condition, participants underestimate the amount of money their representative claimed credit for securing. And the errors are larger when legislators claim credit for more money—both in magnitude and in share of the total amount delivered. To demonstrate the magnitude of the errors, the right-hand plot in Figure 5.7 presents the ratio of the funds our participants recall as having been claimed to the actual funds claimed (in total). Participants in the small award/single message condition—the bottom line of the plot—underestimated the amount claimed by $10,282—estimating that legislators claimed credit for only 31% of the total money announced. The numerous announcement of small awards appears to increase slightly the accuracy of assessments. Participants in the small award, five message condition were the most accurate across all four conditions, estimating that their legislators claimed credit for 41% of the total announced amount. The accuracy of the estimates suffered substantially when large amounts of money were announced numerous times. Participants in the large award, five message condition—the top line—had an extremely poor estimate of the total amount claimed. Participants in this condition underestimated the total amount claimed by $15.2 million—estimating their legislator claimed credit for only 13.5% of the total funds actually claimed.

Constituents, then, not only struggled to contextualize and evaluate the amount of money claimed. They also systematically underestimated the amount legislators claimed to direct to the district, because they struggled to tally the amount delivered. The variance in the percentage of funds recalled in the right-hand plot of Figure 5.7 also rules out an alternative and nonpsychological mechanism to explain the effectiveness of sending several messages. It may be that sending multiple messages may increase the probability that a participant actually reads the credit claiming statement, or that multiple messages make it more likely that our participants receive the treatment. But if the differences were explained by probability of reading an email, then we would expect there to be equal rates of recall across the conditions. And yet, the right-hand plot in Figure 5.7 shows substantial differences across conditions. Therefore, multiple messages do more than simply raise the probability that a constituents receives a message.

Our experimental results show that legislators can regularly claim credit for relatively small amounts of money to build an impression of influence over spending. In the next section, we show that our experimental results correspond with the credit legislators actually received when they claimed credit for spending.

5.5 CREDIT CLAIMING AND THE CULTIVATION OF SUPPORT OUTSIDE OF EXPERIMENTS

Our experiments have provided precise estimates of how constituents respond to legislators' credit claiming messages. And legislators appear to know, at least intuitively, that they can receive credit for relatively small allocations and for credit throughout the expenditure process. But we may remain concerned that the credit allocation we observe in our experiments differs from how constituents actually allocate credit. In this section, we show that there is a relationship between legislators' credit claiming efforts and constituents' evaluations. This is evidence that the credit claiming process that we describe in press releases and experiments actually matters for representation.

To demonstrate the relationship between legislators' credit claiming efforts and constituents' evaluations we combine our measures of representatives' credit claiming rates in Chapter 3 with a survey of constituents that assesses their existing attitudes towards their representative without an experimental manipulation. We collected this new survey using a Survey Sample International (SSI) sample, census matched to correspond to the United States. To assess the external validity of our interventions, we replicate the questions we asked in our survey experiments in this

TABLE 5.9
The Observational Effect of Legislator Credit Claiming.

	Effective Delivering Money	Feeling Thermometer
Overall	0.13	2.1
	[0.00, 0.25]	[0.07, 4.20]
Copartisans	0.06	1.68
	[−0.1, 0.22]	[−1.02, 4.34]
Opposing	0.22	2.71
Partisans	[0.03, 0.41]	[−0.47, 5.91]

new survey. We ask constituents to evaluate how effective their legislator is at delivering federal money to the district and to provide an overall assessment of their representative.[21] We then regress the responses to this question on legislators' credit claiming rates.

While this design allowed us to assess actual behavior from legislators with the response of their constituents, it came at the cost of experimental control over the credit claiming messages. We attempt to minimize the potential bias in our estimates by conditioning on characteristics of constituents that might affect how they evaluate their representative. While this design includes constituents' socioeconomic status, whether they are from the same party as the representative, and constituent ideology. To account for several of respondents sharing the same representative we estimated a multilevel model that allowed the intercept to vary across legislators. Of course, this design does not completely eliminate potential bias in the estimate of the effect of legislator credit claiming on constituent evaluations, but it does provide a robust model for assessing the covariance between credit claiming and evaluations.

The left-hand column in Table 5.9 shows the relationship between representatives' credit claiming rates and constituents' evaluations of their effectiveness at delivering federal money to the district. The top row in the plot shows the overall relationship between legislators' credit claiming efforts and constituents' evaluations, revealing that legislators who engage in more credit claiming are viewed as more effective at delivering money to their district. The increase in credit claiming leads to a predicted increase in effectiveness of 0.13 points—about 10% of the size associated with the increase in effectiveness from having a copartisan as a representative (95 percent confidence interval, [0.00, 0.25]). The next two rows in the left-hand column show that this increase is particularly large for opposing partisans: legislators' credit claiming

---

[21] This survey contained only partisans—that is, constituents who identified with either the Republican or Democratic Party.

rates appear to be best at cultivating an impression of influence among those who would otherwise not want to vote for the legislator. A 15-percentage point increase in credit claiming rate leads to a predicted increase of effectiveness of 0.22 points.

Legislators' credit claiming efforts also appear to affect their overall evaluations with constituents. The right-hand column in Table 5.9 shows that this credit claiming is effective: legislators with higher credit claiming rates have higher evaluations among constituents. The top row shows that the same 15-percentage point increase in a legislator's credit claiming rate increases a feeling thermometer evaluation 2.1 points (95 percent confidence interval, [0.1, 4.2]). Again, this increase in strongest among opposing partisans, with the increase in credit claiming rate associated with an increase of 2.7 points, while associaed with only a 1.7-point increase among copartisans.

This observational evidence shows that legislators' credit claiming rates appear to affect constituent evaluations—both of how effective legislators are at delivering money to the district and overall evaluations of the legislator. Legislators who engage in higher rates of credit claiming are evaluated as more effective at delivering money to their district and have a higher overall evaluation. This result demonstrates that the credit claiming process that we examine in this chapter is not an artifact of our experimental setup—it actually matters for the politics of representation. This finding does not, however, imply that all legislators should just claim credit for spending in all their press releases. This implication does not follow, in part, because the credit allocated depends on whom legislators represent. Legislators' credit claiming is most effective at cultivating support with opposing partisans. This helps explain why legislators who are marginal allocate more effort to credit claiming. The observed credit claiming rates are also part of a broader rhetorical strategy for legislators.[22] Even marginal legislators must appeal to their partisan base when presenting their work, limiting the potential to abandon completely nonparticularistic issues.

5.6 CONCLUSION: REPRESENTATION AND REFORM WITH INTUITIVE CONSTITUENTS

We have shown how constituents allocate credit in response to legislators' credit claiming messages. Constituents reward legislators for the report of an action and evaluate the type of expenditure, but have

---

[22] Grimmer (2013).

a limited response to the dollar amount legislators claim credit for directing money to the district. Legislators appear responsive to this type of credit allocation, claiming credit for expenditures throughout the appropriations process and for relatively small amounts of money. And we have shown that our results are, at least in part, externally valid. Legislators who claim credit for spending at a higher rate are viewed as more effective at delivering money to their district and have a higher overall evaluation.

How constituents allocate credit in response to credit claiming messages complicates their task of holding legislators accountable for spending in the district. But this complication need not make it harder to hold legislators accountable, nor need it harm representation. Indeed, the ways constituents allocate credit to legislators may lead to outcomes that constituents prefer over outcomes that may occur if they rewarded legislators based on the size of actual expenditures as they occur in the district.

Rather than exercising direct control over legislators, the credit claiming, credit allocation process enables constituents to exercise indirect control over their representatives. And this interaction may yield positive outcomes for constituents. When constituents reward legislators throughout the appropriations process, they may incentivize legislators to produce greater spending for the district. This is a basic insight from principal-agent models of accountability.[23] Securing expenditures for a district often requires legislators to expend effort, but even if legislators work dutifully to direct funds to the district some projects may fail. For example, spending bills may be revised before passage, removing funds that a legislator earmarked for a district. Or executive agencies may redirect earmarked funds or projects may be revised, negating the impact of the spending.[24] This uncertainty about spending can dampen legislative effort to direct funds to the district. If legislators only receive credit for expenditures that actually occur, then effort spent on projects that do not yield spending in the district is wasted. The risk that that effort may be wasted may push legislators into other activities. But rewarding the act of requesting, in addition to securing, the expenditure makes pursuing spending more attractive to legislators. It ensures that legislators can receive immediate benefits from requesting the expenditure, in addition to the benefits from delivering the money. This additional reward may encourage legislators to expend more effort in the appropriations process, directing more money to the district.

---

[23] Bolton and Dewatripont (2005); Ashworth (2012).
[24] Frisch and Kelly (2011).

Constituents' responsiveness to the type of expenditure and unresponsiveness to the size of the project may dampen incentives that lead to budget deficits. A persistent concern in models of distributive politics in legislatures is that representatives' electoral incentives cause overspending. Single-member districts, such as House districts, concentrate the benefits of particularistic spending in a single district and spread the costs across all districts. The diffused cost causes legislators to spend more on their individual districts than they would if serving a national constituency, resulting in overspending.[25] But when constituents reward legislators for the type of expenditure or the number of messages, they blunt the mechanism that drives overspending. If constituents reward the type of expenditure and the number of messages, then legislators can cultivate support with many smaller projects. This behavior eliminates the need for excessive spending in the district. So, by evaluating the type of expenditure and the number of projects, constituents create incentives to align the optimal political allocations with the optimal economic allocations.

The credit claiming, credit allocation process also creates incentives for legislators to secure and claim credit for projects that are responsive to constituents unstated spending priorities. Of course, legislators may secure money for an unpopular recipient and simply neglect to announce that expenditure to constituents. But the process that we document in this chapter shows that there are additional costs to delivering unpopular spending to the district. Not only will legislators have to expend effort in the institution to deliver money to the recipient. They will also pay an electoral opportunity cost: every project directed to unpopular recipients is one less project that could be used for claiming credit with constituents and building popular support. This downside creates incentives to create expenditures for popular projects in the district.

Yet there are potential risks to accountability as well. If legislators receive credit for merely requesting expenditures and not for actual expenditures, they may shirk or provide insufficient funds for the district. Taken to the extreme, legislators may regularly claim credit for requesting money for the district, but fail to actually deliver that money. The potential result is that legislators create an impression of influence over expenditures and yet deliver no money to the district. A related concern is that legislators may take a free ride on the work of their colleagues. House members and senators may collaborate to announce a project, when the effort in delivering the project is more evenly split.

In both cases, legislators deceive constituents—that is, they lead constituents to believe something that differs from the truth. We believe,

---

[25] Weingast, Shepsle, and Johnsen (1981).

however, that this deception would be difficult to sustain for long. Other political actors have an incentive to ensure that legislators actually deliver projects to the district. Local officials often depend on federal expenditures to secure their budgets. Congressional colleagues are unlikely to tolerate representatives who contribute little to actually delivering the projects. And constituents do reward legislators slightly more for securing money for the district, providing slight additional incentives to deliver money. So shirking is certainly possible, but it is unlikely to be sustainable for more than a short period of time.

Rewarding legislators for the act of requesting, however, creates incentives for legislators to make requests more readily accessible and salient to the public. This outcome suggests a different interpretation of recent reforms to the appropriations process. After the 2006 midterm elections and a series of lobbying-related scandals, both the House and Senate adopted reforms to the earmarking process in spending bills. The hope was to increase transparency, ensuring that members of Congress could be easily held accountable for securing spending for campaign donors. To do this, an earmark database was created and the member responsible for requesting the earmark was identified.

The reforms did have an effect on earmark transparency. As Stephen Slivinski of the Cato Institute explains, before the reform, "numerous congressmen could often take credit for a single project. There was no official way to verify who was really the main supporter of the earmark."[26] Slivinski goes on the explain that the reform created a way to identify the person who requested an expenditure, comparing it to "intellectual property protection for government waste."[27] After the reform, those who merely requested an expenditure got an official record of the request and a guarantee that they would be clearly associated with the spending.

The attempt to eliminate corruption in the earmarking process instead created a prominent place for legislators to broadcast that they requested money for constituents, perhaps making the earmarking process more electorally valuable than before the reform.

The potential for subtle deception is a persistent concern when constituents allocate credit in response to legislators' credit claiming efforts. In the next chapter we show how a subtle linguistic deception causes constituents to reward legislators for projects they had little role in securing. And we explain why constituents may prefer to be deceived.

[26] Slivinski (2007).
[27] Slivinski (2007).

CHAPTER 6

Credit, Deception, and Institutional Design

OUR EVIDENCE THUS FAR SHOWS THAT CONSTITUENTS ARE responsive to the actions legislators claim credit for performing. Constituents evaluate projects based on who receives the money and who claims credit for the spending, but are much less responsive to the amount spent. In this chapter we show that the value of claiming credit for actions and the opportunity to *imply* influence over expenditures helps explain a long standing puzzle in American political economy. Federal expenditures occur through a large number of federal programs, with each of the many programs administered by a small number of bureaucrats.[1] While this structure of federal spending has evolved for diverse reasons, we show in this chapter that legislators' strategic credit claiming and their constituents' response to it help explain how many of the programs survive. Strategic bureaucrats create opportunities for legislators to imply they deserve credit for spending, which legislators value because constituents reward legislators implications' nearly as much as when credit is explicitly claimed. Legislators value these opportunities because they know that constituents give them nearly as much credit for implying as for explicitly claiming a role in these awards. In return for the credit claiming opportunities, legislators reward bureaucrats with continued funding for their program. The result is that the many federal programs are maintained and that legislators have a broader set of activities to claim credit for securing.

We provide direct evidence for each stage of this process. Using a case study, we demonstrate how bureaucrats create credit claiming opportunities to cultivate support. We examine the Assistance to Firefighter Grant Program (AFGP), a competitive grant program administered through the Federal Emergency Management Association (FEMA) in the Department of Homeland Security. We show that bureaucrats at the AFGP funnel information to representatives' offices, providing members of Congress the opportunity to announce the grants before notifying the actual grant recipients. Using comprehensive data sets of agency announcements and

---

[1] Lowi (1969); Stein and Bickers (1997).

legislator press releases, we show that legislators regularly take advantage of the opportunity, with representatives' press releases occurring about two days prior to the formal agency announcement.

Even though legislators are unable to claim credit directly for the spending from executive agencies, it is valuable to legislators because they are able to cultivate an impression of influence over the expenditures by merely implying they are responsible for the spending. We show how legislators use language to encourage constituents to infer that their representative is responsible for the spending. To do this, legislators *announce* an expenditure, rather than stating they explicitly secured the money. We use a pair of survey experiments to show that this implication works: whether legislators say they explicitly secured an expenditure or simply announce a grant, constituents infer that legislators are responsible for securing the money. Our experiments show that this inference occurs because constituents infer that legislators who announce expenditures are responsible for securing the money—insuring that legislators can create an impression of influence, even without literally claiming credit for money. If we make explicit, however, that legislators had only an indirect role in obtaining an expenditure they receive substantially less credit from constituents.

The credit claiming opportunities the AFGP creates help insulate the program from budget cuts. Even though the AFGP is regularly criticized as inefficient,[2] members of Congress continue to protect the agency's budget. Using roll call votes on a pair of amendments that saved the AFGP's budget from massive cuts, we show that legislators who take advantage of the AFGP's credit claiming opportunities are systematically more likely to favor protecting the agency's budget. Bureaucrats at the program create credit claiming opportunities and legislators value the opportunity to appear influential. Legislators express their appreciation by continuing to fund the program.

We may be tempted to label the process we describe in this chapter as bad for representation. After all, legislators are deceiving constituents, causing them to believe something that is only partially true. Deception may have a corrosive effect on the relationship between representatives and their constituents,[3] may violate widely held ethical standards,[4] or may allow legislators to shirk and provide few projects to the district and still maintain an impression of influence. We may justify the deception, however, because it leads to better policy outcomes. The mere opportunity to claim credit for expenditures—and deceive

---

[2] Staff (2006*b*); Muhlhausen (2009, 2012).

[3] Mansbridge (2003).

[4] Kant (1983).

constituents—insulates more efficient expenditure programs from criticism and budget threats. This deception solves a problem in institutional design, but at the cost of sustained deception.

The institutional-design problem is to devise robust institutions that spend money efficiently. A large literature argues that legislators' political influence in Congress will cause economically inefficient expenditures in districts. One solution may be to delegate the authority to allocate grants to an outside agency, but this fix eliminates the potential political benefit from legislators' ability to direct spending to their district. And it might undermine congressional support for the program. But when bureaucrats create credit claiming opportunities for legislators they create value for the politicians. The mere opportunity to announce expenditures cultivates congressional support for the more efficient allocation of grants, solving a challenge in institutional design.

This chapter shows one way that the credit claiming, credit allocation process affects the ways that the federal government disburses money. The value of credit claiming alone ensures programs can cultivate support when they might otherwise be politically vulnerable. We begin the chapter by explaining how federal agencies allocate money and how bureaucrats cultivate support for their programs.

6.1 THE STRUCTURE OF FEDERAL SPENDING AND THE INCENTIVE TO CULTIVATE BUREAUCRATIC SUPPORT

As scholars have long observed, there are an abundance of federal programs that determine how the federal government spends large amounts of money.[5] The numerous and diverse programs create a risk for bureaucrats: members of Congress may forget why programs were created or, worse yet, may perceive the programs to be wasteful. Older programs may serve problems that the current Congress views as less pressing—particularly when the ideological composition of Congress changes dramatically.[6] The risk has been amplified recently. For example, in February 2011, the House passed a continuing resolution to continue to fund the federal government. During the process, members of the Tea Party (and some Democrats) submitted a series of earmarks to cut funding for programs. Some of the cuts were arbitrary. Robert Draper describes how Tea Party freshman, Jeff Duncan (R-SC), "also wanted a piece of the [program cutting] action. He sent his legislative director, Joshua Gross, on a mission to find some program to cut so that he

---

[5] Lowi (1969); Stein and Bickers (1997).
[6] Berry, Burden, and Howell (2010*a*).

[Duncan] could introduce an amendment."[7] While an extreme example, the cutting amendments are indicative of what causes bureaucrats' broader concern: that their program will be targeted for funding cuts and that they will lack congressional allies to defend their agency's budget.

Bureaucrats, then, have a basic goal: to defend their program and its budget. To do this, bureaucrats need to clarify their value to members of Congress. Many bureaucrats are well positioned to cultivate this support by exploiting their ability to offer members of Congress the opportunity to claim credit for agency grant expenditures. Outside of earmarks and formulas in spending bills, legislation rarely details exactly how to spend money for a program. The legislation leaves disbursement decisions to bureaucrats.[8] Strategic agency officials can exploit this discretion to achieve their goal of sustaining their agency and increasing its budget. When bureaucrats at funding programs have discretion over spending decisions, such as the Army Corps of Engineers,[9] they can strategically manipulate funding decisions to build support for their programs.[10] Bureaucrats funnel money to legislators' districts, creating opportunities for legislators to claim credit for increased funding in their district. Legislators, in turn, ensure that the agency survives authorization votes and receives a larger budget.[11]

Officials at competitive grant programs share the same goals as bureaucrats who have more discretion over spending decisions. Like other agency officials, bureaucrats at competitive grant programs want their program to continue and to expand their budget.[12] But bureaucrats at competitive programs lack the tools that other bureaucrats often employ to build support for their program. Enacting legislation often

---

[7] Draper (2012).

[8] Arnold (1979); Berry, Burden, and Howell (2010b).

[9] Ferejohn (1974).

[10] Arnold (1979); Wildavsky (1984); Hird (1991); Grose and Bertelli (2009).

[11] Ferejohn (1974); Arnold (1979). Another mechanism that explains agency survival is the calculated behavior of interest groups who, coupled with bureaucrats, ensure that representatives remember that a program is valuable. Stein and Bickers argue that the structure of spending programs, and the constituencies the programs serve, insulate programs from cuts and defend bureaucrats' jobs (Stein and Bickers, 1997). This occurs because some programs serve motivated interest groups who benefit substantially from the programs. For example, police groups closely track funding levels for the Edward Byrne Memorial grant program—money that is used to hire and train new police officers. The motivated interest groups, according to Stein and Bickers' (1997) theory, apply pressure to Congress if funding levels or the overall program is threatened. But even if interest groups can defend some programs, risk-averse bureaucrats are unlikely to rely solely upon outside groups to defend their programs. Instead, we expect that bureaucrats will pursue further assurances that their program will be protected from potential cuts.

[12] Personal Interviews, Wildavsky 1984.

constrains bureaucrats at competitive programs, making it difficult for them to target money to specific congressional districts. Many of the programs have constraints written into the authorizing legislation and the Code of Federal Regulations that limit bureaucratic discretion over where the grants are allocated. In some cases, the laws and regulations make it exceedingly difficult, perhaps impossible, for bureaucrats to direct funds at legislators crucial to the agency's survival. This structure places them at a disadvantage when trying to build support with their congressional principals.

But bureaucrats at competitive programs have other tools available to build support for their program. As we have shown, legislators receive credit for actions performed throughout the appropriations process. And bureaucrats that oversee competitive programs know that legislators value the opportunity to announce grants allocated to their district, even if legislators have only an indirect role in influencing the expenditure. To build support bureaucrats at competitive grant programs manipulate how grants are announced, creating credit claiming opportunities to cultivate congressional support.

Perhaps the most effective manipulation is delaying the official agency announcement of an award, providing members of Congress the right of first announcement. Agency officials funnel information about a new grant award to congressional offices after the official award decision is made, but before the agency announces the new grant. This delay (and advance notice) ensures that local officials receiving the grants learn the good news from their members of Congress and that local news coverage of grant disbursements will focus on the representative's announcements. Agency officials view this manipulation as one of the most effective tools for building support. One agency official told us in an interview that it was essential for achieving her goal of making "sure that legislators remember that this program is valuable *to them* [members of Congress] during authorization votes" (Personal Interview). Indeed, the delay in announcing an expenditure is sufficiently important to be codified in official agency policy. As we detail in the Conclusion of this chapter, easily acquired minutes from meetings in agencies clarify that agency officials dictate delays in agency grant announcements as part of official policy.

Bureaucrats create the credit claiming opportunities for legislators because representatives value the opportunity to announce the grant awards. Announcing an expenditure is valuable because it allows legislators to *imply* they were influential over the expenditure—even if they never explicitly claim credit. This implication is possible, in part, because of the basic structure of language. To fully understand the content of a conversation or statement, inferences must often be made, based on both the logical content of a sentence and the context in which it is spoken.[13] These inferences, called implicatures, make language more efficient, allowing sentences to have meaning based on their context and the identity of the speakers. But the use of implications creates the possibility for subtle deceptions. A speaker may imply that she is responsible for performing some action—even when her actual influence is minute. This subtle deception allows legislators to avoid accusations of lying while still effectively claiming credit for an outcome on which they had only limited influence.

Implicatures are all the more effective because our brains strive to find causal relationships when reading statements from legislators.[14] Hassin, Bargh, and Uleman document the occurrence of spontaneous causal inferences—that is, causal inferences that are made even though "people are unaware of the intention to make the causal inference ... and unaware of the inference itself."[15] Spontaneous causal inferences are especially likely when reading texts. When reading causally our brains attempt to find a coherent sequence of events, even when this coherence is not explicitly provided. And psychologists have found that "one of the main factors that determines coherence is causality."[16]

Even if not explicitly, legislators and their staff intuitively understand how to exploit language to claim credit, even when the actual influence over the expenditure is indirect or small. This understanding is apparent in how legislators claim credit for grants allocated to their district. Consider Frank LoBiondo (R-NJ), who regularly claims credit for small grants awarded to local fire departments in his districts. For example, on August 9, 2007, LoBiondo "announced that the Bargaintown Volunteer Fire Company in Egg Harbor Township was awarded $64,273 in federal funding for the purchase of new portable radios."[17] On January 17, 2006, LoBiondo announced that the "Laureldale Fire Department in Hamilton Township was awarded $114,000 ... for the purchase of new air packs."[18] And on December 29, 2005, he "announced that the Longport Volunteer Fire Department was awarded $51,661 ... to help them with their continued fire operations and safety programs."[19] LoBiondo explained that the fire departments deserve the support because "day in and day out, the men and women of our fire and rescue units are the first responders to emergency events in our communities."

[13] Grice (1989).
[14] Hassin, Bargh, and Uleman (2002); Van Berkum (2008); Kahneman (2011).
[15] Hassin, Bargh, and Uleman (2002), 515.
[16] Hassin, Bargh, and Uleman (2002), 516.
[17] LoBiondo (2007).
[18] LoBiondo (2006a).
[19] LoBiondo (2005).

LoBiondo's credit claiming reflects a broader pattern in how members of Congress claim credit for federal grants. This pattern is present in both what he claimed credit for obtaining—grants to local fire departments—and how he claimed credit for those grants. For each grant, LoBiondo announced that the grants had been awarded. This language is carefully chosen to imply that LoBiondo was responsible for the grant awards. And similar language is frequently used by other members of Congress: representatives from both parties regularly announce that grants have been allocated. For example, Kenny Hulshof (R-MO) "announced today that the Fulton Fire Department has been awarded a grant for $198,561";[20] Nick Rahall (D-WV) "announced today that the Rhodell Fire Department has been awarded $147,689";[21] Spencer Bachus (R-AL) "announced that federal fire grants have been awarded to the Stewartville Volunteer Fire Department and to Maplesville Fire and Rescue";[22] Aaron Schock (R-IL) "announced today Pittsfield Fire Rescue Department and Beardstown Fire Department will be receiving Assistance to Firefighters Grants (AFG)";[23] David Davis (R-TN) "announced today a U.S. Department of Homeland Security Assistance to Firefighters Grant to the Kingsport Fire Department for $97,200"; and Elijah Cummings (D-MD), John Sarbanes (D-MD), Ben Cardin (D-MD), and Barbara Mikluski (D-MD) "announced Howard County Fire and Rescue Services have been awarded more than $1.3 million in federal funding."[24] In each of these examples the member (or members) of Congress never explicitly claims credit for the expenditure.

Legislators also announce other types of grant awards to the district, with the same goal of implying they are responsible for the expenditures. On August 20, 2010, Jerry Costello (D-IL) "announced today that the City of Marion has received a $10,277 Edward Byrne Memorial Justice Assistance grant."[25] When announcing the grant, Costello assured his constituents that he would "continue to work to make this funding a priority in the federal budget." On March 7, 2010, Bart Stupak "announced that the Federal Aviation Administration (FAA) has awarded more than $6.7 million in grants to six airports in Michigan's First Congressional District."[26] And Pete Visclosky (D-IN) issued a press release titled "Visclosky Announces $279,586 for Valparaiso University," which explains that "Congressman Visclosky announced that Valparaiso

---

[20] Hulshof (2006).
[21] Rahall (2008).
[22] Bachus (2008).
[23] Schock (2009).
[24] Cummings (2009).
[25] Costello (2010).
[26] Stupak (2009).

University received a grant from the National Science Foundation (NSF) to support Science, Technology, Engineering and Math (STEM) programs."[27]

A quick and superficial reading of the press releases leaves us with the impression that each of the legislators is responsible for the spending. Yet, a closer and more literal examination of the statements reveals that in each press release the legislators only announce the spending and never explicitly claim credit for having secured the expenditure. Rather, it is up to the reader to infer that the representative is responsible for the expenditure, based on the implications in the press release and the brain's pursuit of coherence through causality. The distinction between credit implied and credit claimed is even more obvious when examining how legislators talk about expenditures secured through earmarked funds in the appropriations process. For example, consider how David Obey (D-WI) claimed credit for money that he earmarked to construct a building in his district. After attending a groundbreaking ceremony, Obey explained that he "*secured* $1.5 million in last year's federal budget to help the Village construct the new facility."[28]

Legislators and their press secretaries, then, carefully use language to encourage constituents to infer that their representative is responsible for directing money to the district. Constituents are more likely to infer that a legislator who announces spending is responsible for securing it because of contextual cues from their own personal experiences.[29] Most constituents know that representatives can direct money to the district, even if constituents only have an approximate understanding of how this process occurs. Representatives include extraneous facts to make the automatic causal attribution more likely. For example, legislators often suggest that their committee assignments were important for securing a grant, even when the committee has little role in grant oversight. When Ben Cardin (D-MD) announces grants, he reminds constituents that he "is on the Budget Committee," even though the Budget Committee has no role in appropriating funds for, or oversight of, the program that disburses the particular grant he announces.[30] Richard Shelby (R-AL) begins his grant announcements by describing himself as "a senior member of the Appropriations committee"[31] and both Barbara Mikulski (D-MD) and Arlen Specter (R-PA) point out their position on the Homeland Security Appropriations Subcommittee.[32]

[27] Visclosky (2013).
[28] Obey (2006) (emphasis added).
[29] Van Berkum (2008).
[30] Cardin (2007).
[31] Shelby (2005).
[32] Specter (2007); Mikulski (2007).

The credit claiming, credit allocation process explains how creating credit claiming opportunities help bureaucrats cultivate support for their programs. Constituents' rapid evaluation of credit claiming statements causes them to attribute credit to legislators for expenditures, even when those legislators never explicitly claim credit for the spending. Legislators enhance this implication with additional facts to make the causal inference more plausible. The implication, then, makes the opportunity to claim credit for an expenditure that occurs with only indirect influence from the legislator as valuable as funding that legislators are more directly responsible for securing. And the result is that bureaucrats can cultivate support for their program through the creation of credit claiming opportunities.

6.2 STUDY 1: INFERENCES ABOUT INFLUENCE AND THE VALUE OF ANNOUNCEMENTS

The credit claiming, credit allocation process explains why legislators value announcing grants because they need only imply that they are responsible for an expenditure in order to receive credit from constituents. We expect this credit allocation will occur because constituents quickly evaluate the content of legislators' statements, inferring that legislators caused the expenditure to occur. We test these predictions with an experimental design that allows us to isolate how legislators claim credit for the expenditures and what information constituents have available about how their legislator secured the grant.

We conducted this experiment twice, replicating the same finding in different populations and with different information about the representative provided to participants. In the first instance of the experiment, we recruited 316 participants from Amazon's Mechanical Turk. We told our participants that we were evaluating how the public feels about local funding and then presented the subjects with a news article about a hypothetical representative, where the content varied by the participant's randomly assigned conditions.

To assess whether constituents infer that a representative is responsible for an expenditure that she announces, our experiment simultaneously varied the action that legislators report and the *information* constituents have to interpret the action. We summarize our treatment in Table 6.1. The action conditions vary the verb representatives use to report the grant allocation. Participants in the secured condition read a newspaper article with the headline "Representative Secures Vital Funding for Local Fire Departments." And the main body of the article states that "[t]he representative secured the money to replace

TABLE 6.1
Article Content across Conditions.

Headline: Representative [Secures/Announces] Vital Funding for Local Fire Departments

Body: A representative announced $250,000 in funding for local fire departments yesterday. [The representative secured the money to replace aging equipment/ No additional content if announce condition].

"Firefighters and emergency service personnel dedicate themselves to protecting the health and safety of our district," said the legislator. "This funding will help our local fire departments by providing them the means to obtain the best equipment and training available."

Secured and Civics Lesson: The Homeland Security Appropriations bill passed out of the House of Representatives. The representative inserted funding for the fire departments directly into the bill. Specifically, the representative inserted a provision that directs FEMA's Assistance to Firefighter Grant Program (AFGP) to award $250,000 to local fire departments.

Announced and Civics Lesson: Government watchdog groups hail the program for its lack of influence from members of Congress. A computer scoring algorithm initially evaluates each application. For those scored sufficiently high, a committee of expert fire chiefs evaluates the proposals for effectiveness, appropriateness, and overall community need. The representative was informed of the awards after the committee finalized its decisions.

Treatments

Actions: [Secures/Announces]

---

aging equipment." We use the verb secure to replicate how legislators claim credit for earmarking money for the district and to provide a clear meaning to the sentence when read literally: the representative is responsible for delivering the money to the district. Participants in the *announced* condition read a newspaper article where the representative merely announces the expenditure. Participants in this condition see a headline that declares that the "Representative Announces Vital Funding for Local Fire Departments." This condition, replicates the implication that legislators use to receive credit for spending without explicitly claiming credit.

The second condition varies the information that participants have available to interpret the legislator's credit claiming effort. Delivering this information allows us to explicitly affect what our participants conclude after reading the newspaper article. We deliver this information in the form of a civics lesson—that is, a brief paragraph that explains how the program allocates funds. Participants who are assigned to the *no civics* condition see no additional information and simply receive the treatment described in the previous paragraph. Participants who are assigned to the *civics* condition and are also assigned to the secured condition learned that the "representative inserted funding for the fire departments directly into the bill." This information reinforces the conclusion that the representative is primarily responsible for delivering the money to the district. Participants in the civics condition and also assigned to the announced condition were provided with a paragraph that explained that "[g]overnment watchdog groups hail the [fire grant] program for its lack of influence from members of Congress," and that "[t]he representative was informed about the awards after the committee finalized its decisions." This information prevents participants from inferring that the legislator was responsible for securing the expenditure and instead informs participants that the legislator is *only* announcing that the expenditure was made.

After randomly assigning participants to conditions and providing them with the treatment, we asked them to assess how responsible the representative and the agency was for the award, with the responsibility score ranging from 0 to 100. We use this scale to obtain an impressionistic assessment of how constituents allocate credit in response to the subtle differences across our treatments.

The left-hand plot in Figure 6.1 shows that participants infer that legislators are responsible for an expenditure, even when the representative merely announces the spending. The lines in the left-hand plot present the difference between the credit participants allocate the representative and agency under the announced condition to the credit allocated under the secured condition. The bottom pair of lines presents the difference without a civics lesson, while the top pair of lines presents the difference when we provide the civics lesson. The point is the average difference and the line is a 95 percent confidence interval.

Without a civics lesson, representatives receive nearly the same credit for announcing or securing a grant. Participants in the announced condition allocate 6.5 points less credit to the legislator than participants in the secured condition, but the relatively small number of participants in our study make for a wide confidence interval, (95 percent confidence interval, [−15.52, 2.61]). While legislators receive slightly less credit, they still receive the majority of credit for the expenditure when announcing the expenditure. Participants allocated 67.6% of the credit to representatives in the secured condition, while participants allocated 61.1% of the credit in the announce condition. The verb that legislators use to report the grant also does not affect the credit that our participants allocate to the agency. We find essentially no difference in the agency's credit (0.5 points more credit when announced, 95 percent confidence interval, [−6.6, 7.6]).

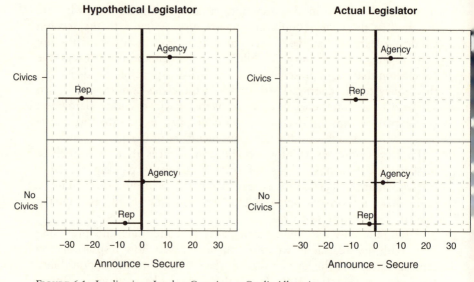

FIGURE 6.1. Implications Lead to Constituent Credit Allocation.
This figure shows the results of our study, which we conducted twice. The left-hand plot shows the results of our study conducted on a group of Mechanical Turk participants, using a hypothetical representative. The right-hand plot shows the results of our study for a more representative and larger sample of participants, using an actual representative. In both experiments, we show that constituents infer their representative is responsible for securing a grant—even when that credit is only implied in legislators' statements.

Representatives who merely announce funding receive almost the same amount of credit as legislators who secured the expenditures. Providing the civics lesson shows that this near-equal attribution occurs because participants infer that legislators who announce an expenditure are *responsible* for obtaining the spending. The second line from the top shows the difference in the credit allocated to legislators by participants in the announce and secured conditions when the civics lesson is provided. Participants in the announce condition allocated 23.7 points less credit when legislators announce the expenditure than when legislators secured the expenditure (95 percent confidence interval, [−32.9, −14.7]).

This change occurs because the civics lesson causes participants in the announce condition to substantially lower the credit allocated to the legislator—evidence that the participants no longer infer that their representative is responsible for the spending. Participants in the announce condition who receive a civics lesson allocate 44.7% of the credit to the representative—that is, 16.4 fewer points than participants in the announce condition allocate to the representative when no civics information is provided [−25.6, −7.3]). The effect of the civics lesson on participants in the announce condition is substantial, but the civics lesson has no effect on participants in the secured condition. Participants in the secured condition who receive the civics lesson increase the credit allocated to the representative only 0.9 percentage points, an increase that is neither substantively nor statistically significant (95 percent confidence interval, [−5.6, 7.4]). This result is evidence that constituents have already inferred that the representative is primarily responsible for securing the expenditure and so additional information reinforcing this point fails to change the conclusion reached.

This experiment shows that announcing an expenditure causes constituents to infer that the representative is responsible for the expenditure—nearly as responsible as when the legislator secures the expenditure. Revealing additional information disrupts the inference and prevents the legislator from receiving credit, causing a substantial drop in the representative's responsibility for securing the grant.

The results of this iteration of the study are clear. But concerns may linger about our conclusion. One concern is that the use of a hypothetical legislator amplifies the effect of the civics lesson. Additional information that is provided when using an actual representative may dampen the responsiveness to the intervention. A second concern is that we have a relatively small sample size, making more precise inferences difficult to make.

To address these concerns we replicated our first study, but included actual legislators rather than hypothetical representatives and used a more representative and larger sample of participants. In the second iteration of this study, we used 1,048 participants from the Survey Sampling International (SSI) panel, matching on census characteristics. Using participant zip codes we identified the participant's congressional district and corresponding House member. We then replaced "A representative" in Table 6.1 with the name and party affiliation of each respondent's representative. The rest of the study proceeded as in the other conditions: we randomly assigned participants to one of the four conditions and then assessed the credit allocated to the legislator and agency.

The right-hand plot in Figure 6.1 contains the results of this second experiment, demonstrating that this second study replicates our findings. As in the first study, we see that participants find only small differences between legislators who announce a grant and legislators who secure an expenditure. Participants in the announced condition, without additional information, allocate only 2.4 percentage points less credit than participants in the secured condition (95 percent confidence interval, [−6.9, 2.2]). Again, we find that announcing or securing a grant causes constituents to reach the same conclusion: the representative is responsible for the expenditure.

As in the first experiment, including civics information causes participants to revise their inference. Participants in the announced condition who receive the civics lesson allocate 7.9 percentage points less credit to their representative than participants in the secured condition who also receive the civics lesson (95 percent confidence interval, [−12.50, −3.21]). Again, the decrease occurs because participants with context no longer infer that legislators are deserving of credit: the civics information undermines the legislator's implication that they were influential.

The differences in credit allocation affect other assessments of the legislator. In both instances of our study, we asked our participants if they agree that their representative "works hard to bring federal money to the district." In our Mechanical Turk sample, there was only a small difference in perceptions of hard work between the announce and secure conditions when no civics information was provided. Participants in the announced condition were only 3.4 percentage points less likely to agree that their representative was hardworking, a difference neither statistically nor substantively significant (95 percent confidence interval, [−0.14, 0.07]). But there are substantial differences in perceived effectiveness when constituents are provided contextual information from the civics lesson. When this information is provided, participants in the announced condition are 23.3 percentage points less likely to identify their representative as hardworking (95 percent confidence interval, [−0.38, −0.08]). Our more representative survey replicates the finding. When no civics lesson is provided, we find that representatives in the announced condition are rated only slightly less hardworking without context (3.3 percentage points, 95 percent confidence interval, [−0.13, 0.06]), but when the civics lesson is provided, the representatives in the announced condition are rated substantially less hardworking (9.3 percentage points, 95 percent confidence interval, [0.01, 0.18]).

6.3 CREATING CREDIT CLAIMING OPPORTUNITIES: EVIDENCE FROM FIRE DEPARTMENT GRANTS

Our experimental evidence shows that legislators have incentive to seek opportunities to announce expenditures in their district. Announcing gives legislators the opportunity to imply that they are responsible for spending and this causes constituents to infer that the representative is responsible for the expenditure. Strategic bureaucrats recognize the value that legislators attach to the announcements and create credit claiming opportunities to cultivate legislator support.

To demonstrate how bureaucrats cultivate support with announcements, we use an extended case study: we analyze the previously

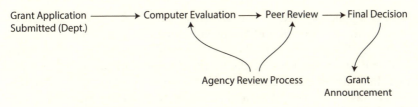

FIGURE 6.2. The Assistance to Firefighter Grant Application Process, as described in the Code of Federal Regulations.

discussed Assistance to Firefighters Grant Program (AFGP). Created with an amendment in the fiscal year 2001 National Defense Authorization Act and reauthorized during the fiscal year 2005 appropriation process, the AFGP has distributed billions of dollars to fire departments. The money is allocated for the purchase of equipment and the creation of wellness and fitness programs. Each year tens of thousands of fire departments from across the country apply for awards, with a small percentage (about 13%) actually receiving awards.[33]

We selected the AFGP because the rules of how grants are allocated make it difficult for legislators or bureaucrats to influence directly where the grants are awarded. The process that the AFGP uses to allocate the grants affords bureaucrats few opportunities to exercise discretion over who receives an award and provides few opportunities for legislators to intervene directly. The intention to insulate the grant awards from bureaucratic or legislative influence is found in the authorizing legislation, which mandates that the program allocate "grants on a competitive basis directly to fire departments of a State" (15 U.S.C. 2229 (b)(1)(A)). Each stage of the grant program—from application to final award—limits the potential for meddling. We now detail the grant allocation process. In order to guide our discussion of how the grants are awarded, we include Figure 6.2, which describes how the grants are awarded. We created the figure using the *Code of Federal Regulations* (44 CFR Part 152) and interviews we conducted with agency officials.

Moving through the application process presented in Figure 6.2, it is clear that legislators are able to exert only indirect influence over how the grants are disbursed. The application begins with local fire departments, who initiate the application process by submitting an extensive application to the grant program. There are two possibilities for congressional influence at this stage and both are indirect. Members of Congress can use their staff to assist local fire departments in the preparation of an application or a legislator can send a letter of support

[33] Kruger (2009).

with an application. Representatives do publicize the AFGP, attempt to increase the participation of fire departments, and even hold workshops to inform fire departments about the expenditures. But agency officials said that any influence over the grant allocation process is narrow and rare. In an interview, one agency official told us that congressional offices would have to invest substantial resources to help departments because the applications are "very specific and technical... congressional staff wouldn't be much help." He also cited the need to create a "departmental narrative" that would require substantial investment from departments to write. Perhaps indicative of the lack of congressional support are the private companies who help fire departments prepare grants. An employee of one of these companies told us that their business exists because congressional offices are rarely able to help in the preparation of the AFGP grants. And yet another official at the agency explained that letters of support would not help much in the evaluation process. This, she explained, is because "letters from senators [or representatives] are sent to the central agency office in Washington, applications are sent to the regional offices for evaluation" (Personal Interview). The regional centers make it harder for the bureaucrats to affect the decision, because the program's director and other top officials are stationed in Washington. Therefore, the officials who will make the final decision about grants will never see letters of support from members of Congress.

Once submitted, grant applications are sent to one of the regional evaluation centers. There, they are subjected to an initial screening that is insulated from all forms of influence (Personal Interview, 44 CFR Part 152.5). The applications are evaluated using an automated (computerized) routine that scores them according to predetermined (and publicized) criteria (44 CFR Part 152.5 (a), Personal Interview). Only those applications given a sufficiently high score from the computerized evaluation make it to the next round. The score from the initial screening algorithm cannot be modified–the score is final. This procedure leaves little room for strategic bureaucratic action at this stage.

After the first evaluation, a second evaluation occurs in order to identify the grants that will be awarded funding. At this stage, a team of "non-Federal experts with a fire service background" (44 CFR Part 152.5 (b)) evaluate the applications. One agency official described the panel as "fire chiefs from around the [geographic] region" who score the applications after a brief training session. The score from this panel cannot be altered and is then used to determine who receives applications. The final step in the application process is the selection of departments to receive grants. Once again, there is little opportunity for bureaucratic influence. In the Code of Federal Regulations, the agency states that, "we will fund the highest scored applications before considering lower scored applications": departments are ordered according to their score and this order is used to disburse the grants (44 CFR Part 152.6 (b)).

According to agency policy, officials are *technically* allowed some discretion at the final stage of this evaluation procedure (44 CFR Part 152.6 (c)). But this discretion is limited and can only be used to ensure that the applications satisfy the geographic distribution requirements that accompany the enacting statute. This rule states that, while the grants are to be allocated competitively, fire departments from across the country are expected to receive awards. The effect of the geographic requirement appears to be limited. One agency official was quite clear about the lack of discretion. He told us that, "we haven't used these geographic considerations in our decisions and follow the panel scores."[34]

While the application process provides few opportunities for either congressional or bureaucratic influence, the announcement stage provides ample opportunity for manipulation. After the award recipients are selected, agency officials are required to inform the departments. While the announcements are required in the CFR, there are few explicit regulations governing how the announcements should occur. Indeed, they seem to be described as a formality with little policy consequence. But it is the first place in the application process where agency officials have complete discretion. In interviews, several officials told us that they recognized the opportunity that the announcement stage provided. It was the only step where they would be able to increase support for their program among members of Congress effectively.

To create the credit claiming opportunities, agency officials send the award decisions to members of Congress who are encouraged to make the award announcement before the agency. One agency official was very clear about the manipulation. She told us that "we give the information about the grant awards to congressional offices two or three days before the agency makes the announcement."[35] A second agency official told us that, "we give legislators the opportunity to announce grants before the agency."[36] Officials do this, they said, "to ensure that the legislators *remember us around appropriations time.*"[37]

The evidence from qualitative interviews shows that agency officials believe that representatives value the chance to claim credit for grants. The interviews provide this important insight, but we are limited in the conclusions we can draw just from our small set of conversations with agency officials. Because we only talked to a few officials, we may

[34] Personal Interview.
[35] Personal Interview.
[36] Personal Interview.
[37] Emphasis added.

have had the misfortune of selecting bureaucrats who engage in an odd practice. Further, the agency officials may have provided an idealistic account of how their agency works—while they may believe they create many of these opportunities, it may be because of motivated (biased) reflections.

To provide a more comprehensive test of whether agency officials create announcements opportunities for members of Congress, we collected data on agency announcements. Using the AFGP website, we created a database of all grant announcements from 2005, 2006, and 2007—the three years with the most comprehensive and easily accessed announcement data. We combined data on agency grant announcements with our collection of House press releases about fire grants and a collection of Senate press releases about fire department grants.[38] Together, the three data sets facilitate direct tests of whether the agency creates credit claiming opportunities for members of Congress.

If bureaucrats create credit claiming opportunities for representatives in the way that the bureaucrats detailed to us in interviews, then we would expect a sharp increase in the number of press releases claiming credit for fire grants two to three days prior to the official agency release of a grant. Figure 6.3 focuses on a brief two-month period at the end of 2006: from November 1 to December 31, 2006. During this period, the AFGP announced their grants on Saturday of each week and before each announcement both senators and representatives took advantage of the AFGP's announcements. For example, the AFGP announced a round of grants on November 4 (the first gray line in both the left-hand and right-hand plot in Figure 6.3. And on November 2 and 3, there were ten press releases from representatives and senators announcing grants, but zero press releases announcing grants from November 5 and 6, after the official announcement. This pattern persists over the two months: representatives announce before the agency. The early announcements in this two-month period are indicative of a more general pattern. A Granger Causality test shows that legislators' grant announcements tend to occur before agency announcements.

Figure 6.3 shows that legislators take advantage of the opportunity that the bureaucrats at the AFGP identified as the primary tool to cultivate support. To further demonstrate that members of Congress announce press releases immediately prior to the AFGP, we manually read a sample of press releases to ensure that the press releases announced grants that the agency had yet to announce. To perform the validation, we sampled 50 fire department press releases issued in the three days prior to an agency announcement. We then read each press

---

[38] Grimmer (2013).

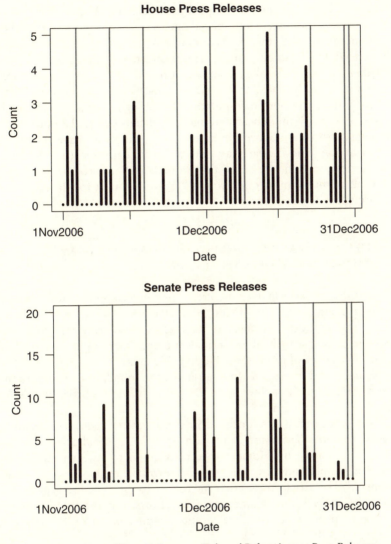

FIGURE 6.3. Congressional Press Releases are Released Before Agency Press Releases. This figure shows that House and Senate press releases are released prior to the official agency announcement. This figure shows specific weeks in November and December 2006, demonstrating that the number of press releases from representatives is highest immediately before the agency announcement date.

release, identifying the grants discussed in the press release, including the fire department awarded the grant and the dollar amount. Using the announcement data we compiled from the AFGP program, we validated that the grant discussed in the press release was in fact announced one to three days later. Among the sampled press releases, 95.2% of the grants in the press releases were announced one to three days prior to the AFGP announcement. The other 4.8% announced grants were announced after the official AFGP announcement. This is direct, and strong, evidence that members of Congress take advantage of the AFGP's offer of assistance.

Our case study, then, shows one method a strategic bureaucrat can use to cultivate support: manipulating the timing of press releases. By delaying an official announcement, agency officials create the opportunity for legislators to announce the expenditure. And as we have shown, the act of announcing is nearly as valuable as actually securing the grant. In the next section, we show that bureaucrats' efforts are successful: creating credit claiming opportunities creates support for the Assistance to Firefighter Grant Program.

6.4 DEFENDING AND EXPANDING THE GRANT PROGRAMS: EVIDENCE THE AFGP IS SUCCESSFUL

Bureaucrats at the AFGP create credit claiming opportunities to bolster support among members of Congress. One reason that the bureaucrats create this support is to insulate themselves from criticism and threats to their budget. Much of this criticism comes from right-leaning think tanks. In a series of reports, the Heritage Foundation criticized the AFGP as wasteful and ineffective. In one report, the foundation concludes that the Assistance to Firefighter Grant Program is "a grant program that has significant shortcomings."[39]

This sentiment is often echoed in conservative media. For example, the *Washington Times* ran a story on April 20, 2006 alleging that "fire departments are using Homeland Security grants to buy gym equipment, sponsor puppet and clown shows, and turn first responders into fitness trainers." The article argues that the money to the local fire departments could be better spent on anti-terrorism efforts, arguing that "Congress has ignored pleas" to "redirect grant spending based on the risk of a terrorist attack."[40]

Perhaps not surprisingly, then, the program has a history of proposed cuts. For example, in his fiscal year 2005 budget, President Bush proposed a $250-million cut to the program—reducing funding from $750 million to $500 million. In response to the proposed cut, members of Congress rallied to defend the program. A group of bipartisan legislators wrote a letter to Bush "to express ... deep concern over the

---

[39] Muhlhausen (2012).
[40] Staff (2006*b*).

treatment of the Assistance to Firefighters Grant Program in your fiscal year 2005 budget submission."[41] The legislators go on to dispute "the findings of a Program Assessment Rating Tool, that the Fire Grant program 'is unfocused and has not been able to demonstrate its impact on public safety.'"[42] The legislators were successful in rallying support and prevented $150 million in cuts. Steny Hoyer (D-MD) added an amendment to the Homeland Security Appropriations Bill to set the AFGP funding at $650 million. Another $65 million was allocated for the related Staffing for Adequate Fire and Emergency Response Firefighters (SAFER) grant, which was to be administered by the same bureaucrats. In total, then, the president's attempt to cut the program's budget by $250 million was met with an actual cut of only $35 million.

Attentive members of Congress again saved the program from cuts in 2011. The Obama administration requested $670 million for the AFGP and the SAFER grants, but the House Appropriations committee reported a bill that included only $350 million for the program—a 47% decrease over Obama's budget request.[43] But as Kruger explains, two amendments on the House floor successfully restored funding.[44] One amendment, from Steve LaTourette (R-OH) and Bill Pascrell (D-NJ) increased the funding of the program to $670 million, the amount Obama requested. On the floor, Pascrell declared that "those who say that the Federal Government bears no responsibility about public safety, they are absolutely wrong. On one side of our mouth, we say that we must protect and defend our first responders; on the other side of our mouth we say that we have no responsibility whatsoever in talking about our firefighters and our police officers." A second amendment, from David Price (D-NC), allowed the grants to be used to hire laid-off firefighters—a major use of previous grants.

The floor votes provide an opportunity to see who voted to defend the AFGP when its funding was threatened. Table 6.2 regresses votes on both amendments on either a measure of legislators' credit claiming rate (Column 1) or the proportion (Prop.) of press releases claiming credit for fire department grants (Column 2). To ensure that our conclusions are not based on obvious confounding factors, we include whether a representative is a Democrat and their DW-Nominate score, a measure of legislators' previous roll call history that corresponds roughly to her ideological orientation.[45] Because we collect the two votes into a single

[41] Hoyer (2004).
[42] Hoyer (2004).
[43] Kruger (2013).
[44] Kruger (2013).
[45] Poole and Rosenthal (1997).

TABLE 6.2

Legislators Who Claim Credit for Fire Grants Vote to Restore Agency Funding.

Covariate	Overall	Fire Grant
Intercept	0.94	0.91
	(0.07)	(0.07)
Prop. Credit Claiming	0.28	-
	(0.14)	-
Prop. Fire Grants	-	1.02
	-	(0.48)
Democrat	−0.21	−0.04
	(0.11)	(0.11)
Ideal Point	−0.65	−0.43
	(0.10)	(0.10)
Waiver Amendment	−0.13	−0.10
	(0.02)	(0.02)
Rep. Random Effects	Yes	Yes

This table shows that representatives who take advantage of opportunities to claim credit for fire grant expenditures vote to increase funding on the House floor. It appears, then, that bureaucrats' efforts to build support are successful.

model, we include an indicator for each amendment and also legislator random effects.[46]

Table 6.2 shows that representatives who claim credit for spending, and crucially, fire department grants, are the most likely to vote to increase funding for the program. A shift from the tenth percentile of proportion of press releases allocated to credit claiming to the ninetieth percentile increases a legislator's probability of voting to increase the AFGP funding 8.7 percentage points (95 percent confidence interval, [0.01, 0.17]). Likewise, a similar shift in proportion of press releases allocated to claiming credit for fire department grants increases the probability of support for the AFGP amendments 4.1 percentage points (95 percent confidence interval, [0.00, 0.08]).

The roll call votes provide evidence that the AFGP has cultivated congressional support simply through the creation of credit claiming opportunities. And as fiscal battles in Washington continue, the program continues to receive support from representatives. For example, Aaron Schock (R-IL), who allocates about 12.7% of his press releases to claiming credit for fire grants, introduced an amendment to restore funding for the AFGP in a continuing resolution (a bill to continue funding the federal government without an Appropriations bill).

[46] Gelman and Hill (2007).

After the amendment passed, Schock (R-IL) declared that "these grants provide vital funding to the nation's first responders to help adequately staff firehouses and to provide the necessary specialized equipment to protect those that put themselves in harm's way."[47] The grants do help recipient fire departments prepare for fires in the town, but they also help legislators cultivate support with constituents.

While we have focused on a single program, the bureaucratic strategy for cultivating support with members of Congress is implemented across many federal agencies. Indeed, several agencies put the policy in publicly available writing. For example, when announcing the recipients of Head Start grants, the Department of Health & Human Services' (HHS) policy is that

> [t]he Congressional Liaison Office (CLO) relays information on ACF [Administration of Children and Families] awards to the senators and representatives in whose states and districts the projects are awarded. The responsible grants office will provide a copy of the FAA to the CLO and allows the CLO a 72-hour waiting period to notify the appropriate congressional delegation. The FAA will not be mailed to the grantee agency until the waiting period has expired (Staff, 2013)

This document is indicative of a more general HHS policy, which states that "generally, a 72-hour waiting period will be required between CLO [Congressional Liason Office] notification and mailing the NGA [Notification of Grant Award]."[48] Similarly, in meeting minutes posted from a National Institute of Health (NIH) board meeting, a board member "reminded the group that a 72-hour waiting period is required between CLO [Congressional Liason Office] notification and mailing the Notification of Grant Award (NGA). He asked group members to ensure that everyone... is following this policy and releasing the NGA in the proper amount of time."[49] The seemingly narrow focus of our study identifies a more general relationship between legislators and bureaucrats.

6.5 CONCLUSION: DECEIVING CONSTITUENTS TO DEFEND A PROGRAM

This chapter has shown how the credit claiming, credit allocation process shapes the way that the federal government spends money. The mere

---

[47] Schock (2012).
[48] Staff (1999).
[49] Staff (2003).

opportunity to claim credit makes possible grant programs that may be otherwise politically vulnerable. Bureaucrats give members of Congress the opportunity to claim credit for agency grant decisions and members of Congress take advantage of this opportunity, regularly announcing new expenditures. Even though legislators never explicitly claim credit for the spending, merely announcing expenditures leads constituents to infer that legislators are responsible for expenditures. The inference occurs, in part, because of psychological processes that cause constituents to identify a causal relationship between announcing and securing funds, even when the relationship is only implied and never explicitly stated. These conditions make merely announcing an expenditure valuable to legislators, because announcing gives them the opportunity to imply that they are responsible for an expenditure. And legislators appear to repay bureaucrats for the chance to announce grants by supporting the program when it is threatened.

When bureaucrats funnel announcements to legislative offices, they affect congressional representation, though in subtle ways. We may be worried that bureaucrats are facilitating deception.[50] Legislators' announcements, created with the help of bureaucrats, may lead constituents to believe something that legislators know to be untrue, or at least partly untrue. The potential deception we identify in this chapter is closely related to other concepts in ethics and political science. Arthur Applbaum, for example, describes *redescription*—the act of describing something again "to bypass certain evaluative and prescriptive questions."[51] In a study of lying in international politics, John Mearsheimer identifies *spinning* as "when a person telling a story emphasizes certain facts and links them together in ways that play to his advantage, while, at the same time, downplaying or ignoring inconvenient facts."[52] And without politicians having the same overriding intent to mislead constituents, Lawrence Jacobs and Robert Shapiro describe how politicians use *crafted talk* to influence public opinion.[53]

While subtle, legislators deceive constituents when they announce expenditures that they had only an indirect role in securing. One might object that legislators are not deceiving constituents at all. We might say that legislators deserve credit because Congress continues to authorize expenditures for the program and, subsequently, to appropriate funds for the grant program to continue. Even when legislators vote against increasing funding to the agency, they still may correctly say that they

---

[50] Mansbridge (2003).
[51] Applbaum (1999), 92.
[52] Mearsheimer (2011), 16.
[53] Jacobs and Shapiro (2000).

support the existence of the program by supporting a budget the funds the grant program. In this way, they can claim, they support the program that ultimately leads to the expenditure in the district. Legislators help the program, but it is a very limited sort of help: it is passive and requires little effort. What is more, changing the actions of a single legislator is unlikely to affect the fate of a grant directed to a district. Contrast this effort with the effort legislators dedicate to earmarking or other methods of intervening directly in the expenditure process. Inserting an earmark requires legislators to pursue funds actively, requires more direct effort, and in many instances the earmark is a necessary cause of the expenditure—without the earmark the project would never occur. Even if legislators deserve some credit for the grant expenditure, their language causes constituents to allocate credit as if legislators had secured the money through earmarking. And our experiments show that constituents would not allocate this credit if they had more information about how the grant was secured. By implying they deserve credit, legislators deceive their constituents.

How troubling we find this deception, though, depends on our standards for representation. If we prioritize citizens' direct control over their representative, then this deception is problematic because it undermines direct accountability. Citizens might want to reward and punish their representatives for the money actually spent in the district—with more money spent yielding greater reward. Deception makes this direct control more difficult to exercise. Rather than rewarding the legislators for the actual spending that a legislator is responsible for securing, citizens will reward legislators for a much wider array of spending. The deception, then, would allow legislators to avoid the direct sanction of constituents.

Deception may also be objectionable on ethical grounds. A Kantian view of ethics would condemn it as corrosive to the standards necessary for legitimate representation.[54] Immanuel Kant advocated an absolutist view of truth telling—asserting it is always inappropriate to deceive or lie to an interlocutor. Christine Korsgaard summarizes the Kantian logic, "we must tell the truth so others may reason freely... in telling them the truth, we are inviting them to reason together with us, to share in our deliberations."[55] Legitimate representation, then, requires that constituents have the opportunity to reason about government actions and decide the credit legislators are owed. Deception is problematic for Kantians because it eliminates constituents' opportunity to reason. Rather, when legislators use deception, they also make a decision

[54] Kant (1983); Korsgaard (1997); Applbaum (1999).
[55] Korsgaard (1997), xxiii.

for constituents: representatives decide they still deserve credit for the expenditures and that the spending program should persist.

Deliberative democrats raise a similar objection to deception. They assert that deception is a tool to achieve manipulation, ensuring political elites use communication to achieve their preferred outcome—credit for the spending and the continuation of the program—rather than a tool to exchange ideas and reasons with the public.[56] Kantians and deliberative democrats would instead ask that legislators explain more carefully their role in the process and why constituents should reward them nonetheless. Constituents can then decide if they prefer the competitive grant programs and if legislators deserve credit. The necessary risk is that constituents will choose a less efficient system for spending money.

If we examine the deception as consequentialists, however, we may find that the deception is justifiable because constituents may prefer that their legislator continue to deceive them about their role in securing the expenditure. This preference arises because deception may lead to more efficient allocations of projects. A large literature has examined how political factors can affect the districts that receive expenditures.[57] If our only goal is to allocate funding to the objectively most economically efficient projects, then the political influence induces inefficiencies[58] and even budget overruns.[59] Competitive grant programs are an institutional innovation that is intended to limit the role of political influence in the allocation of grants and eliminate the accompanying inefficiencies. Rather than allocating expenditures by who has the greatest political power, a competitive process directs spending to the projects most deserving of the expenditure. The focus on objective, rather than political, considerations may, however, undermine support for the grant program. When allocating grants competitively, influential legislators lose the ability to direct funds to their district.

When bureaucrats create credit claiming opportunities for legislators, they solve this institutional design problem, creating political support for a program that allocates expenditures through an explicitly nonpolitical process. The credit claiming opportunities build support with legislators, who continue to support the program because it provides them with the opportunity to claim credit regularly for popular expenditures with little effort exerted. Bureaucrats continue to create the credit claiming opportunities for legislators to sustain their program. The result is that

---

[56] Gutmann and Thompson (1996); Mansbridge (2003).

[57] Ferejohn (1974); Weingast, Shepsle, and Johnsen (1981); Berry, Burden, and Howell (2010*b*).

[58] Ferejohn (1974).

[59] Weingast, Shepsle, and Johnsen (1981); Chen and Malhotra (2007).

a program that allocates expenditures using more criteria, and that will likely lead to more efficient allocations of money, also has the support necessary to sustain the efficient expenditures.

A consequentialist justification for an expenditure is that it helps sustain the competitive grant process, an institution that constituents prefer to a more political allocation. Of course. there are many potential objections to this conclusion. Perhaps one of the most salient objections is that the deception is still self-serving for legislators and the use of consequentialist or utilitarian logic does not preclude the application of more absolutist ethical standards.[60] For example, we might suspect that this deception, if systematically revealed and explained to constituents, could further undermine trust in government. When considering even more morally troubling situations, Michael Walzer has advocated that legislators atone for their misdeeds in public after the deception or other morally dubious action has been conducted.[61] This is not an option available for legislators making use of the fire grants, because revealing the deception would undermine the entire point: constituents would no longer attribute credit to legislators and the program would be politically vulnerable. So to sustain the competitive grant institution, we must tolerate legislators receiving credit for projects they had only an indirect role in securing.

The credit claiming, credit allocation process complicates the process of representation around spending. It can create policy benefits, but also undermine how legislators communicate with constituents. In describing this process thus far, we have focused on how legislators use rhetoric around spending to build constituent support. In the next chapter, we examine how opponents can use criticism to undermine legislators' credit and how this rhetoric helps to explain the large decrease in Republican credit claiming rates that we documented in Chapter 3.

[60] Kymlicka (2002).
[61] Walzer (1973).

CHAPTER 7

Criticism and Credit: How Deficit Implications Undermine Credit Allocation

ON FEBRUARY 17, 2009 IN DENVER COLORADO, BARACK OBAMA signed the American Recovery and Reinvestment Act, a large-scale infusion of "stimulus" cash into the American economy, into law. At the ceremony, Obama declared that "The American Recovery and Reinvestment Act that I will sign today ... is the most sweeping economic recovery package in our history." The massive stimulus spending was an attempt to stop the massive layoffs after the fiscal crises of late 2008, to allay growing fears about the economy, and to cease the momentum of the foreclosure crisis. As the law was signed, unemployment was rapidly increasing—jumping from 6.8% when Obama was elected in November to 8.3% in February. Keeping close pace with the rising unemployment was public anxiety about the economy. Consumer confidence plummeted from 61.4 in September 2008 to 25.3 in February 2009. And as home prices tumbled, it was estimated that 1.8% of homeowners had received at least one notice that foreclosure proceedings on their home had begun.[1]

Obama promised at the ceremony that "[t]oday does not mark the end of our economic troubles. Nor does it constitute all of what we must do to turn our economy around. But it does mark the beginning of the end." He had good reason to be optimistic. The stimulus injected a massive amount of cash into the stagnant economy: $787 billion in total. While liberal economists warned that the spending was too little, the scope of the cash infusion was impressive. Consider transportation spending alone—constituting $48.1 billion total—including $27.5 billion for the construction and maintenance of highways. The stimulus also included money to bolster energy, waste, and communication infrastructure. With only slight exaggeration, Obama declared that "we are remaking the American landscape with the largest new investment in our nation's infrastructure since Eisenhower built an interstate highway system in the 1950s."

---

[1] Staff (2009b).

The stimulus spending also included a modest program to stop home foreclosures before they began. The "Home Affordable Modification Program" provided incentives to loan companies to revise the terms of mortgages whose owners may face foreclosure in the future, but have yet to miss a payment. The relatively small expenditure was intended to avoid the substantially more costly—to both governments and citizens—process of foreclosing on homes.

This small and seemingly uncontroversial foreclosure-prevention program catalyzed one of the largest—and most impactful—social movements in recent American political history. Two days after Obama signed the Recovery Act into law, CNBC reporter Rick Santelli crystallized conservative frustration with the Keynesian stimulus spending. Santelli, while participating in a seemingly mundane discussion about the mortgage assistance program at the Chicago Mercantile Exchange, declared that "the government is promoting bad behavior." He went on to ask "if we really want to subsidize the losers' mortgages?" or if instead the government should "buy houses in foreclosure and give them to people who might have a chance to actually prosper down the road?" The exchange traders accompanying Santelli joined in the criticism of the program. While Santelli was speaking, a trader burst on-screen and shouted "how about we all stop paying our mortgage?" Near the end of the rant, Santelli declared that "we're thinking of having a Chicago Tea Party in July. All you capitalists that want to show up to Lake Michigan, I'm going to start organizing."

Long before July, Santelli's Tea Party movement was beginning.[2] On April 15, Tea Party groups across the country held well attended rallies, with prominent news coverage broadcasting the message even further.[3] At one rally a protester, Mary Wojnas, told a CNN reporter that "our government's out of control with spending."[4] A Tea Party protester in Sacramento declared that she rallied "to oppose socialism and anyone who supports it." At the same rally, a protester carried a sign declaring that "my piggy bank ain't your pork barrel."

After the rallies on April 15, Tea Party groups continued to be a presence in American politics. During the summer of 2009, as Congress was crafting the Affordable Care Act—popularly known as Obamacare—Tea Party members railed against a perceived government takeover of the health care system. Particularly offensive to the Tea Party members was the particularistic spending used to win the support of moderate Democrats in the Senate. The Tea Party members lambasted the

[2] Skocpol and Williamson (2011).
[3] Skocpol and Williamson (2011).
[4] Cooper et al. (2009).

"Cornhusker Kickback" (which funded Nebraska Medicaid recipients in exchange for Ben Nelson's (D-NE) support) and the "Louisiana Purchase" (which provided $200 million in Medicaid funds for Louisiana to win Mary Landrieu's vote) as unjust "bribes" used to obtain "cloture on the government health care takeover."[5]

The Tea Party's anger was focused on the types of particularistic spending that we have shown legislators use to build support. And it is this criticism that undermined support for legislators. The Tea Party movement—and conservative political pundits—broadcasted criticism about government spending, often citing the sorts of projects that legislators regularly claim credit for obtaining. As the Tea Party movement rose in prominence, Republicans changed how they talked about spending. Not only did Republicans substantially reduce their credit claiming propensity in 2009 and 2010, as we have documented in Chapter 3. Republicans also increased and amplified their criticism of government spending—particularly Republican representatives from districts with a large concentration of Republicans, where the Tea Party was especially strong.

This criticism is important for understanding credit allocation, because it causes constituents to consider the potentially negative budget consequences of particularistic spending in the district. Constituents, as we have shown in the previous chapters, think intuitively when evaluating legislators' credit claiming statements and allocating credit. This means that the public can simultaneously hold contradictory preferences. Constituents not only have a preference for spending in their district, they also prefer to eliminate budget deficits and lower the national debt.[6] Spending criticism reminds constituents of their preferences for reduced overall spending and directly affects the credit legislators receive from claiming credit for particularistic spending. Deficit criticism causes constituents to punish legislators whom they would otherwise reward. Building off of research in political behavior about how citizens process competing messages,[7] we use a pair of experiments to show that providing budgetary information about otherwise popular expenditures negates the positive credit legislators receive for the expenditure. Instead, introducing criticism decreases approval ratings, thermometer scores, and perceptions of fiscal responsibility. And the budgetary information that critics illuminate also undermines overall support for government spending in the district.

[5] Malkin (2009).
[6] Hansen (1998).
[7] Zaller (1992).

Our experimental evidence coupled with our analysis of congressional speech helps explain how the Tea Party rhetoric diminished the personal vote-building effect of the stimulus spending. While constituents normally do not consider the budget implications of spending,[8] the Tea Party rhetoric raised the salience of the deficit spending that supported the stimulus, a message regularly reiterated in sympathetic media coverage. The rhetoric caused constituents to identify spending as an example of the type of "pork barrel project" that Tea Party activists and television hosts assured the public was ruining the federal budget.[9] We show that the criticism was particularly effective among constituents who likely hold preferences for a reduced budget:[10] criticism reduced support for spending among everyone but strong liberals who actually increased support for legislators in response to the budget criticism. The criticism also affected how constituents evaluated their representative's actual credit claiming behavior. Without criticism, there is a positive relationship between a legislators' actual credit claiming rates and constituents' perceptions of their actual representatives' ability to deliver money to the district. But when we introduce criticism of government expenditures this relationship is reversed: legislators who claim credit at a higher rate are viewed more negatively overall and as being less effective advocates for their constituents. Criticism of spending, then, is an effective strategy for undermining legislators' credit claiming efforts and for attacking legislators' impression of influence.

The pervasive budget criticism undermines the value of credit claiming for legislators. And so too, we believe, does this criticism dampen the value of particularistic spending for creating consensus in legislative institutions. Both political scientists[11] and politicians have argued that legislative earmarks are often instrumental in assembling legislative coalitions, but political pressure from transparency and conservative groups have lead to bans on earmarked funds in Appropriations bills. Some observers have argued that the bans make forming legislative coalitions more difficult. They argue that removing the ban could help solve some of the legislative paralysis that lead to brinksmanship over the debt ceiling in 2011 and 2013 and a government shutdown in the fall of 2013. Our evidence shows, however, that earmarks alone are likely insufficient for overcoming the legislative divisiveness that plagues Congress. This is because the budget criticism causes legislators to place lower value on the credit claiming opportunities that earmarks provide.

---

[8] Hansen (1998).
[9] Skocpol and Williamson (2011).
[10] Zaller (1992).
[11] Evans (2004); Frisch and Kelly (2011).

For particularistic spending to again "grease the wheels" of the legislative process, a change in rhetoric must also accompany the ability to earmark funds.

The evidence we present in this chapter demonstrates how legislators' statements—credit claiming and criticism—affect the credit legislators receive for spending. We begin with an examination of how Republicans adopted antispending language as the Tea Party rose to prominence. To show this, we start with Zach Wamp, a Tennessee Republican who converted from appropriator to deficit hawk.

7.1 THE DECLINE OF REPUBLICAN CREDIT CLAIMING AND THE RISE OF TEA PARTY RHETORIC

Before the Tea Party's rise in the Republican Party, Zach Wamp (R-TN) was a powerful appropriator who used his position on the Appropriations Committee to direct spending and projects to his East Tennessee district. After joining the Appropriations Committee in 1997, Wamp regularly claimed credit for spending in his district. For example, in 1998 Wamp claimed credit for an $8 million education grant, stating that the grant "should mean better teaching, more challenging courses and a much more creative learning environment for thousands of Hamilton County students."[12] In 2000, Wamp claimed credit for a $1 million earmark to improve water in his district, because Wamp said "in the foothills of Appalachia there are still people that are without the basic necessities"[13] and in 2001 he pushed for funds to improve Tennessee tourism. One news story—that looks suspiciously like a press release—describes a "$1.2 million funding package moving through Congress" to promote tourism—a proposal sponsored by Wamp.[14]

Wamp's prowess in securing money continued throughout the 2000s, becoming an integral component of how he defined his tenure in Washington to constituents. In one profile he described himself as "a heat-seeking missile on behalf of Tennessee and my district."[15] Wamp even defended his efforts against antispending criticism. The Citizens Against Government Waste issued a report in 2003 that was critical of an increase in pork barrel spending in Tennessee. Tom Schatz, then president of the group, criticized appropriators like Wamp, asking them to "look in the mirror and decide whether your parochial pork project is

---

[12] Press (1998).
[13] Press (2000).
[14] Press (2001).
[15] Staff (2010c).

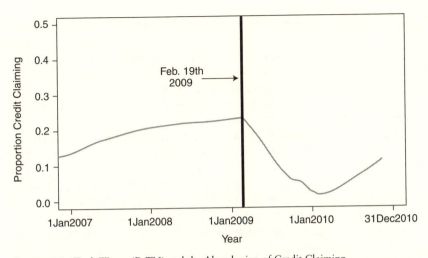

FIGURE 7.1. Zach Wamp (R-TN) and the Abandoning of Credit Claiming.
This figure shows that after the Santelli Tea Party rant, Zach Wamp abandoned his focus on credit claiming.

really more important than protecting the United States of America."[16] Wamp struck back sharply at Schatz's rhetoric. Wamp made clear that he had "no hesitancy to tell you that I regularly look myself in the mirror, and I'm very proud of the work we're doing on the House Appropriations Committee for our state, our region and our nation."[17]

With Wamp's considerable power in Tennessee—based in part on his well-cultivated impression of influence over the appropriations process—he declared his candidacy for governor on January 5, 2009.[18] Yet, with the rise of the Tea Party, it became clear that Wamp would have to distance himself from his particularistic past. Part of this distancing was a shift in his credit claiming propensity. Figure 7.1 shows Wamp's propensity to claim credit in the two years prior to the Tea Party movement—2007 and 2008—and the two years after—2009 and 2010. The gray lines are estimates of the daily probability of an issued press release claiming credit for money and the thick black line represents February 19, the day of Santelli's rant. In 2007 and 2008, Wamp allocated a large share of his press releases to claiming credit: about 19% of his press releases immediately before the emergence of the Tea Party. But after the Tea Party emerged, Wamp abandoned credit claiming, decreasing his credit claiming propensity by *11 percentage points*.

[16] Press (2003).
[17] Press (2003).
[18] Press (2009).

Wamp's sharp decline in credit claiming propensity reflects Republicans' broader movement away from credit claiming that we documented in Chapter 3. In response to the Tea Party, Republicans abandoned credit claiming as a strategy to cultivate support. But Wamp, like other Republicans, went further and became a harsh critic of particularistic spending. Wamp, who defended particularistic spending in Tennessee from the Citizens Against Government Waste, adopted Tea Party language to criticize spending and actively avoided being associated with spending projects in his district. For example, on December 12, 2009, Wamp issued a press release titled "Mall Energy Project Funded Without Congressional Help." In the release, Wamp declared that, "Core Properties, owner of the Oak Ridge mall, did not request congressional help on its competitive grant from the U.S. Department of Energy. Congressman Zach Wamp did not play any role in this grant."[19]

Wamp's adoption of Tea Party rhetoric went even further than merely distancing himself from spending in the district. Wamp suggested that the intrusive federal government and taxes may warrant secession. In one interview, Wamp expressed "hope that the American people will go to the ballot box in 2010 and 2012 so that states are not forced to consider separation from this government."[20]

Wamp's shift from avid appropriator to spending critic reflects a broader shift in the Republican Party. In Chapter 3, we documented the decline in credit claiming propensity, with Republicans reducing their credit claiming over 13 percentage points after the Tea Party's rise. As Chapter 3 showed, Republican credit claiming rates were declining before the Tea Party movement—a decline that paralleled antispending rhetoric in the McCain campaign and conservative concerns about budget deficits during the Bush administration. But the decline in credit claiming rate was hastened after Obama was elected and Santelli's rant crystallized conservative objections to stimulus spending. Before February 19, 2009, the daily rate of Republican credit claiming was declining by about 0.6 percentage points every three months. After February 19, Republicans decreased their daily credit claiming rate by 1.1 percentage points every three months, nearly doubling the rate of decline.

While Republicans like Zach Wamp were avoiding credit claiming, they became increasingly vocal critics of federal spending: Republicans adopted the language of the Tea Party activists. Figure 7.2 shows the incidence of six examples of antispending rhetoric over the six years of

[19] Wamp (2009).
[20] Kolawole (2010).

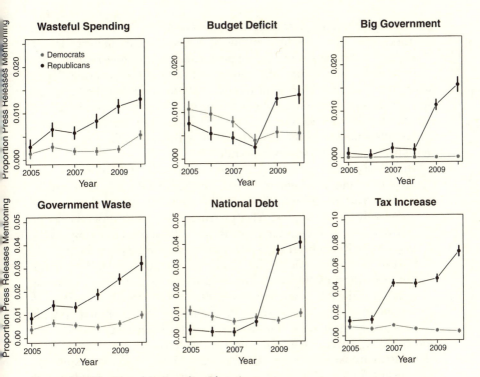

FIGURE 7.2. The Rise of Antispending Rhetoric.
This figure shows the rise of antispending, or tea party, rhetoric among Republicans. The plot shows the proportion of House press releases in which particular key words appear, in each year (horizontal axis), from Democrats (gray line) and Republicans (black line). The points are the measures of proportions, the thick lines are 95 percent confidence intervals. There is a rise in the proportion of press releases from Republicans that use the key words, indicative of the general rise in antispending rhetoric.

press releases included in this study. Each plot represents the proportion of times a particular term appears in press releases (vertical axis) over the six years of study (horizontal axis) for Democrats (gray line) and Republicans (black line).

As an illustrative example, consider the plot in the top right corner. This shows the proportion of press releases from each party that make use of the term "big government." Big government has a long history of being used as a pejorative description of an expanding federal bureaucracy by both Democrats and Republicans. Ronald Reagan famously quipped that "you can't be for *big government*, big taxes, and big bureaucracy and still be for the little guy" (emphasis added). And Bill Clinton declared in his 1996 State of the Union Address that "the era of *big government* is over" (emphasis added). Anger against "big government" became a regular component of Tea Party rhetoric. At an appearance early in the movement, former House majority leader Dick Armey declared that "we oppose bailouts, *big government*, and bad economic policy that threatens the health of the economy."[21] A Washington Times editorial on July 4, 2009 declared that the "popular uprising against oppressive *big government* is in the best tradition of the American independence movement."[22] And one Tea Party protester in Pittsburgh summarized the purpose of a Tax Day rally when he declared that "[i]t's an anti-*big government* rally."[23]

The top right plot in Figure 7.2 shows the increase in Republicans' use of the phrase "big government" after 2009. Before Obama's election, the term "big government" was rarely used in press releases: the phrase appeared in only 0.07% of press releases. After Obama's election, the use of "big government" among Republicans increased substantially. By 2010, over 1.5% of Republican press releases refer to big government. This number included Republicans like John Culberson (R-TX) declaring that "[i]t is clear that his [Obama's] reckless spending and big government policies have failed."[24] John Sullivan (R-OK) reacted to Obama's State of the Union address by stating that "the American people are fed up with what is going on in Washington—they are not buying the tax, borrow and spend big government solutions that the President, Nancy Pelosi and Harry Reid are selling."[25] And Bill Shuster (R-PA) criticized the stimulus as "a near trillion dollar grab-bag of big government social spending and pet projects from the political left."[26] There is no similar increase for Democrats—the increase in the use of the phrase "big government" is exclusive to Republicans.

Other antispending phrases saw a similar increase after Obama's election. For example, Republicans became more likely than Democrats to use the phrase "National Debt"—displayed in the bottom center panel of Figure 7.2—after Obama's election. Republicans also became more likely to discuss the "budget deficit" and "tax increases." Republicans clearly adopted the language of the Tea Party after Obama's election, while Democrats avoided the antispending rhetoric.

We aggregate the incidence of the six spending phrases in Figure 7.2 to create an antispending rhetoric index. We first record whether any of the six phrases in Figure 7.2—determined using Tea Party manifestos

---

[21] Armey 2009 (emphasis added).
[22] Editorial (2009) (emphasis added).
[23] Conte (2009).
[24] Culberson (2009).
[25] Sullivan (2010).
[26] Shuster (2010).

and websites—occur in legislators' press releases. We then measure the proportion of press releases for each legislator in which the antispending rhetoric occurs. To create a final measure, we use a multilevel model to smooth this proportion, borrowing information when legislators issue only a few press releases.[27]

Our measure of antispending rhetoric has a great deal of face validity—even though it is not based on a formal coding scheme and is built on only a small set of antispending phrases. The highest rate of antispending rhetoric is from Virginia Foxx (R-NC). *The National Journal* ranks Foxx as the most conservative member of Congress and is a well known vocal critic of President Obama's policies and of Democrats in general. Other vocal members of the Tea Party caucus— including Ander Crenshaw (R-FL), John Kline (R-MN), Pete Sessions (R-TX), and John Culberson (R-TX)—all are among the representatives with the highest rate of antispending rhetoric in their press releases. Overall, Republicans in 2009 and 2010 have antispending rhetoric in about 9.5% of their press releases. But Democrats, who had substantially less incentive to criticize spending than Republicans, have antispending rhetoric in only 3.2% of their press releases.

Figure 7.3 shows the explosion in Republican antispending rhetoric. This increase occurs in two major shifts. The first shift occurred after the Democrats won the majority in the House of Representatives. At this point, the remaining Republicans began to be more critical of spending—increasing the proportion of antispending press releases 2.1 percentage points (95 percent confidence interval, [0.01, 0.03]). The biggest increase, however, occurred after Barack Obama is elected. In 2008, Republicans had an antispending phrase in about 6% of their press releases, but in 2009 Republicans allocated 9.3% of their press releases to antispending rhetoric, a substantial 3.3 percentage point increase (95 percent confidence interval, [0.02, 0.04]).

The adoption of the Tea Party rhetoric appears to be a response, in part, to Republican incumbents inoculating themselves against potential primary challengers.[28] We demonstrated in Chapter 3 that Republicans from the most conservative districts decreased their attention to credit claiming more than Republicans from more moderate districts. Republicans from conservative districts—those most likely to have Tea Party activists—had the largest increases in antispending rhetoric. Republicans from districts where McCain received 65% of the two-party vote in the 2008 presidential election increased the allocation of their press releases to antispending rhetoric 1.6 percentage points more than Republicans

---

[27] Gelman and Hill (2007).
[28] Mayhew (1974); Brady, Han, and Pope (2007).

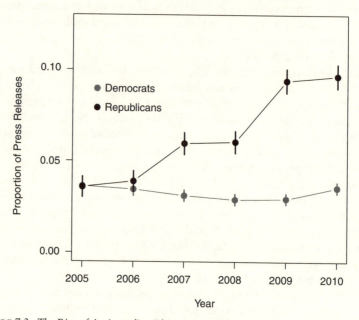

FIGURE 7.3. The Rise of Antispending Rhetoric among Republicans.
This figure shows how Republicans allocated a much larger share of their press releases to antispending rhetoric than Democrats, with a large increase after Obama is elected.

from districts where McCain received 55% of the two-party vote (95 percent confidence interval, [0.01, 0.3]).

When Republicans lob the antispending critiques, they attack a major Obama administration policy goal. But they also attempt directly to undermine the electoral benefit of the stimulus spending for all members of Congress. Perhaps no attack was more direct on the ability to claim credit for spending than Republican efforts to eliminate funds for signs that mark stimulus projects. Ander Crenshaw issued a press release characteristic of the attack. In his press release, Crenshaw explained that he "voted to save American taxpayers millions of dollars by eliminating federal funding for signage that promotes the Obama Administration's stimulus bill." He went on to explain that "across the country, signs have been erected to alert citizens that certain projects are being funded by last year's stimulus bill. These signs, often along highways, provide no meaningful information, create no jobs, and have been criticized as taxpayer-funded advertisements for the stimulus bill."[29] He concludes

[29] Crenshaw (2010).

with a case against the stimulus, stating that "Americans are sick and tired of Washington's spending spree and are calling for an end to big government spending."[30]

Other Republicans set out to explicitly undermine the content of the spending package. Ed Royce (R-CA) leveled criticism when the stimulus package was proposed. He stated that:

> Americans around our nation are suffering. They deserve legislation that spurs investment and creates jobs back home. Instead I have to tell my constituents that the Democrat Leadership decided the solution to this crisis included giving billions to ACORN, a special interest group that has been accused of voter fraud and is reportedly under federal investigation.... What started out as an economic stimulus bill turned into an omnibus spending spree.[31]

Republicans encouraged constituents to join in the criticism, inviting them to identify spending programs worthy of cutting. As Howard Coble (R-NC) explained "House Republican Whip Eric Cantor launched YouCut one week ago and invited viewers to vote on one of five spending cuts that Republicans would bring to the House floor for an up or down vote each week. More than 280,000 people voted in just the first week."[32] While some criticized the YouCut program as frivolous, it provided Republicans with the opportunity to identify individual projects and criticize the expenditures.

Republican criticism of the stimulus affected how the spending package was covered, ensuring that legislators' credit claiming efforts were coupled with criticism of the spending. For example, one report touted that Charlie Melancon's (D-LA) district in Louisiana would receive "more than $5 billion over three years."[33] But Bill Cassidy (R-LA) criticized the spending, stating that "[a] better bill would focus on providing tax relief for working families and small businesses and strengthening our infrastructure.... This is the vision originally laid out by President Obama, and this is the kind of package I could potentially support. Unfortunately, that vision has been weighed down with irresponsible and ineffective spending."[34]

Chet Edwards' (D-TX) opponent in the 2010 congressional election expressed a similar sentiment. Edwards was a long time representative

---

[30] Crenshaw (2010).
[31] Royce (2009).
[32] Coble (2010).
[33] Deslatte (2009).
[34] Deslatte (2009).

of a Republican-leaning district—in part because of his ability to secure money and claim credit for it in the district. As one newspaper report summarizes, "political experts have credited Edwards' sustained political success in a district that is heavily Republican in part to his ability to bring in federal pork."[35] That same article, which covered Edwards' claiming credit for a $16.5 million earmark for Fort Hood, also explained why Edwards' credit claiming was increasingly difficult. The article argued that Edwards' Republican challenger, Bill Flores, "has dinged Edwards for being a big spender in a conservative-leaning district," explicitly arguing that the expenditures that Edwards secured contributed to the national debt.[36] Jeb Hensarling (R-TX) expressed a similar sentiment when stumping for Flores. Hensarling argued that "Obama, Pelosi and Edwards have put the nation on the road to bankruptcy, and they're pressing on the pedal. They're spending us into oblivion at a time when tax revenues are down because the economy is on its back."[37] The Tea Party's criticism, then, directly undermined Edwards' primary strength: the impression of influence over expenditures that he had cultivated with his constituents.

The Republican Party's budget rhetoric coincided with an increasing awareness of the budget deficit among Americans. By the midterm elections in November 2010, 9% of voters identified the budget deficit as the most important problem facing America—up from nearly 0% throughout the Bush administration.[38] When prompted, voters were more united in their expression of budget concerns. In March 2010, Gallup asked the voters to rate the importance of a series of issues for the 2010 congressional elections. When asked, 45% of respondents identified the federal budget deficit as extremely important for their vote. The concern for the deficit extended beyond Republicans. The budget deficit was the second most important issue for independents, with 52% identifying the deficit as extremely important for their vote.[39]

The Tea Party movement created public opposition to spending projects, raised the salience of budget concerns, and undermined legislators' credit claiming efforts. This criticism, we show in the next section, undermined support for spending projects and causes constituents to revise how they view their legislators' credit claiming efforts.

---

[35] Benning (2010).
[36] Benning (2010).
[37] Smith (2010).
[38] Newport (2010).
[39] Jones (2010).

7.2 Study 1: Rewarded for Spending, Punished for Deficits

To examine how Tea Party-style budget criticism affects constituent credit allocation, we conducted a pair of experiments. While voters often have little reason or incentive to connect expenditures in the district to broader budget concerns,[40] political elites—like the representatives who articulated the Tea Party rhetoric we examined in the previous, section—can make the connection explicit and undermine legislators' credit claiming efforts. A robust public opinion literature shows that this kind of contrasting information will affect constituent evaluations.[41] But, as we will show, our experiments allow us to assess who is responsive to the criticism and how this responsiveness has a broader effect on evaluations of legislators.

Our first experiment examines the effect of budget criticism from a nonpartisan source, the Congressional Budget Office. Using this source allows us to isolate the effect of the budget information, separate from any partisan signals that may occur as party officials attack a legislator. For this experiment, we recruited a census-matched sample of 702 self-identified partisans from the SSI panel. We told participants that we had identified a recently written newspaper article about their actual representative in the House and then provided the participant with the experimental manipulation. The use of the actual representative and newspaper stories increases the ecological validity of our treatment, while also ensuring that our participants do not easily identify our manipulation.

Our experiment provides participants with one of two versions of the article, which we summarize in Table 7.1. The *credit claiming* condition presents participants with a legislator claiming credit for an $84-million highway expenditure in the district. To customize the paragraph about each participant's legislator, we include the representative's name at |representativeName and the participant's state at |state.

The *CBO Budget Information* condition includes this same credit claiming about a highway expenditure, but pairs it with information about the budget consequences of the expenditure from the nonpartisan Congressional Budget Office (CBO). We chose the CBO to deliver the information because the CBO is a trusted source that both parties cite regularly. This choice allows us to isolate the explicit effect of budget information from the effect of budget information with partisan content. We also include overall cost of the program, providing information that

---

[40] Hansen (1998).
[41] Zaller (1992).

TABLE 7.1
Content across Conditions, Experiment 1.

Headline: Representative |representativeLastName Announces $84 Million for Local Road Projects

Body: Representative |representativeName (|party - |state) announced that the Department of Transportation Federal Highway Administration has released $84 million for local road and highway projects. Representative |representativeName said 'I am pleased to announce that we will receive $84 Million from the Federal Highway Administration. It is critical that we support our infrastructure to ensure that our roads are safe for travelers and the efficient flow of commerce.' This funding will add lanes to |state highways.

CBO Budget Information: The nonpartisan Congressional Budget Office reported that the spending bill is wasteful and contributes to the growing federal deficit. "This bill contributes to federal spending without identifying a new source of revenue or off-setting budget cuts. Accounting for the total cost of this program across all Congressional districts, the bill costs taxpayers $36.5 billion, all of which is added to the deficit and compounded with interest."

Key
|representativeName: Representative's name
|party: Representative's party
|state: Represenative's state

the expenditure allocates equal money to all districts: $435 \times \$84$ million = $36.5 billion. With these multiple elements, this condition provides constituents with information about the consequences of the project for their district and the consequences of the expenditure for the national budget. We randomly assigned our participants to the two conditions and then first asked them about their representative and next about the program.

Information about the budget consequences of the expenditures from the CBO severely undermines legislators' credit claiming efforts. Including information about the budget consequences of an expenditure causes a severe drop in our participants' evaluations of their legislators. The left-hand column of Table 7.2 presents the average feeling thermometer evaluations across the two conditions, with the 95-percent confidence interval presented below each average. The budget information from the CBO causes participants to decrease their evaluation of their representative 3.97 units (95 percent confidence interval, $[-8.04, 0.10]$). This same decrease is found in legislators' approval ratings. The second column from the left shows the proportion of participants who approve of their legislator across the two conditions. After providing the budget

TABLE 7.2
Budget Information Undermines Support from Credit Claiming.

Condition	Legislator Feeling Thermometer	Approve	Fiscally Responsible	Delivering Money	Passing District Legislation
Credit Claiming	55.26	0.57	0.52	4.77	4.54
	[52.40, 58.13]	[0.52, 0.62]	[0.47, 0.57]	[4.61, 4.92]	[4.38, 4.70]
Budget	51.30	0.45	0.41	4.50	4.33
	[48.40, 54.19]	[0.40, 0.50]	[0.35, 0.46]	[4.34, 4.65]	[4.17, 4.49]

information, legislators' approval ratings drop 12 percentage points (95 percent confidence interval, [−0.19, −0.05]).

The budget information decreases legislators' overall evaluations, in part, because it causes constituents to perceive their representative as wasteful. We asked participants if they agreed that their representative is fiscally responsible. The middle column shows that 52% of participants in the credit claiming condition rated their representative as fiscally responsible, but only 41% of participants in the budget condition agreed that their representative was fiscally responsible—a decrease of 11 percentage points (95 percent confidence interval, [0.35, 0.46]). That this decrease occurs only after the budget information is provided is evidence that constituents, unprompted, do not associate expenditures in the district with waste. But when the criticism is included in the story— as in the Edwards' story in the previous section—the same expenditure is viewed as wasteful. And the legislators' credit is undermined.

The effects of the undermined expenditures extend beyond overall evaluations: constitutents' impression of their legislator's influence over spending is harmed when budget information is provided. The second column from the right shows the average evaluation of a legislator's effectiveness at delivering money to the district, on a seven-point scale. Providing information causes constituents to view their representative as 0.27 points less effective at delivering money to the district (95 percent confidence interval, [−0.49, −0.05]). The budget information also causes legislators to appear less effective at passing legislation that is beneficial for the district (−0.21 decrease, 95 percent confidence interval, [−0.43, 0.01]).

The first iteration of our experiment demonstrates that providing budget information—the kind of information that became salient with the Tea Party movement—undermines the credit that legislators receive from constituents after they announce expenditures. The result is that legislators seem less effective and more wasteful. And most important for understanding how the Tea Party criticism affected credit claiming for the stimulus, legislators' overall evaluations suffer as a result.

This experiment demonstrates that legislators have an incentive to avoid public disclosure if spending contributes to the deficit. But the use of the trusted nonpartisan source—the CBO—may overstate our results. Most of the criticism of particularistic spending came from Tea Party candidates, Tea Party leaders, or from Republican members of Congress. And these partisan sources are likely to be viewed as less trustworthy. This is especially true for Democrats, who are likely to use a partisan heuristic to discount the criticism from the opposing party, because Democratic party officials have argued against the Tea Party rhetoric.[42] Even nonpartisan respondents may dismiss attacks from partisan officials as simple bickering, rather than credible information.

In the second iteration of our experiment, we created a condition that approximated this more contentious source of budget information. In our second experiment, we maintained our credit claiming condition and the CBO Budget Information condition in Table 7.3. To introduce the more contentious information we added a *Partisan Budget Information* condition. Participants in this condition receive budget information from a political figure likely to criticize the participant's member of Congress: the opposing party's national chairperson. For participants whose representative was a Democrat, we included a statement from Reince Priebus, chair of the Republican National Committee. And for participants whose representative is a Republican, we included a statement from Debbie Wasserman-Schultz—chair of the Democratic National Committee. Both the Democratic and Republican National Committees regularly criticize opposing partisans for actions in Congress, ensuring that our treatments replicate the kind of criticism that occurred in response to the stimulus. The statements from the opposing party chairpersons are harsher and more critical of the expenditure than the statement from the CBO. In addition to the CBO information on the budget consequences of the bill, the opposing party chairpersons also assert that "the spending bill is wasteful." We administered this second iteration of our study to 1,166 participants—this time including nonpartisans—census matched to the US sample from the SSI panel. We assigned participants to conditions, administered the treatment, and then collected information in a post-survey.

The results of the second iteration of our experiment replicate our first iteration, while also revealing that the source of the budget information has only a small effect on respondents. Whether the information comes from the CBO or opposing partisans, it undermines constituents' impression of their legislators' influence and harms constituents' overall evaluations. This result is evident in the first column of Table 7.4,

[42] Zaller (1992).

TABLE 7.3
Content across Conditions, Experiment 2.

Headline: Representative |representativeLastName Announces $84 Million for Local Road Projects

Body: Representative |representativeName (|party - |state) announced that the Department of Transportation Federal Highway Administration has released $84 million for local road and highway projects. Representative |representativeName said "I am pleased to announce that we will receive $84 Million from the Federal Highway Administration. It is critical that we support our infrastructure to ensure that our roads are safe for travelers and the efficient flow of commerce." This funding will add lanes to |state highways.

CBO Budget Information: The nonpartisan Congressional Budget Office reported that the spending bill is wasteful and contributes to the growing federal deficit. "This bill contributes to federal spending without identifying a new source of revenue or off-setting budget cuts. Accounting for the total cost of this program across all Congressional districts, the bill costs taxpayers $36.5 billion, all of which is added to the deficit and compounded with interest."

Partisan Information: [Debbie Wasserman-Schultz, Chair of the Democratic National Committee/Reince Preibus, Chair of the Republican National Committee] said that the spending bill is wasteful and contributes to the growing federal deficit. "This bill contributes to federal spending without identifying a new source of revenue or off-setting budget cuts. Accounting for the total cost of this program across all Congressional districts, the bill costs taxpayers $36.5 billion, all of which will be added to the deficit and compounded over time with interest."

Key
|representativeName: Representative's name
|party: Representative's party
|state: Represenative's state

---

which shows the effect of the budget information on legislators' feeling thermometer evaluations. Information from the CBO caused a 3.3-point reduction in average feeling thermometer evaluations (95 percent confidence interval, [−7.69, 1.09]), while the more strongly-worded partisan attack reduced evaluations 5.15 points (95 percent confidence interval, [−9.49, −0.83]). The two sources of information also have a nearly identical effect on approval ratings—the budget information from the CBO caused an 8.2-percentage point decrease in approval ratings (95 percent confidence interval, [−0.16, −0.01]) and the budget information from the party chairperson decreased approval ratings 7.7 percentage points (95 percent confidence interval, [−0.15, −0.00]). Not only do both conditions that provide budgetary information cause a similar drop

TABLE 7.4

Regardless of Source, Budget Information Undermines the Impression of Influence.

Condition	Legislator Feeling Thermometer	Approve	Fiscally Responsible	Delivering Money	Passing District Legislation
Credit Claiming	54.56	0.51	0.44	4.69	4.56
	[51.48, 57.63]	[0.45, 0.56]	[0.39, 0.50]	[4.53, 4.85]	[4.39, 4.72]
Budget	51.25	0.43	0.39	4.40	4.30
	[48.13, 54.38]	[0.37, 0.48]	[0.33, 0.44]	[4.24, 4.56]	[4.13, 4.46]
Partisan Attack	49.40	0.43	0.37	4.53	4.36
	[46.34, 52.45]	[0.38, 0.48]	[0.32, 0.43]	[4.37, 4.68]	[4.19, 4.52]

in overall evaluations of legislators, the decrease we find in the second study is quite similar to the decreased evaluations in the first study, further evidence of the detrimental effects of the budgetary information on the credit legislators receive for spending.

The budgetary information from the partisan source affected perceptions of the legislator's fiscal responsibility and ability to deliver money to the district—an effect that is indistinguishable when the CBO provides the information. The proportion of respondents who agreed that their representative is fiscally responsible decreases 5.9 percentage points when respondents are provided with information from the CBO (95 percent confidence interval, $[-0.13, 0.02]$) and the proportion decreases 7.1 percentage points when respondents are provided with the budget information in a partisan attack (95 percent confidence interval, $[-0.14, 0.00]$). And the budget information from the party chairperson affects constitutents' perceptions of their legislator's influence in Congress. Providing participants with nonpartisan budget information caused a 0.29-point reduction in the average evaluation of a legislator's ability to deliver money to the district (95 percent confidence interval, $[-0.51, -0.06]$), a reduction indistinguishable from the reduction that occurs after participants receive information from a partisan source.

Tables 7.2 and 7.4 show that budget criticism undermines the effect of credit claiming on constituent evaluations, whether the source is the Congressional Budget Office or a member of the opposing party with an incentive to attack. And the negative effects are pervasive, causing constituents to view their legislator more negatively. But the effects of criticism extend well beyond evaluations of legislators. The budget information also undermines support for government spending, causing constituents to express opposition to the program funding the highway expenditure. Table 7.5 shows how budget information affects program support across both iterations of our experiment.

TABLE 7.5
Budget Information Erodes Support for the Spending Program.

Condition	Experiment 1		Experiment 2	
	Oppose Program	Worth Money	Oppose Program	Worth Money
Credit Claiming	0.13	0.61	0.08	0.63
	[0.09, 0.17]	[0.56, 0.66]	[0.03, 0.12]	[0.58, 0.68]
Budget	0.32	0.47	0.25	0.55
	[0.28, 0.37]	[0.42, 0.52]	[0.21, 0.29]	[0.49, 0.60]
Partisan Attack	–	–	0.24	0.52
	–	–	[0.20, 0.28]	[0.47, 0.57]

In both experiments, we asked our participants if they opposed the spending program that allocated funds to the district. And in both experiments including the budget information caused a sharp increase in opposition to the program. In our first experiment, budget information from the CBO caused a 21.2-percentage point increase in opposition to the program, (95 percent confidence interval, [0.14, 0.28]). A similar effect is found across both conditions in the second iteration: the CBO causes a 17.3-percentage point increase in opposition, (95 percent confidence interval, [0.11, 0.23]) and partisan budget information causes a 16.5-percentage point increase in opposition (95 percent confidence interval, [0.11, 0.22]). The budgetary information also causes constituents to perceive the program as wasteful. We asked our participants if they agreed that the program was "worth the money." In our first iteration, the CBO information causes a 14.0-percentage point decrease in the proportion of respondents who would agree that the program was worth the cost (95 percent confidence interval, [−0.21, −0.07]). Our second iteration replicates this finding with information from the CBO (8.4-percentage point decrease, 95 percent confidence interval, [−0.16, −0.01]) and party chairpersons (11.1-percentage point decrease, [−0.19, −0.04]) less likely to perceive the program as valuable.

Budget criticism and labeling expenditures as wasteful, then, undermine the effect of legislators' credit claiming efforts on their constituents' impression of their influence over spending. Credit claiming is undermined because most ideologues have a negative reaction to the budget criticism. Figure 7.4 shows how the effect of criticism varies for constituents with different ideologies (left-hand vertical axis) for the CBO and partisan criticism (right-hand vertical axis), with the effect measured on legislators' approval rating. To determine the heterogeneous treatment effects—how the effect of the intervention varies with respondent characteristics—we used a weighted ensemble, as described in

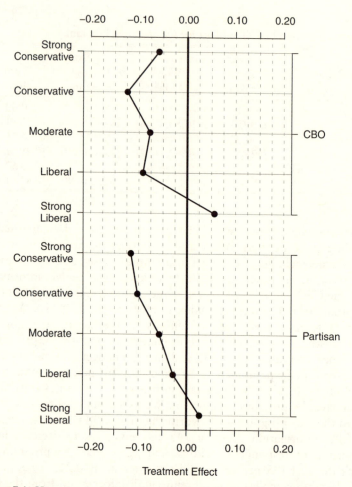

FIGURE 7.4. Heterogeneity in Response to Credit Claiming.
Constituents' response to the budget criticism varies with their ideology. Strong liberals have a positive response to the criticism, which is consistent with a rejection of the criticism about spending from Tea Party representatives. More conservative constituents, however, have a negative response to the criticism, punishing legislators when they learn about the budget consequences of spending.

Grimmer, Messing, and Westwood (2013). For both treatments, strong liberals actually have a positive response to the criticism, while all other ideologues have a negative response. That strong liberals respond positively is perhaps expected, as many progressive and liberal pundits— such as Paul Krugman—responded to Tea Party rhetoric by asserting that budget deficits were not a pressing problem and that particularistic

TABLE 7.6
The Consequences of Budget Criticism for Legislators' Credit Claiming Efforts.

	Effective at Delivering Money	Feeling Thermometer
Credit Claiming	0.09	1.94
	[0.05, 0.14]	[1.08, 2.81]
Budget Criticism	−0.17	−2.09
	[−0.31, −0.03]	[−4.53, 0.36]

spending is only a small contributor to budget overruns.[43] All other ideologues, however, had a much more negative response to the budget criticism. Liberals (who are not strong liberals), moderates, and all conservatives allocated less credit to legislators after the criticism was announced. This is consistent with Zaller's (1992) model of public opinion, where citizens reject messages that contradict their ideological views.

Criticizing the budget implications of the expenditures undermines legislators' credit claiming efforts in our experiment. The effect of the criticism, though, extends well beyond the immediate evaluations we capture in our experiment. The criticism also causes constituents to revise the credit that legislators receive for actual credit claiming messages outside of our experiment. In Table 7.6, we present the relationship between legislators' actual credit claiming rates and constituents' evaluations of their representative. To calculate this relationship, we aggregated across all of our experiments involving actual House members and used our measures of credit claiming calculated in Chapter 3, after controlling for a number of potentially confounding covariates. In the top row of Table 7.6, we present the relationship between legislators' credit claiming rates and the dependent variables when we provide constituents with a credit claiming message alone. The left-hand column, for example, shows how legislators' actual credit claiming rates affect constituents' evaluations of their representative's effectiveness at delivering the money to the district. As we would expect from Chapter 5, there is a positive relationship—legislators who claim credit for more spending are perceived as more effective at delivering money.

The bottom row of Table 7.6 shows there is a negative relationship between legislators' credit claiming rates and their perceived effectiveness at delivering money when the budget implications of spending are criticized. After criticism, legislators who claim credit more often are viewed as less effective by constituents. Criticism also undermines the

[43] Krugman (2010).

effect of credit claiming on overall support. In credit claiming conditions, legislators who actually have a higher credit claiming rate are evaluated more highly overall. But when budget criticism is introduced, legislators who claim credit more often are evaluated more negatively.

The evidence reveals the power of Tea Party criticism to undermine legislators' efforts to cultivate an impression of influence. Not only does the criticism undermine the credit legislators receive for spending, it also causes constituents to revise their assessment of their representative. This turns a representative's strength—a personal vote that is based on perceptions as effective at delivering money to the district—into a liability. And as we now explore in the conclusion, the persistence of this criticism has broad implications for the possibility of using particularistic spending to build legislative coalitions.

7.3 CRITICISM, THE TEA PARTY, AND CONSENSUS

This chapter demonstrates the potential downsides to credit claiming performed in order to cultivate a personal vote. When legislators engage in credit claiming, they create an impression of influence over expenditures that go to the district. At the same time, they associate themselves with expenditures that other legislators may label as wasteful, particularly when projects are financed by deficit spending. We show that Republicans are particularly likely to make this criticism. After Obama was elected and Democrats passed a large Keynesian stimulus, Republican legislators amplified their criticism of government spending and dampened their own credit claiming rates. This strategy undermined legislators' ability to create an impression of influence over spending and, consequently, to cultivate a personal vote. Not only did the criticism affect how constituents respond to one message, it also caused constituents to change their evaluations of legislators' previous credit claiming.

The increase in budget criticism also suggests limitations to institutional reforms aimed at solving congressional gridlock. When the Republicans reclaimed the majority in 2011, they also instituted a ban on earmarked funds in appropriations bills. This ban was intended to create transparency in government spending projects, forcing bureaucrats to vet all federal spending. The ban has been criticized by both politicians and political scientists. Politicians have argued that removing the ability to earmark funds cedes power to executive agencies. When legislators lack power over spending, they often find themselves frustrated that they cannot advance spending priorities in their district, no matter how popular the spending projects might be.

But the most common reason given for lifting the earmark ban is that including federal spending may alleviate the partisan gridlock that has lead to government shutdowns and near breaches of the debt ceiling. In high-profile opinion pieces, political scientists have argued that earmarks "if doled out strategically" can "provide an efficient way for presidents and congressional leaders to build coalitions for broad-based national legislation."[44] Journalists seized on research in political science to make the same point. Matthew Yglesias has written that "[t]he judicious application of lard emerged over the years as a time-honored means of greasing the wheels of government."[45] Leon Nayfakh argues that "in demonizing pork Congress accidentally gave up something deeply valuable: a tool for reaching compromise."[46] Politicians have expressed similar sentiment. Tom Cole (R-OK) has argued that, with a ban on earmarks, "you're removing all incentive for people to vote for things that are tough."[47]

Our evidence in this chapter suggests, however, that earmarks alone are insufficient to induce compromise in Congress. This is because criticism undermines the value that legislators attach to claiming credit for spending. Consider, for example, the Republican majority as they attempt to piece together a coalition on key votes. Even if the leadership were able to distribute pork to its members, it is unclear that the most conservative legislators—who are also the most vocal critics of expenditures—would be willing to accept the earmarks in exchange for their votes. Given the vocal objections to particularistic spending, it seems, in fact, unlikely. Standard-bearers for the Tea Party movement had previously refused earmarked funds. For example, Tom Coburn (R-OK) writes in his memoir about turning down a $15 million earmark to support a federal highway Appropriations bill. He asserts that "when we were asked to trade our vote for absolute control over $15 million, we refused to participate in a process that had little integrity and was damaging to the country."[48] Coburn articulates a more general argument: when legislators cultivate support by objecting to spending, they have little reason to trade their votes for projects in their district.

More liberal Republicans and Democrats are also likely to be less willing to trade their votes for earmarked funds. This is because legislators who trade their votes for earmarks are likely to face vocal criticism, which we have shown may undermine the value of earmarked money.

---

[44] Patashnik (2013).
[45] Yglesias (2013).
[46] Neyfakh (2013).
[47] Greeley (2013).
[48] Coburn (2003).

Consider, for example, how the 60-vote coalition was pieced together in the Senate for legislation that would eventually become the Affordable Care Act, or Obamacare. While not in the final legislation, Ben Nelson (D-NE) and Mary Landrieu (D-LA) both received substantial financial concessions for their states in return for voting for the legislation. And both Nelson and Landrieu faced vocal criticism from opponents of the bill for the deal. Conservative media were quick to label the special concessions for Nebraska's medicaid contribution the "Cornhusker Kickback" and additional medicaid funds sent to Louisiana to entice Landrieu's support was labeled the "Louisiana Purchase." Conservative media equated the particularistic concessions for the senators' states with bribes. For example, the conservative blogger Michelle Malkin listed recipients of concessions in an article titled "Cash for Cloture: Demcare Bribe List Part II."[49] The vocal criticism eroded the value of the medicaid exceptions for the two senators, exactly the kind of criticism that our results show undermines the value of credit claiming for legislators.

For both Republicans and Democrats, the criticism of spending makes the opportunity to claim credit for future expenditures in the district less valuable. This hinders the ability of earmarks to "grease the wheels" and solve gridlock. The problem is not just that earmarks are unavailable. It is also that legislators attach substantially less value to any particularistic spending. So even if earmarks become available, it may still be difficult to assemble coalitions to support legislation, because earmarks may erode support for legislators.

The detrimental effects of criticism may also help explain why legislative coalitions tend to be universalistic. For example, a large literature in the study of Congress has attempted to explain the extremely large coalitions in distributive spending bills—coalitions that are so large they are called "universalistic."[50] We think the detrimental effect of budget criticism for the credit *individual* legislators receive provides strong incentives for party leaders to co-opt potential critics and create large coalitions.[51] Rather than simply attempting to defend a party brand,[52] legislators, it seems, also attempt to defend the value of particularistic spending in their own district. And this may also explain why party leaders are so harsh towards those who refuse to participate in the large coalitions: the leaders are attempting to dampen detrimental criticism. William Proxmire, for example, regularly criticized particularistic spending in Appropriations bills. In response, Proxmire's colleagues had

---

[49] Malkin (2009).
[50] Weingast (1979).
[51] Weingast (1979); Groseclose and Snyder (1996); Balla et al. (2002).
[52] Balla et al. (2002).

the Senate showers removed, which he regularly used after running to work. After Jim DeMint (R-SC) and Tom Coburn (R-OK) joined the Senate in 2005, they introduced a series of amendments to embarrass Appropriators. In response, the Republican leadership removed funding for their offices.

This chapter has shown that the effect of credit claiming is contingent: it depends not just on how closely legislators associate themselves with spending in the district, but also on how other actors talk about expenditures. This demonstrates yet another way that the rhetoric on spending affects representation around spending. Dollars in the district alone are insufficient to cultivate support; constituents also have to believe that those expenditures are worthwhile investments in order for legislators to receive credit. And if other politicians are successful at convincing constituents that expenditures are wasteful, then an incumbent's strength—that is, constituents' impression of his or her influence over spending—can become a weakness.

CHAPTER 8

Representation and the Impression of Influence

PETE VISCLOSKY (D-IN) EASILY WON REELECTION IN 2012, defeating an upstart Republican challenger. One newspaper editorial endorsed Visclosky because of his "excellent record of service to the district"[1] and because the spending he directed to the district "helped the region move forward in multiple ways."[2] Visclosky had built a reputation as an effective advocate for the interests of his district—specifically, he had built an impression of influence over government expenditures. Visclosky directed spending to the district to cultivate this reputation. He also engaged in a sustained and public marketing campaign, to make certain constituents know that he was responsible for spending. When in his district, Visclosky regularly cut ribbons at new facilities, attended groundbreaking ceremonies at new projects, and issued press releases about his efforts to direct new projects to the district.

When legislators like Visclosky claim credit for a project, they ensure that constituents learn about their representative's work in Washington. This credit claiming solves a problem for representatives—namely, that inattentive constituents may fail to reward them for expenditures in the district. It also creates an opportunity for legislators to receive credit for much more than spending as it occurs in the district. This book has shown how the credit claiming, credit allocation process works and how it matters for representation. Representatives engage in credit claiming to cultivate a personal vote, claiming credit for projects and expenditures likely to bolster support with constituents.[3] Constituents, in turn, react to these messages, evaluating them based on the actions that legislators claim to perform and the types of expenditures they claim credit for obtaining. But constituents are much less responsive to the amount of money allocated to the project. Even though constituents lack strong preferences over spending, they can still exercise indirect control

---

[1] Ross (2012).
[2] Ross (2012).
[3] Arnold (1992); Ashworth (2012).

over legislators and indirectly hold legislators accountable. But rather than being responsive to constituents' stated preferences, legislators are responsive to the types of projects they anticipate will bolster their standing with constituents. This behavior complicates accountability and forces us to consider how we might trade off more efficient outcomes with greater potential for deception.

We have characterized when and how legislators use spending to cultivate a personal vote. Legislators' credit claiming rates depend on the composition of their district. Representatives who need to cultivate support with independents and opposing partisans tend to claim credit for spending at higher rates than legislators who rely on their own partisans to win reelection. When legislators engage in credit claiming, they claim much more than expenditures as they occur in the district. We show that legislators regularly claim responsibility for spending long before it reaches the district and for projects that representatives might have only had an indirect role in securing. And legislators claim credit for relatively small amounts of money, with typical expenditures providing small contributions to the district.

Constituents are responsive to legislators' credit claiming messages. Claiming credit not only increases name recognition, it also cultivates an impression of influence over expenditures. The impression of influence, in turn, leads to an increase in overall support for legislators—an increase larger than other nonpartisan messages. When constituents evaluate credit claiming messages they tend to focus on the action legislators report and the recipient of the expenditure, rather than the amount that legislators claim credit for securing. The result is that repeated opportunities to engage in credit claiminga are more valuable for legislators than an increase in the amount of money legislators claim in any one message.

Legislators value the opportunity to claim credit for spending because it helps them to build support among constituents. This motivation affects the institutions that disburse federal money. We show how the credit claiming, credit allocation process makes some grant programs politically robust, even though legislators have little control over how the expenditures are allocated. The political security rises because bureaucrats at the programs recognize the value that legislators attach merely to announcing a project. So bureaucrats create opportunities for legislators to make an announcement, even if the legislator had only an indirect role in securing the grant. Legislators take advantage of the opportunity by implying they deserve credit for the grant, although without explicitly claiming credit for it. The opportunities work for bureaucrats, too. Legislators who most regularly announce the expenditures defend the program from cuts. And these opportunities help legislators with their constituents, who reward them for merely implying they deserve credit for an expenditure.

Our evidence also shows the contingent value of credit claiming messages. Legislators create an impression of influence with their credit claiming messages, but how constituents allocate credit depends on what other political actors say about expenditures. If other legislators say spending is wasteful, this dampens the benefits of credit claiming. Merely explaining that spending will contribute to a budget deficit is sufficient for constituents to view particularistic expenditures as wasteful, rather than beneficial. And this criticism affects constituents' overall evaluations of a legislator and his or her effectiveness. Recent political history shows that the risk of being criticized is real for many legislators. After Barack Obama's election, Republicans avoided credit claiming and instead attacked particularistic expenditures as wasteful, undermining other legislators' credit claiming efforts.

In this book, we have shown that to understand how legislators use spending to build support, we must consider legislators' credit claiming efforts. In this concluding chapter, we explore what our evidence implies for political representation. Evaluating the implications of the process that we describe in this book depends on our priorities in representation. If we prioritize citzens' direct control over legislators or the truthful, reasoned exchange of ideas, then the credit claiming process we describe is detrimental because in it legislators regularly deceive their constituents. And assuming that we care about this exchange, we propose some remedies that could increase the clarity in legislators' messages. But if we prioritize the policy outcomes and believe that indirect control is compatible with effective representation, then the credit claiming process is beneficial. It may encourage legislators to work harder to direct spending to the district and lead to more efficient expenditures.

The credit claiming, credit allocation process we describe occurs outside of Congress as legislators attempt to cultivate support in their districts. But the process also matters for the design of political institutions in Washington because it affects how the federal government disburses funds and how funds can be used to create legislative coalitions. And while our argument has focused on how members of Congress make the case that they deserve credit for spending as it occurs in the district, our logic applies more broadly to other components of representation. Within the United States, a similar logic may help explain when and how legislators engage in other activities, such as oversight on congressional committees. Outside of the United States, our logic may help explain the conditions in which officials may need to engage in credit claiming to remove ambiguity about who is responsible for government actions.

This chapter reveals the broad implications of narrow district spending. With seemingly small expenditures, legislators are able to cultivate support. In this way, the credit claiming, credit allocation process illuminates how representation is about much more than just the ideological alignment of legislators with their constituents.

8.1 REPRESENTATION WITH ENTREPRENEURIAL LEGISLATORS

Legislators create support with credit claiming messages, acting like entrepreneurs to build political support. Representatives produce messages for constituents, encouraging them to allocate credit for projects that occur in the district. And constituents, in turn, are responsive to this encouragement, allocating credit to legislators for projects. Legislators' anticipation of constituents' reaction makes indirect control and accountability over spending possible, even though constituents may struggle to articulate their spending priorities. Legislators will enact constituents' spending priorities if the representatives are effective at anticipating constituent reaction and cultivating support. This interaction creates a dynamic accountability.[4]

This mechanism of accountability is qualitatively different than the notion of accountability and representation usually advanced in the empirical literature on political representation. Beginning with Miller and Stokes[5] scholars have equated political representation with ideological agreement between constituents and representatives.[6] Recent studies of ideological representation have provided even more precise insights into how legislators and constituents agree about expenditures, introducing tools for placing legislators and constituents into the same policy space. These tools facilitate a direct comparisons of preferences.[7] The new studies provide insights into how the policy views of constituents are aggregated into political tools in Congress.

The same techniques and standards, however, are unlikely to be useful for studying representation on district expenditures. These tools cannot help because constituents lack the strong and well-formed preferences to be situated in a "policy space." In other words, a constituent's evaluations of policies tend to be in response to legislators' credit claiming statements, rather than the result of reflecting on how some expenditure delivered to the district or proposed project align with her

[4] Arnold (1992); Mansbridge (2003); Ashworth (2012).
[5] Miller and Stokes (1963).
[6] Achen (1978); Bafumi and Herron (2010).
[7] Bafumi and Herron (2010); Tausanovitch and Warshaw (2013); Bonica (2014).

deeply held beliefs. This different mechanism for accountability creates different risks for representation and different potential benefits. And how we even think about accountability in this setting depends on our priorities in representation.

8.1.1 The Potential for Deception to Harm Representation and Undermine Accountability

Perhaps the most obvious risk to accountability is that legislators will engage in a broad and systematic deception of their constituents. That is, legislators may simply lie about the work that they have done in Washington or the efforts to direct spending back to the district. As we explain in Chapter 2, however, outright lies are very risky for legislators and exceedingly unlikely. Members of Congress and their staff know that simply fabricating actions can undermine legislators' prior credit claiming efforts and perhaps even derail a reelection campaign.[8] Similarly, local political officials will recognize if expenditures rarely arrive in the district. This makes it difficult for legislators to claim credit for requesting expenditures and and then shirk in providing expenditures for their district.

Legislators do, however, engage in deception. Representatives regularly imply that they deserve credit for expenditures, even though they might have exercised only an indirect role in delivering the expenditure. These deceptive implications are successful: constituents reward legislators who imply they deserve credit at about the same rate as they reward legislators who explicitly state that they deserve credit for the expenditure. Arthur Applbaum argues that this action is a redescription— an intentional focus on certain facts to cause an interlocutor to reach a false conclusion.[9] Participants in our experiments appear to agree that this behavior is a deception. When legislators' implications are revealed, participants decrease the credit allocated to legislators for the expenditure.

If we equate representation with citizens exercising direct control over legislators, then the credit claiming process is detrimental to representation. Legislators' credit claiming causes constituents to reward their representatives for much more than spending as it happens in the district and for many more projects than those legislators are directly responsible for securing. This dynamic undermines citizens' ability to react to their representative's actions and to hold them accountable based on those actions. As a result, we might say that representation suffers.

---

[8] Arnold (1992).
[9] Applbaum (1999).

The deception is also problematic if we believe that deliberation and the reasoned exchange of ideas are inherently important for representation. Philosophers in this tradition view deception as an action of unsanctioned authority by legislators. Kantian philosophers, for example, argue that for two individuals to be treated like equals they must each be truthful with each other.[10] Deceiving constituents is tantamount to making a decision for them—an exercise in autocratic authority. Deliberative democrats take a similar stand against deception. As Mansbridge (2003) explains, deception is a form of "manipulation", inducing constituents to support a legislator when they would be less supportive if given full information.[11] Other theorists argue that combining diverse ideas together can lead to better public decisions.[12] When legislators engage in deception, however, they undermine conditions that can lead to reasoned exchange of ideas and new policies.

If we worry about deception because of this corrosive effect, we may naturally ask how to limit legislators' deceptions. This is no small task. Legislators' vague language creates plausible deniability for any accusation of lying. Legislators can accurately say they were not deceiving constituents if an opponent or other politician accuses the representative of being deceitful. After all, a legislator is never actually lying. This makes simple institutional changes—such as empowering opponents or opposing party officials—unlikely to work.

Perhaps the greatest potential change would be to encourage newspapers to avoid reprinting legislators' press releases. Grimmer shows that local newspaper outlets regularly reprint legislators' press releases under a "Staff" or "Associated Press" by-line.[13] By providing legislators the chance to write their own news stories, newspapers and other media outlets repeat and amplify the deception. Simple changes in press offices could diminish the effect of this amplification. Reporters might still cover the announcement, but instead offer a more realistic account of how the expenditure was allocated to the district. Of course, this requires that reporters be educated on the appropriations process and sufficient newspaper budgets to engage in this effort. Given the current constraints on budgets among local media, this reform would be difficult to implement. And, as we explain in the next section, there are potential reasons not to want to stop legislators from implying they deserve credit for spending.

---

[10] Korsgaard (1997).
[11] Mansbridge (2003).
[12] Page (2007); Ober (2010).
[13] Grimmer (2013).

8.1.2 *The Potential for Deception to Improve Representation and Accountability*

If we prioritize the outcomes of the process—that is, the allocation of expenditures across districts—and recognize that indirect control may be sufficient to induce legislator effort and responsiveness, then the deception may be justifiable. As we describe in Chapter 5, rewarding legislators for their work throughout the appropriations process, and not just spending as it occurs in the district, may cause legislators to work harder at delivering spending to the district. If legislators are only rewarded for spending as it occurs, then directing money to the district is risky. The most prominent risk is that executive-branch officials may fail to disburse funds that representatives secure for their district, either at any time or before a critical election for a representative. If constituents only evaluate legislators based on spending in the district, then any unspent funds are wasted effort for legislators. For representatives, the higher the probability that funds go unspent or are delayed until after a critical election, the less attractive that directing spending to the district will be. The results are dampened incentives to work on directing funds to the district.

Rewarding legislators throughout the appropriations process lowers the risk of unspent funds and this lower risk increases the reward from working on directing money to the district. Rather than receiving a reward once when the spending occurs, the credit claiming process ensures that legislators receive credit for requesting funds, seeing them through the Appropriations Committee, and verifying that the money is included in the final bill. The increased reward creates incentives for more legislators to work harder to direct money to their district. The result is that credit claiming creates incentives to increase, not decrease, the effort allocated to directing funds to the district.

Another reason that constituents may prefer to be deceived is that the credit claiming process may offer a solution to persistent problems in government budgets. For three decades, scholars of government budgeting have worried that political consideration will cause inefficient allocations of expenditures.[14] Political power moves expenditures away from the projects that have the greatest economic return, instead moving them to districts represented by the most influential representatives. Such projects are commonly referred to as pork-barrel projects. Antispending politicians have also argued that political influence in spending decisions exerts a corrupting influence. In one floor speech, Senator John McCain (R-AZ) asserted that "the corruption which stems from earmarking has

---

[14] Ferejohn (1974); Weingast, Shepsle, and Johnsen (1981).

resulted in current and former members of both the House and Senate either under investigation, under indictment, or in prison."[15]

One way to purge political influence from spending decisions is to delegate authority to an executive agency: members of Congress could write legislation that provides executive agencies with authority over disbursement decisions. This alone, however, is insufficient to remove political influence. Bureaucrats may try to cultivate congressional support by directing expenditures to congressional districts.[16] Or, executive officials may be responsive to political pressure from the presidential administration.[17] So, in addition to the delegation of authority, legislators can also put in place rules that limit bureaucratic discretion, forcing an agency to award grants based on clear criteria that would be difficult to manipulate. One example of such rules are those in competitive grant programs, where scoring of applications is based on clearly defined criteria or conducted by experts not officially in the agency. In Chapter 6, we describe a competitive grant program that disburses fire department grants, where funding decisions are made through an automated scoring process and a team of expert reviewers not affiliated with the agency.

Delegating authority with rules to limit discretion reduces the opportunity for political influence to affect disbursements. But insulating the program from political manipulation may also make it politically fragile. We have shown how legislators value the opportunity to announce that they have requested an expenditure for their district and then claim credit for securing that expenditure. If the competitive grant program is unable to provide these opportunities to legislators, members of Congress may see little value in the program. And this may make it more susceptible to budget cuts or even termination.

Creating credit claiming opportunities provides a solution to a program's political fragility. They enable bureaucrats at competitive grant programs to bolster congressional support. And, by increasing this support, the program makes itself politically robust. When the agency provides credit claiming opportunities, it provides a reminder that it is valuable to reelection-oriented members of Congress who want to create an impression of influence over expenditures. The value, however, comes at the cost of facilitating deception. When legislators claim credit for the spending, they imply that they are responsible for the expenditure, even though both the legislator and bureaucrat know full well that the legislator had, at best, an indirect role in securing the expenditure.

---

[15] McCain (2010).

[16] Ferejohn (1974); Arnold (1979).

[17] Berry, Burden, and Howell (2010b).

This deception may make constituents materially better off and, if given a choice between institutions, constituents might prefer a representational system in which legislators actively engage in deception. This preference seems counterintuitive at first: why would constituents prefer a legislators who exerts little effort for an expenditure to a legislator who works hard to deliver a project to the district? Constituents make the choice for deception, however, because the *system* of expenditures may be more efficient. Programs may be more likely to allocate expenditures to more efficient projects when deception is possible and budgets are less susceptible to budget overruns. The benefits of this system may override any potential negative material costs from having a shirking representative who exerts little actual effort. The dual of this argument is also true: having a legislator exert effort to deliver spending to a district may be beneficial to the district, but may impose systemic costs that dampen the local benefits.

If given a choice between institutions, then, constituents may choose a system where they are deceived rather than a system where expenditures are broadly decided on a political basis. It should be emphasized, however, that this choice is only a theoretical possibility, which limits the power of the consequentialist justification for deception. If the deception is revealed to constituents, our evidence shows, legislators will no longer receive credit for the expenditure (see Chapter 6). This forces legislators and bureaucrats to decide that constituents are better off being deceived; the very political elites who benefit from the deception are also deciding if the deception is justified. So we might have reason to justify the deception, but constituents are never able to choose to be deceived. Rather elites who benefit from the deception, must make the choice. This creates a new risk: legislators may deceive constituents, even if the deception is not economically justified.[18]

8.2 CONTINGENT VALUE OF PARTICULARISTIC SPENDING AND ITS IMPLICATIONS FOR INSTITUTIONS

Throughout this book, we have emphasized that legislators receive credit for spending if they make the case that they deserve credit. In the absence of this credit claiming effort, constituents struggle to attribute projects

---

[18] We may be worried that expenditures constitute only a small portion of the federal budget. While this is an important objection, we think its force is dampened by two considerations. First, legislators are able to exert political influence on formula grants (Martin, 2012). Second, even small expenditures in the district may be consequential for local budgets or for local organizations.

in the district to their member of Congress. The value of spending, then, depends on legislators' efforts to be associated with the projects in their district. The same project in two congressional districts could have very different electoral consequences, depending on how hard legislators work to be associated with it.

For legislators to be rewarded for expenditures, they not only need to make the case that they deserve credit. They also need others to not criticize the expenditures—the value of credit claiming depends on what other legislators say about particularistic expenditures. If other legislators and political elites criticize particularistic expenditures, then the credit that legislators receive for those expenditures is diminished. And the criticism causes constituents to reconsider legislators' prior credit claiming efforts. In this way, the introduction of budget criticism creates a negative relationship between higher rates of credit claiming and legislator approval.

The force of this criticism is particularly relevant given the recent rise in antispending rhetoric among members of the Republican Party. After the election of Barack Obama, the passage of a massive stimulus-spending bill, and the emergence of the Tea Party, Republican House members began avoiding claiming credit for spending. Instead, they became more vocal in their criticism of government expenditures. Rather than claiming credit for money going to their districts, Republicans became more likely to decry the rise of "big government," the increase in "national debt," or cite specific expenditures in districts as "wasteful spending."

That the value of spending depends on the absence of criticism from legislators not only matters for understanding how legislators use particularistic spending to cultivate a personal vote. It also helps us understand how particularistic expenditures can be used to create legislative coalitions. Political scientists have argued that the ability to direct particularistic expenditures to the district facilitates the formation of legislative coalitions.[19] The key insight is that legislators are willing to cast votes that they might otherwise be reluctant to cast, if they can offset some of the electoral risk with the opportunity to claim credit for expenditures in the district. And recently, politicians and political scientists have argued that a return to earmarking may be key to overcoming some of the gridlock that has characterized Congresses after the ban of earmarked funds.

Our evidence suggests, however, that as long as the Republican Party continues to criticize government expenditures, lifting the earmark ban will be insufficient to overcome legislative gridlock. This is because

---

[19] Lee (2003a); Evans (2004).

Republican criticism substantially dampens the value of particularistic projects. Rather than offsetting the electoral risks of casting controversial votes, this criticism may introduce new electoral risks, particularly for Republicans. For party leaders to use spending effectively as a tool to build legislative coalitions, then, party leads need more than the ability to distribute funds. The use of spending to build support also requires a change in how legislators talk about spending—a shift in the expressed attitudes towards expenditures in the district. A reform that requires much more than a change in the House rules.

8.3 IMPRESSIONS IN OTHER CONTEXTS

Legislators create an impression of influence in order to receive credit for expenditures in the district. While we have focused on how credit claiming affects representation around spending, legislators' impressions are likely to affect representation in other areas of policy. For example, legislators may attempt to create an impression of oversight when participating in congressional hearings. This may explain why legislators are quick to participate in very prominent televised committee hearings. Participating in the hearings provides legislators with an opportunity to appear in local news and to give the impression they provide careful oversight as a member of Congress. This high visibility provides legislators an electoral incentive to participate in oversight, perhaps alleviating a collective-action problem for members of Congress in the provision of oversight. Similarly, we might expect that legislators will attempt to create impressions that they were instrumental in the passage of new legislation. As Mayhew argued, legislators' credit claims must be plausible: in other words, they must have a reasonable claim to have affected policy in some way.[20] But legislators may have ample opportunity to imply they were influential in a policy process, or to claim credit for one small component of a policy.

The impression of influence over expenditures may occur in other contexts as well. For example, Cruz and Schneider show how elected officials in the Philippines imply they deserve credit for disaster aid allocated by foreign governments.[21] Indeed, we might expect that any situation where elected officials face the representative's problem— namely, that inattentive constituents are unlikely to notice activities legislators do to cultivate support—politicians have an incentive to create an impression of influence. Understanding the impression of influence in

[20] Mayhew (1974).
[21] Cruz and Schneider (2013).

a comparative context can better illuminate when and how legislators use rhetoric to receive credit for projects in the district.

There remains much work to be done in order to understand how legislators cultivate an impression of influence and how this matters for representation. Some of this work could examine how legislators cultivate an impression of influence in other policy areas and in comparative contexts. Future work should also explore how what others say about spending affects the credit legislators receive. In Chapter 7, for example, we show that criticism about spending undermines legislators' credit claiming efforts. There might be competition between members of Congress over credit for expenditures Shepsle et al.[22] Future studies may examine how constituents divide credit across multiple representatives and how members of Congress and other politicians compete over credit for the same project. But rhetoric from other politicians could help members of Congress create an impression of influence. For example, endorsements from local officials may cause constituents to view their representative as even more effective at delivering money. And other work could address some of the limitations of our analysis. We examine legislators' credit claiming statements in press releases, but constituents might have a very different reaction when they encounter credit claiming in other mediums. For example, constituents may feel even more positive about a legislator after attending a groundbreaking or ribbon-cutting ceremony. We also show that legislators' actual credit claiming rate is related to their impression of influence among constituents. Other studies could seek to explain this finding, examining how likely it is that constituents will learn about their representative's work by evaluating the kinds of information available to constituents about their representative.

8.4 THE IMPRESSION OF INFLUENCE

Legislators solve the representative's problem with their credit claiming statements. This solution ensures that legislators are able to use the tools of office to cultivate support. It also ensures that entrepreneurial legislators are able to be accountable to constituents. But the credit claiming, credit allocation process creates new risks for representation and new opportunities for disbursement. To understand how and why the federal government distributes money, we need to study more than just spending as it occurs to congressional districts. We also need to understand how legislators create an impression of influence over expenditures.

---

[22] Shepsle et al. (2009).

CHAPTER 9

Text as Data: Methods Appendix

IN THIS APPENDIX WE PROVIDE MORE DETAILS ABOUT HOW WE classify the nearly 170,000 House press releases that we use in this study as credit claiming or not. Our strategy will be to make use of recent Text as Data methods,[1] while also utilizing methods from other fields to improve upon the classification.

As we discussed in Chapter 3, our goal is to provide a label for each of the press releases as claiming credit for spending or not. We begin with 800 triple-hand-coded documents, which we will use to *supervise* statistical models for text. To classify the texts we use *supervised* learning techniques. The idea is that we will learn a relationship between the hand-coded labels and the words (or other features) in the texts. We will then use this relationship between labels and features to predict the label for all the remaining documents. The result of the process is that all the press releases will be labeled.

As with all Text as Data methods, we need to make a series of simplifying assumptions that make statistical modeling of the texts feasible.[2] Because we are performing supervised learning, choices about which assumptions to make are guided by our simple goal: accurately replicating hand coding. Our particular set of assumptions were chosen to optimize out-of-sample classification performance. We begin with the bag of words assumption—discarding information about the order of words in a document. While this may be a strong assumption in other contexts,[3] our assessments showed that additional information on word order failed to increase our classification accuracy. We also discarded placeholder words (like the or a), and words that appeared in fewer than three documents. While common in other large collections of text, we did not *stem* the words in our documents—remove the ends of words in order to return the *stem* of the word[4]—because

---

[1] Grimmer and Stewart (2013).
[2] Grimmer and Stewart (2013).
[3] Spirling (2012).
[4] Porter (1980).

stemming words decreased our classification accuracy. The result of the preprocessing steps is that each of our documents is a vector of word counts.

We use this representation of our press releases and our hand-coded documents to train a model to classify the remaining press releases as credit claiming or not. There are a number of well-established statistical methods for performing this classification, such as: support vector machines,[5] LASSO,[6] elastic-net,[7] random forests,[8] and Kernel Regularized Least Squares (KRLS),[9] among many others. Each of the individual classifiers are likely to perform well on particular problems, but there are other problems where the classifiers are likely to be less useful. We could instead apply all the methods individually and then choose the method with the highest out-of-sample performance.[10] This takes advantage of the methods that performs well on this problem, but this fails to exploit the power from the other methods.

To exploit the advantages of all the methods, we adapt the *super learner* ensemble method for text classification.[11] The training procedure for super learning proceeds in two steps. First, we replicate our coding task and assess how well our constituent methods can predict a document's label, using our hand-labeled documents. We include five methods in our ensemble: a support vector machine (SVM), LASSO, elastic net, random forests, and KRLS. The result of this first step is a set of weights that we attach to our methods. Second, with the weights in hand, we then use our entire set of hand-labeled documents to train our classification algorithms and make predictions about the probability of each unlabeled document being a credit claiming press release. We then generate a weighted average of the predicted probability, using the weights from the first step.

Specifically, we use ten-fold cross-validation[12] to generate predictions for our hand-coded labels. We then use the predictions to fit a regression of the true label on the hand-coded labels. We constrain this regression to have the coefficients all be greater than zero and sum to one, so the coefficients are interpretable as weights. We then fit the set of methods to

---

[5] Tong and Koller (2002).

[6] Hastie, Tibshirani, and Friedman (2001).

[7] Hastie, Tibshirani, and Friedman (2001).

[8] Breiman (2001).

[9] Hainmueller and Hazlett (2014).

[10] Hastie, Tibshirani, and Friedman (2001).

[11] van der Laan, Polley, and Hubbard (2007).

[12] Hastie, Tibshirani, and Friedman (2001); van der Laan, Polley, and Hubbard (2007).

the entire collection of training documents and use the weights from this first step.

In Chapter 3, we evaluate this method with ten-fold cross-validation. To perform this evaluation, we perform this entire procedure within each fold of the cross-validation. This ensures all our evaluations are out of sample.

Bibliography

Achen, Christopher. 1978. "Measuring Representation." *American Journal of Political Science* 22(3): 475–510.

Adler, E. Scott, and John S. Lapinski. 1997. "Demand-Side Theory and Congressional Committee Composition: A Constituency Characteristics Approach." *American Journal of Political Science* 41(3): 895–918.

Ansolabehere, Stephen, Marc Meredith, and Erik Snowberg. 2013. "Asking About Numbers: Why and How." *Political Analysis* 21(1): 48–69.

Applbaum, Arthur Isak. 1999. *Ethics for Adversaries: The Morality of Roles in Public and Professional Life*. Princeton University Press.

Ariely, Dan. 2000. "Controlling the Information Flow: Effects on Consumers' Decisions and Preferences." *Journal of Consumer Research* 27(2): 233–248.

Armey, Richard. 2009. "Dick Armey Brings Small Government Message to Florida; Armey a Guest at Tampa, Tallahassee Taxpayer Tea Parties." FreedomWorks Press Release.

Arnold, R. Douglas. 1979. *Congress and the Bureaucracy: A Theory of Influence*. Yale University Press.

Arnold, R. Douglas. 1992. *The Logic of Congressional Action*. Yale University Press.

Ashworth, Scott. 2005. "Reputational Dynamics and Political Careers." *The Journal of Law, Economics, and Organization* 21(2): 441–466.

Ashworth, Scott. 2012. "Electoral Accountability: Recent Theoretical and Empirical Work." *Annual Review of Political Science* 15(183–201).

Ashworth, Scott, and Scott Bueno de Mesquita. 2006. "Delivering the Goods: Legislative Particularism in Different Electoral and Institutional Settings." *Journal of Politics* 68(1): 168–179.

Associated Press. 1998. "Hamilton County Schools Win $8 Million Federal Grant." Associated Press State & Local Wire. September 2nd, 1998.

Associated Press. 2000. "Federal Bill Provides $1 Million for Water Service to Rural Communities." Associated Press State & Local Wire.

Associated Press. 2001. "Congressmen Push for $1.2 million to Boost Ocoee Rafting." Associated Press State & Local Wire.

Associated Press. 2003. "Tennessee Pork Barrel Spending Up, Group Says." The Associated Press State & Local Wire. April 10th, 2003.

Associated Press, 2009. "Wamp Says He Will Run for Governor." The Associated Press State & Local Wire. January 5th, 2009

Bachus, Rep. Spencer. 2008. "Rep. Bachus Announces Fire Grants for Stewartsville and Maplesville Departments." Representative Press Release.

Bafumi, Joseph, and Michael Herron. 2010. "Leapfrog Representation and Extremism: A Study of American Voters and Their Members of Congress." *American Political Science Review* 104(3): 519–542.

Balla, Steven, Eric Lawrence, Forrest Maltzman, and Lee Sigelman. 2002. "Partisanship, Blame Avoidance, and the Distribution of Legislative Pork." *American Journal of Political Science* 46(3): 515–525.

Benning, Tom. 2010. "Rep. Chet Edwards Touts $16.5 Million Earmark for Fort Hood Facility." *The Dallas Morning News*.

Berinsky, Adam J., Gregory A. Huber, and Gabriel S. Lenz. 2012. "Evaluating Online Labor Markets for Experimental Research: Amazon.com's Mechanical Turk." *Political Analysis* 20(3): 351–368.

Berlyne, D.E. 1970. "Novelty, Complexity, and Hedonic Value." *Perception & Psychophysics* 8(5): 279–286.

Berry, Christopher R., Barry C. Burden, and William G. Howell. 2010a. "After Enactment: The Lives and Deaths of Federal Programs." *American Journal of Political Science* 54(1): 1–17.

Berry, Christopher R., Barry C. Burden, and William G. Howell. 2010b. "The President and the Distribution of Federal Spending." *American Political Science Review* 104(4): 783–799.

Bickers, Kenneth et al. 2007. "The Electoral Effect of Credit Claiming for Pork Barrel Projects in Congress."

Blei, David, Andrew Ng, and Michael Jordan. 2003. "Latent Dirichlet Allocation." *Journal of Machine Learning and Research* 3: 993–1022.

Bolton, Patrick, and Mathias Dewatripont. 2005. *Contract Theory*. Massachusetts Institute of Technology Press.

Bonica, Adam. 2014. "Mapping the Ideological Marketplace." *American Journal of Political Science*.

Brady, David, Hahrie Han, and Jeremy Pope. 2007. "Primary Elections and Candidate Ideology: Out of Step with the Primary Electorate?" *Legislative Studies Quarterly* 32(1): 79–105.

Breiman, Leo. 2001. "Random Forests." *Journal of Machine Learning* 45(1): 5–32.

Brokaw, Chet. 2010. "Herseth-Sandlin, Noem Squabble About Attacks in Last Televised Debate." *Rapid City Journal*. http://rapidcityjournal.com/news/herseth-sandlin-noem-squabble-about-attacks-in-last-televised-debates/article_3ccd6d90-e27f-11df-bad8-001cc4c03286.html

Buhrmester, Michael, Tracy Kwang, and Samuel D. Gosling. 2011. "Amazon's Mechanical Turk A New Source of Inexpensive, Yet High-Quality, Data?" *Perspectives on Psychological Science* 6(1): 3–5.

Cain, Bruce, John Ferejohn, and Morris Fiorina. 1987. *The Personal Vote: Constituency Service and Electoral Independence*. Harvard University Press.

Camp, David. 2005. "Rep. Camp Secures $2.5 Million for M-72 Project." Representative Press Release.

Campbell, Angus, Philip E. Converse, Warren E. Miller, and Donald E. Stokes. 1960. *The American Voter*. John Wiley & Sons.

Campbell, Margaret C., and Kevin Lane Keller. 2003. "Brand Familiarty and Advertising Repetition Effects." *Journal of Consumer Research* 30(2): 292–304.

Canes-Wrone, Brandice, David Brady, and John Cogan. 2002. "Out of Step, Out of Office: Electoral Accountability and House Members' Voting." *American Political Science Review* 96(1): 127–140.

Canes-Wrone, Brandice, Michael C. Herron, and Kenneth W. Shotts. 2001. "Leadership and Pandering: A Theory of Executive Policymaking." *American Journal of Political Science* 45(3): 532–550.

Cardin, Sen. Ben. 2007. "Cardin, Mikulski Announce Federal Funding for Prince George County Firefighters." Senator Press Release.

Caughey, Devin, and Jasjeet Sekhon. 2012. "Regression Discontinuity Designs and Popular Elections: Implications of Pro-Incumbent Bias in Close US House Races." *Political Analysis* 19(4): 385–408.

Census. 2013. "Census Quick Facts, Shannon County." http://quickfacts.census.gov/qfd/states/46/46113.html.

Chen, Jowei. 2010. "Electoral Geography's Effect on Pork Barreling in Legislatures." *American Journal of Political Science* 54(2): 301–322.

Chen, Jowei, and Neil Malhotra. 2007. "The Law of k/n: The Effect of Chamber Size on Government Spending in Bicameral Legislatures." *American Political Science Review* 101(4): 655–674.

Cheves, John. 2005. "Prince of Pork: Hal Rogers Hauls Home Tax Dollars by the Billions." *Lexington Herald-Leader*.

Cleveland, William S. 1979. "Robust Locally Weighted Regression and Scatterplots." *Journal of the American Statistical Association* 74(368): 829–836.

Coble, Howard. 2010. "Rep. Coble Adds GOP YouCut Program to His Website." Representative Press Release.

Coburn, Tom A. 2003. *Breach of Trust: How Washington Turns Outsiders into Insiders*. WND Books.

Conlisk, J. 1996. "Why Bounded Rationality?" *Journal of Economic Literature* 34(2): 669–700.

Conte, Andrew. 2009. "'Tea Party' Attendees Tired of Big Government." Pittsburgh Tribune Review. April 15th, 2009.

Cooper, Aaron et al. 2009. "Nationwide 'Tea Party' Protests Blast Spending." http://www.cnn.com/2009/POLITICS/04/15/tea.parties/.

Costello, Jerry. 2010. "Marion Receives Department of Justice Grant." Representative Press Release.

Cramer, Robert E. 'Bud'. 2005. "North Alabama to Receive over $23 million for Road Projects." Representative Press Release.

Crenshaw, Ander. 2010. "Rep. Crenshaw Votes to Prohibit Taxpayer Funding for Stimulus Bill Promotional Signage." Representative Press Release.

Cruz, Cesi, and Christina J. Schneider. 2013. "The Politics of (Undeserved) Credit-Claiming in Poor Quality Information Environments." University of California, San Diego Mimeo.

Cuellar, Henry. 2005. "Rep. Cuellar Announces $25,000 in Funds for Jourdanton Police Department." Representative Press Release.

Culberson, John. 2009. "Rep. Culberson Issues Statement on Latest Unemployment Numbers." Representative Press Release.

Cummings, Rep. Elijah. 2009. "Reps. Cummings, Sarbanes, Sens. Mikulski, Cardin Announce $1.3 Million Staffing Award for Howard County Firefighters." Representative Press Release.

Daley, Brendan, and Erik Snowberg. 2011. "Even if it is not Bribery: The Case for Campaign Finance Reform." *Journal of Law, Economics, and Organization* 27(2): 324–349.

Deering, Christopher J., and Steven S. Smith. 1997. *Committees in Congress.* Congressional Quarterly Press.

Deslatte, Melinda. 2009. "Stimulus Bill Includes More than $5 Billion in Louisiana Aid." http://www.houmatoday.com/article/20090128/ARTICLES/901280255.

Dietterich, Thomas. 2000. "Ensemble Methods in Machine Learning." *Multiple Classifier Systems* pp. 1–15.

Disch, Lisa. 2012. "Democratic Representation and the Constituency Paradox." *Perspectives on Politics* 10(3): 599–616.

Downs, Anthony. 1957. *An Economic Theory of Democracy.* Harper.

Draper, Robert. 2012. *Do Not Ask What Good We Do: Inside the U.S. House of Representatives.* Simon & Schuster, Inc.

Dropp, Kyle, and Zachary Peskowitz. 2012. "Electoral Security and the Provision of Constituency Service." *Journal of Politics* 74(1): 220–234.

Dunning, Thad. 2012. *Natural Experiments in the Social Sciences: A Design-Based Approach.* Cambridge University Press.

Editorial. 2009. "Protesting Big Government on Independence Day." *The Washington Times.* http://www.washingtontimes.com/news/2009/jul/03/july-4-tea-parties/.

Erikson, Robert S., and Thomas R. Palfrey. 2000. "Equilibria in Campaign Spending Games: Theory and Data." *American Political Science Review* 94(3): 595–609.

Evans, Diana. 2004. *Greasing the Wheels: Using Pork Barrel Projects to Build Majority Coalitions in Congress.* Cambridge University Press.

Fenno, Richard. 1973. *Congressmen in Committees.* Little Brown and Company.

Fenno, Richard. 1978. *Home Style: House Members in their Districts.* Addison Wesley.

Ferejohn, John. 1974. *Pork Barrel Politics: Rivers and Harbors Legislation, 1947-1968.* Stanford University Press.

Finkel, Jenny Rose, Trond Grenager, and Christopher Manning. 2005. Incorporating Non-local Information into Information Extraction Systems by Gibbs Sampling. In *Proceedings of the 43rd Annual Meeting of the ACL.* Vol. 43 pp. 363–370.

Fiorina, Morris. 1977. *Congress: Keystone of the Washington Establishment.* Yale University Press.

Fiorina, Morris. 1981. "Some Problems in Studying the Effects of Resource Allocation in Congressional Elections." *American Journal of Political Science* 25(3): 543–567.

Flake, Jeff. 2008. "Rep. Flake Spotlights Egregious Earmark of the Week." Representative Press Release.

Frisch, Scott A., and Sean Q. Kelly. 2011. *Cheese Factories on the Moon: Why Earmarks are Good for American Democracy*. Paradigm Publishers.

Gaines, Brian J., James H. Kuklinski, and Paul J. Quirk. 2007. "The Logic of the Survey Experiment Reexamined." *Political Analysis* 15(1): 1–20.

Gelman, Andrew, and Jennifer Hill. 2007. *Data Analysis Using Regression and Multilevel/Hierarchical Models*. Cambridge University Press.

Gerber, Alan. 1998. "Estimating the Effect of Campaign Spending on Senate Election Outcomes Using Instrumental Variables." *American Political Science Review* 92(2): 401–411.

Greeley, Brendan. 2013. "Earmarks: The Reluctant Case for Ending the Ban." *Bloomberg Businessweek*. http://www.businessweek.com/articles/2013-01-10/earmarks-the-reluctant-case-for-ending-the-ban.

Grice, Paul. 1989. *Studies in the Way of Words*. Harvard University Press.

Grimmer, Justin. 2010. "A Bayesian Hierarchical Topic Model for Political Texts: Measuring Expressed Agendas in Senate Press Releases." *Political Analysis* 18(1): 1–35.

Grimmer, Justin. 2013. *Representational Style: What Legislators Say and Why It Matters*. Cambridge University Press.

Grimmer, Justin, and Brandon M. Stewart. 2013. "Text as Data: The Promise and Pitfalls of Automatic Content Analysis Methods for Political Texts." *Political Analysis* 21(3): 267–297.

Grimmer, Justin, Solomon Messing, and Sean J. Westwood. 2013. "Estimating Heterogeneous Treatment Effects and the Effects of Heterogeneous Treatments with Ensemble Methods." Stanford University Mimeo.

Grose, Christian R., and Anthony M. Bertelli. 2009. "Secretaries of Pork: A New Theory of Distributive Public Policy." *Journal of Politics* 71(3): 926–945.

Groseclose, Tim. 2001. "A Model of Candidate Location When One Candidate Has a Valence Advantage." *American Journal of Political Science* 45(4): 862–886.

Groseclose, Tim, and James M. Snyder. 1996. "Buying Supermajorities." *American Political Science Review* 90(2): 303–315.

Gutmann, Amy, and Dennis Thompson. 1996. *Democracy and Disagreement*. Harvard University Press.

Hainmueller, Jens, and Chad Hazlett. 2014. "Kernel Regularized Least Squares: Reducing Misspecification Bias with a Flexible and Interpretable Machine Learning Approach." *Political Analysis*.

Hall, Richard. 1996. *Participation in Congress*. Yale University Press.

Hansen, John Mark. 1998. "Individuals, Institutions, and Public Preferences over Public Finance." *American Political Science Review* 92(3): 513–531.

Hassin, Ran R., John A. Bargh, and James S. Uleman. 2002. "Spontaneous Causal Inferences." *Journal of Experimental Social Psychology* 38(2): 515–522.

Hastie, Trevor, Robert Tibshirani, and Jerome Friedman. 2001. *The Elements of Statistical Learning*. Springer.

Hastings, Doc. 2007. "Rep. Hastings Secures $1.185 Million for Odessa Sub-aquifer." Representative Press Release.

Hastings, Doc. 2008. "Federal Funds Headed to Chelan County." Representative Press Release.

Hatano, Giyoo, and Keiko Osawa. 1983. "Digit Memory of Grand Experts in Abacus-Derived Mental Calculation." *Cognition* 15(1): 95–110.

Herseth-Sandlin, Stephanie. 2008. "Rep. Herseth-Sandlin Announces $620,464 in Low Income Energy Assistance Funding for South Dakota." Representative Press Release.

Herseth-Sandlin, Stephanie. 2009a. "House Approves Funding for Joe Foss Field, Veterans Health Care." Representative Press Release.

Herseth-Sandlin, Stephanie. 2009b. "Rep. Herseth-Sandlin Announces $3 Million Grant for Sisseton-Wahpeton Housing." Representative Press Release.

Herseth-Sandlin, Stephanie. 2009c. "Rep. Herseth-Sandlin Announces More Than $5 Million to Hire, Retain 30 Police Officers in 17 Communities Across South Dakota." Representative Press Release.

Herseth-Sandlin, Stephanie. 2009d. "Rep. Herseth-Sandlin Secures Critical Funding for Indian Country, Economic Development Priorities." Representative Press Release.

Herseth, Stephanie. 2005a. "Rep. Herseth Announces $800,000 in Telemedicine Grants." Representative Press Release.

Herseth, Stephanie. 2005b. "Rep. Herseth Announces Significant Funding for South Dakota Water Projects, Air National Guard." Representative Press Release.

Herseth, Stephanie. 2005c. "Rep. Herseth Supports Meth Prevention, Emergency Response Funds." Representative Press Release.

Herseth, Stephanie. 2006a. "Funds for Water Project Advance." Representative Press Release.

Herseth, Stephanie. 2006b. "Rep. Herseth Announces Funding for South Dakota School of Mines Research Projects." Representative Press Release.

Herseth, Stephanie. 2006c. "Rep. Herseth Announces Key Funding for South Dakota Transportation Needs, Indian County." Representative Press Release.

Herseth, Stephanie. 2006d. "Rep. Herseth Praises Release of Emergency Heating Funds." Representative Press Release.

Higgins, Brian. 2006. "Rep. Higgins Announces $75,259 for Walden Fire District." Representative Press Release.

Hillard, Dustin, Stephen Purpura, and John Wilkerson. 2008. "Computer-Assisted Topic Classification for Mixed-Methods Social Science Research." *Journal of Information Technology & Politics* 4(4): 31–46.

Hinchey, Maurice. 2009. "Rep. Hinchey to Introduce Measure to Block Privitization of Government Jobs at West Point." Representative Press Release.

Hird, John. 1991. "The Political Economy of Pork: Project Selection at the US Army Corps of Engineers." *American Political Science Review* 85(2): 429–456.

Holland, Paul. 1986. "Statistics and Causal Inference." *Journal of the American Statistical Association* 81(396): 945–960.

Hopkins, Daniel J., and Gary King. 2010. "A Method of Automated Nonparametric Content Analysis for Social Science." *American Journal of Political Science* 54(1): 229–247.

Hoyer, Steny. 2004. "House Leadership of Congressional Fire Services Caucus Laments Cuts to Fire Grant Program." Representative Press Release.

Hulshof, Rep. Kenny. 2006. "Rep. Hulshof Announces Fire Grant for Upton." Representative Press Release.

Humphreys, Macartan, Raul Sanchez de la Sierra, and Peter van der Windt. 2013. "Fishing, Commitment, and Communication: A Proposal for Comprehensive Nonbinding Research Registration." *Political Analysis* 21(1): 1–20.

Iyengar, Shanto, and Sean J. Westwood. 2013. "Fear and Loathing Across Party Lines: New Evidence on Group Polarization." Stanford University Mimeo.

Jacobs, Lawrence, and Robert Shapiro. 2000. *Politicians Don't Pander: Political Manipulation and the Loss of Democratic Responsiveness*. University Of Chicago Press.

Jacobson, Gary C. 1978. "The Effects of Campaign Spending in Congressional Elections." *American Political Science Review* 72(2): 469–491.

Jankoviak, Shawna. 2009. "CMU Grant Will Expand Coverage." *Cheboygan News*. http://www.cheboygannews.com/article/20091105/NEWS/311059989.

Johnson, Eddie Bernice. 2008. "Rep. Johnson Announces Grant to Old Red Museum." Representative Press Release.

Jones, Jeffrey M. 2010. "Voters Rate Economy as Top Issue for 2010." Gallup Blog Post. http://www.gallup.com/poll/127247/voters-rate-economy-top-issue-2010.aspx.

Jones, Jeffrey M. 2011. "D.C., Hawaii Most Democratic, Utah Most Republican State in '11." State of the States, Blog Post http://www.gallup.com/poll/148949/hawaii-democratic-utah-republican-state.aspx.

Jurafsky, Danile, and James H. Martin. 2008. *Speech and Language Processing*. Pearson Prentice Hall.

Kahneman, D. 2003. "A perspective on judgment and choice: Mapping bounded rationality." *American psychologist* 58(9): 697.

Kahneman, Daniel. 2011. *Thinking, Fast and Slow*. Farrar, Straus, Giroux.

Kant, Immanuel. 1983. *Ethical Philosophy*. Hackett.

Kasperowicz, Pete. 2013. "GOP Seeks Planned Parenthood Study with Hope to Strip Funding." http://thehill.com/blogs/floor-action/house/284633-gop-seeks-planned-parenthood-study-in-hopes-of-defunding-abortion-providers.

Kirmani, Amna. 1997. "Advertising Repetition as a Signal of Quality: Advertised so Much, Something Must be Wrong." *Journal of Advertising* 26(3): 77–86.

Kokesh, Jessica. 2009. "New Camp Rapid HQ to Reflect Guard's 'Upscale' Rise in Quality." *Rapid City Journal*. http://rapidcityjournal.com/news/local/top-stories/new-camp-rapid-hq-to-reflect-guard-s-upscale-rise/article_e87528e1-7d17-584b-9576-690ffe262993.html.

Kolawole, Emi. 2010. "Tennessee Rep. Zach Wamp Talks of Secession." Post Politics Blog. http://www.washingtonpost.com/wp-dyn/content/article/2010/07/23/AR2010072305420.html.

Korsgaard, Christine M. 1997. *Groundwork of the Metaphysics of Morals.* Cambridge University Press chapter Introduction.

Kriner, Douglas L., and Andrew Reeves. 2012. "The Influence of Federal Spending on Presidential Elections." *American Political Science Review* 106(2): 348–366.

Kruger, Lennard. 2009. "Assistance to Firefighters Program: Distribution of Fire Grant Funding." Congressional Research Service. http://assets.opencrs.com/rpts/RL32341_20080806.pdf.

Kruger, Lennard G. 2013. "Assistance to Firefighters Program: Distribution of Fire Grant Funding." Congressional Research Service. http://www.fas.org/sgp/crs/homesec/RL32341.pdf.

Krugman, Paul. 2010. "Me and the Deficit." http://krugman.blogs.nytimes.com/2010/08/12/me-and-the-deficit/.

Kymlicka, William. 2002. *Contemporary Political Philosophy: An Introduction.* Oxford University Press.

Lammers, Dirk. 2006. "Herseth Re-Elected, Pledges Continued Bipartisanship." *Rapid City Journal.* http://rapidcityjournal.com/news/state-and-regional/herseth-re-elected-pledges-continued-bipartisanship/article_5e37915c-199d-5a44-9e20-0716e2343580.html.

Lauderdale, Benjamin. 2013. "Does Inattention to Political Debate Explain the Polarization Gap Between the U.S. Congress and Public." *Public Opinion Quarterly* 77(1): 2–23.

Laverty, Deborah. 2012. "Hobart Marks Start of Ash Street Drainage Project." *Northwest Indiana Times.* http://www.nwitimes.com/news/local/lake/hobart/hobart-marks-start-of-ash-street-drainage-project/article_90c6ae72-06a3-51aa-bc3f-546d309cb065.html.

Lazarus, Jeffrey. 2009. "Party, Electoral Vulnerability, and Earmarks in the US House of Representatives." *Journal of Politics* 71(3): 1050–1061.

Lee, Frances. 2003a. "Geographic Politics in the US House of Representatives: Coalition Building and Distribution of Benefits." *American Journal of Political Science* 47(4): 714–728.

Lee, Frances E. 2003b. "Geographic Politics in the US House of Representatives: Coalition Building and Distribution of Benefits." *American Journal of Political Science* 47(4): 714–728.

Levitt, Steven D., and James M. Snyder. 1997. "The Impact of Federal Spending on House Election Outcomes." *The Journal of Political Economy* 105(1): 30–53.

Lipinski, Daniel. 2004. *Congressional Communication: Content and Consequences.* University of Michigan Press.

LoBiondo, Frank. 2005. "Rep. LoBiondo Announces New Fire Grant for Atlantic County Fire Department."

LoBiondo, Frank. 2006a. "Rep. LoBiondo Announces Federal Funding for Laureldale Fire Department." Representative Press Release.

LoBiondo, Frank. 2006b. "Rep. LoBiondo Announces Federal Grant for Clayton Volunteer Ambulance." Representative Press Release.

LoBiondo, Frank. 2007. "Rep. LoBiondo Announces New Fire Grant for Bargaintown Volunteer Fire." Representative Press Release.

LoBiondo, Rep. Frank. 2012. "LoBiondo Announces More than $100,000 Fire Grant to Forest Grove Volunteer Fire Company." Representative Press Release.

Lodge, Milton, Kathleen M. McGraw, and Patrick Stroh. 1989. "An Impression-Driven Model of Candidate Evaluation." *American Political Science Review* 83(2): 399–419.

Loewenstein, George F., and Drazen Prelec. 1993. "Preferences for Sequences of Outcomes." *Psychological Review* 100(1): 91–108.

Lowi, Theodore. 1969. *The End of Liberalism*. WW Norton & Company.

Madison, James. 1787. "The Federalist No. 10: The Utility of the Union as a Safeguard Against Domestic Faction and Insurrection (continued)."

Malkin, Michelle. 2009. "Cash for Cloture: Demcare Bribe List, Pt. II." http://michellemalkin.com/2009/12/21/cash-for-cloture-demcare-bribe-list-pt-ii/.

Manning, Christopher et al. 2008. *Introduction to Information Retrieval*. Cambridge University Press.

Mansbridge, Jane. 2003. "Rethinking Representation." *American Political Science Review* 97(4): 515–528.

Martin, Gregory J. 2012. "Dividing the Dollar with Formulas." Stanford Graduate School of Business Mimeo.

Mayhew, David. 1974. *Congress: The Electoral Connection*. Yale University Press.

McCain, John. 2010. "Statement by Senator John McCain on Amendment Number 3475 to Prohibit Earmarks in Years in Which There is a Deficit." Senate Floor Speech.

McCarty, Nolan, Keith Poole, and Howard Rosenthal. 2009. "Does Gerrymandering Cause Polarization?" *American Journal of Political Science* 53(3): 666–680.

McDermott, Jim. 2007. "Lifelong AIDS Alliance's Chicken Soup Brigade Wins National Award." Representative Press Release.

McIntyre, Mike. 2006. "Rep. McIntyre Announces over $1 Million for Robeson County Schools." Representative Press Release.

Mearsheimer, John J. 2011. *Why Leaders Lie: The Truth About Lying in International Politics*. Oxford University Press.

Mettler, Suzanne. 2011. *The Submerged State: How Invisible Government Policies Undermine American Democracy*. University of Chicago Press.

Mikulski, Barbara. 2007. "Senator Mikulski Announces $123,809 in Federal Funding for Wicomico County Firefighters." Senator Press Release.

Miller, Warren, and Donald Stokes. 1963. "Constituency Influence in Congress." *American Political Science Review* 57(1): 45–56.

Moore, Gwen. 2009. "Moore Announces West Allis To Receive First Installment of Energy Efficiency Grants." Representative Press Release.

Muhlhausen, David. 2009. "Do DHS Fire Grants Reduce Fire Casualties?" Heritage Foundation Report. http://www.heritage.org/research/reports/2009/09/do-dhs-fire-grants-reduce-fire-casualties.

Muhlhausen, David B. 2012. "Fire Grants: Do Not Reauthorize an Ineffective Program." The Heritage Foundation Issue Brief, No. 3505.

Munsey, Patrick. 2008. "McGoff Launches Bid to Unseat Burton." *The Kokomo Perspective.* http://kokomoperspective.com/news/mcgoff-launches-bid-to-unseat-burton/article_003c0793-884f-5b1d-9774-d809bd0ed76c.html?mode=jqm.

Newport, Frank. 2010. "Jobs Climb Higher on Americans' Top Problems List." Gallup Blog Post. http://kokomoperspective.com/news/mcgoff-launches-bid-to-unseat-burton/article_003c0793-884f-5b1d-9774-d809bd0ed76c.html?mode=jqm.

Neyfakh, Leon. 2013. "Bring Back the United States of Pork." *Boston Globe.* http://www.bostonglobe.com/ideas/2013/05/11/bring-back-united-states-pork/gsa3RcmD4tXlQPs29ytsXJ/story.html.

Nickerson, David W. 2007. "Does Email Boost Turnout?" *Quarterly Journal of Political Science* 2(2): 369–379.

Ober, Josiah. 2010. *Democracy and Knowledge: Innovation and Learning in Classical Athens.* Princeton University Press.

Obey, David. 2007. "Rep. Obey Applauds Federal Grant to Help Firefighting Operations in Antigo." Representative Press Release.

Obey, Rep. David. 2006. "Rep. Obey Visits Boyd For Grand Opening of New Wastewater Treatment Plant." Representative Press Release.

Olver, John. 2005. "Sens. Kennedy, Kerry, Rep. Olver Announce $650,000 for Silvio O. Conte National Fish and Wildlife Refuge." Representative Press Release.

Orne, Martin T. 1969. *Demand Characteristics and the Concept of Quasi-Controls.* Academic Press.

Page, Scott. 2007. *The Difference: How the Power of Diversity Creates Better Groups, Firms, Schools, and Societies.* Princeton University Press.

Palmer, Anna. 2010. "Herseth-Sandlin Faces Best GOP Opponent." Roll Call. http://www.rollcall.com/issues/56_1/-47993-1.html.

Patashnik, Eric. 2013. "Bring Back Pork Barrel Spending." The Monkey Cage. http://themonkeycage.org/2013/01/14/bring-back-pork-barrel-spending/.

Pickering, Charles. 2005. "Rep. Pickering: House Passes $25 Million for 3rd District Transportation." Representative Press Release.

Pickering, Charles. 2006a. "Rep. Pickering Announces $2.4 Million Grant for Mississippi State University." Representative Press Release.

Pickering, Charles. 2006b. "Rep. Pickering Announces Justice Department Grants." Representative Press Release.

Pickering, Charles. 2007. "Rep. Pickering: $75,392 for Forest Fire Department." Representative Press Release.

Polk, Amy. 2008. "Community Leaders, Hospital Board Take Part in Hospital Groundbreaking." *Mackinac Island Town Crier.* http://www.mackinacislandnews.com/news/2008-05-31/front_page/022.html.

Poole, Keith T., and Howard Rosenthal. 1997. *Congress: A Political-Economic History of Roll Call Voting.* Oxford University Press.

Porter, Martin. 1980. "An Algorithm for Suffix Stripping." *Program* 14(3): 130–137.

Quinn, Kevin et al. 2010. "How to Analyze Political Attention with Minimal Assu mptions and Costs." *American Journal of Political Science* 54(1): 209–228.

Rahall, Rep. Nick. 2008. "Rep. Rahall Announces $79,800 for Quinwood Volunteer Fire Department." Representative Press Release.

Rico, Damian. 2011. "Schereville Breaks Ground for Pennsy Greenway Northwest Trail." *Northwest Indiana Times*. http://www.nwitimes.com/news/local/lake/schererville/schererville-breaks-ground-for-pennsy-greenway-northwest-trail/article_e909f7a6-e34f-546d-b322-0e4b5a29caf2.html.

Rivers, Doug, and Morris Fiorina. 1989. "Constituency Service, Reputation, and the Incumbency Advantage." In *Home Style and Washington Work*, ed. Morris Fiorina, and David Rhode. The University of Michigan Press.

Rogers, Hal. 2009a. "Rep. Rogers Announces Funding for Police Vehicles in Leslie County."

Rogers, Hal. 2009b. "Rep. Rogers Announces Key Committee Approval of $3 million for Martin Flood Control Project." Representative Press Release.

Rogers, Harold. 2008a. "More Drug Treatment Funding Approved for Operation UNITE." Representative Press Release.

Rogers, Mike. 2005. "Rep. Rogers Announces $115,200 Grant for Knightens Crossroad Fire Department." Representative Press Release.

Rogers, Mike. 2007. "Rep. Rogers Announces $9,975 for Daviston Volunteer Fire Department." Representative Press Release.

Rogers, Mike. 2008b. "Rep. Rogers Announces $43,082 in Grants for Randolph County Fire Departments." Representative Press Release.

Rogers, Rep. Harold "Hal". 2009c. "Rogers Secures Funding for McKee Made Army Helicopter Drip Pans." Representative Press Release.

Rokita, Rep. Todd. 2012a. "Rokita Announces Congressional Art Competition." Representative Press Release.

Rokita, Rep. Todd. 2012b. "Rokita Honors 4th District Congressional Art Competition Winner from Lafeyette." Representative Press Release.

Ross, Doug. 2012. "Editorial: Take Our Endorsments to the Polls." *Northwest Indiana Times*. http://www.nwitimes.com/news/opinion/editorial/editorial-take-our-endorsements-to-the-polls/article_d97157bd-ac1c-5029-9a1d-c1f77f9d1b9f.html.

Ross, Mike. 2009a. "Rep. Ross Secures $5,122,000 in House for Millwood Lake." Representative Press Release.

Ross, Mike. 2009b. "Rep. Ross, Sens. Lincoln, Pryor Announce $17,000 for Nevada County." Representative Press Release.

Royce, Ed. 2009. "Rep. Royce Opposes Democrats $825 Billion 'Stimulus'." Representative Press Release.

Schiller, Wendy. 2000. *Partners and Rivals: Representation in US Senate Delegations*. Princeton University Press.

Schock, Aaron. 2009. "Schock Announces Pittsfield Fire Rescue Department and Beardstown Fire Department to Receive Grants." Representative Press Release.

Schock, Aaron. 2012. "Schock Passes Critical First Responder Grant Assistance." Representative Press Release.

Sekhon, Jasjeet S., and Rocio Titiunik. 2012. "When Natural Experiments are Neither Natural nor Experiments." *American Political Science Review* 106(1): 35–57.

Sellers, Patrick. 2010. *Cycles of Spin: Strategic Communication in the US Congress*. Cambridge University Press.

Shelby, Sen. Richard. 2005. "Shelby Announces $42,524 for Alabama Port Volunteer Fire Department in Mobile County." Senator Press Release.

Shepsle, Kenneth A. et al. 2009. "The Senate Electoral Cycle and Bicameral Appropriations Politics." *American Journal of Political Science* 53(2): 343–359.

Shirley, Chad. 2011. "Spending and Funding for Highways." Congressional Budget Office Report. http://www.cbo.gov/publication/22003.

Shuster, Bill. 2010. "One Year Stimulus Anniversary: 365 Days, $862 Billion Later, No Results for American People." Representative Press Release.

Skocpol, Theda, and Vanessa Williamson. 2011. *The Tea Party and the Remaking of Republican Conservatism*. Oxford University Press.

Slivinski, Stephen. 2007. "A Reality Check on Earmark Reform." *Business Week*. http://www.cato.org/publications/commentary/reality-check-earmark-reform.

Smith, Matt. 2010. "Hensarling Stumps for Flores in Cleburne." *Cleburne Times-Review* http://www.cleburnetimesreview.com/local/x583214544/Hensarling-stumps-for-Flores-in-Cleburne/print.

Sniderman, Paul M., and Douglas B. Grob. 1996. "Innovations in Experimental Design in Attitude Surveys." *Annual Review of Sociology* 22: 377–399.

Specter, Arlen. 2007. "Specter Announces Funding for Southwest PA Fire Companies." Senator Press Release.

Spirling, Arthur. 2012. "US Treaty Making with American Indians: Institutional Change and Relative Power, 1784-1911." *American Journal of Political Science* 56(1): 84–97.

Sprouse, Jon. 2011. "A validation of Amazon Mechanical Turk for the collection of acceptability judgments in linguistic theory." *Behavior Research Methods* 43(1): 155–167.

Staff. 1999. "Grant Policy Directives System, Guidelines." Department of Health and Human Services Internal Memo. Avaiable at http://dhhs.gov/asfr/ogapa/aboutog/ogpoe/gpd2-04.pdf.

Staff. 2003. "IMPAC II GM Lead User's Group Meeting Minutes." NIH Meeting Minutes.

Staff. 2006a. "Herseth Party." *Rapid City Journal*. http://rapidcityjournal.com/news/local/herseth-party/article_48deb234-46db-5de7-b501-e6357e4d4c20.html.

Staff. 2006b. "Homeland Security Grants Spent on Clowns and Gyms." *The Washington Times*. http://www.washingtontimes.com/news/2006/apr/20/20060420-110852-8296r/?page=all.

Staff. 2008. "Exit Poll Results, CNN.com."

Staff. 2009a. "Airport to Get Grant for Fire-Rescue Building." *Rapid City Journal*. http://rapidcityjournal.com/news/local/airport-to-get-grant-for-fire-rescue-building/article_c61d4090-a8ee-53d6-b2db-268a6106d1d6.html.

Staff. 2009b. "Foreclosures Rise 6 Percent Between January and February." The News Hour with Jim Lehrer http://www.pbs.org/newshour/updates/business-jan-june09-foreclosures_03-12/.

Staff. 2010a. "Gladwin Receives $65,000 in Grants." *Midland Daily News*. http://www.ourmidland.com/news/gladwin-receives-in-grants/article_bc61863c-c2bf-5b02-add2-529c5ff28d29.html.

Staff. 2010*b*. "Herseth-Sandlin Seeks Stimulus Funds to Help with Timber Management Work." *Rapid City Journal*. http://www.ourmidland.com/news/gladwin-receives-in-grants/article_bc61863c-c2bf-5b02-add2-529c5ff28d29.html.

Staff. 2010*c*. "Rep. Zach Wamp (R), Profile." National Journal Profile.

Staff. 2012. "Harold 'Hal' Rogers, Profile." *The Washington Times*. http://www.washingtontimes.com/campaign-2012/candidates/harold-hal-rogers-208/.

Staff. 2013. "Application and Grant Award Process Narrative." HHS Award Guidelines. Available at http://eclkc.ohs.acf.hhs.gov/hslc/tta-system/operations/fiscal/narrative/ApplicationandG.htm.

Staff, and Associated Press. 2009. "Treasury Official Announces Money for Indian County." *Indian Country News*. http://www.indiancountrynews.com/index.php/news/9-news-from-through-out-indian-country/6886-treasury-official-announces-money-for-indian-areas-of-south-dakota.

Stein, Robert M., and Kenneth N. Bickers. 1994. "Congressional Elections and the Pork Barrel." *Journal of Politics* 56(2): 377–399.

Stein, Robert M., and Kenneth N. Bickers. 1997. *Perpetuating the Pork Barrel: Policy Subsystems and American Democracy*. Cambridge University Press.

Strömberg, David. 2004. "Radio's Impact on Public Spending." *Quarterly Journal of Economics* 119(1): 189–221.

Stupak, Bart. 2005. "North Michigan Receives $3.4 Million in Final Transportation Appropriations Bill." Representative Press Release.

Stupak, Bart. 2007. "Calumet Township Receives $440,000 Loan for Water Infrastructure." Representative Press Release.

Stupak, Bart. 2009. "Northern Michigan Airports Receive More than $6.7 million in Federal Grants." Representative Press Release.

Stupak, Bart. 2010*a*. "Northern Michigan Receives Emergency Food, Shelter Funding." Representative Press Release.

Stupak, Bart. 2010*b*. "Rep. Stupak Announces Economic Impact Grants for Beaverton, Gladwin." Representative Press Release.

Stupak, Bart. 2010*c*. "Rep. Stupak Announces Stimulus Funds for Norther Michigan University Job Training Program." Representative Press Release.

Sulkin, Tracy. 2005. *Issue Politics in Congress*. Cambridge University Press.

Sullivan, John. 2010. "Sullivan Reacts to President Obama's State of the Union Address." Representative Press Release.

Tausanovitch, Chris, and Christopher Warshaw. 2013. "Measuring Constituent Policy Preferences in Congress, State Legislatures, and Cities." *Journal of Politics* 75(2): 330–342.

Tong, Simon, and Daphne Koller. 2002. "Support Vector Machine Active Learning with Applications to Text Classification." *The Journal of Machine Learning Research* 2(1): 45–66.

Tversky, Amos, and Daniel Kahneman. 1974. "Judgment under Uncertainty: Heuristics and Biases." *Science* 185(4157): 1124–1131.

Udall, Tom. 2005. "New Mexico Lawmakers Tackle BRAC Recommendations with Three BRAC Commissioners." Representative Press Release.

Van Berkum, Jos J.A. 2008. "Understanding Sentences in Context." *Current Directions in Psychological Science* 17(6): 376–380.

van der Laan, Mark, Eric Polley, and Alan Hubbard. 2007. "Super Learner." *Statistical Applications in Genetics and Molecular Biology* 6(1).

Vinson, Danielle. 2002. *Through Local Eyes: Local Media Coverage of Congress.* Hampton Press.

Visclosky, Pete. 2007. "Rep. Visclosky Secures $7.25 Million for Northwest Indiana Rail, Transportation Improvements." Representative Press Release.

Visclosky, Pete. 2013. "Visclosky Announces $279,586 for Valparaiso University." Representative Press Release.

Walzer, Michael. 1973. "Political Action: The Problem of Dirty Hands." *Philosophy & Public Affairs* 2(2): 160–180.

Wamp, Zach. 2009. "Mall Energy Project Funded Without Congressional Help." Representative Press Release.

Weingast, Barry, Kenneth Shepsle, and Christopher Johnsen. 1981. "The Political Economy of Benefits and Costs: A Neoclassical Approach to Distributive Politics." *The Journal of Political Economy* 89(4): 642–664.

Weingast, Barry R. 1979. "A Rational Choice Perspective on Congressional Norms." *American Journal of Political Science* 23(2): 245–262.

Wichowsky, Amber. 2012. "District Complexity and the Personal Vote." *Legislative Studies Quarterly* 37(4): 437–464.

Wildavsky, Aaron. 1984. *The Politics of the Budgetary Process.* Brown, Little.

Woster, Kevin. 2010. "Polite Crowd Gives Herseth Sandlin Mixed Review." *Rapid City Journal.*

Yglesias, Matthew. 2013. "Why I Miss Pork-Barrel Politics." Slate.com. http://www.slate.com/articles/business/moneybox/2013/01/fiscal_cliff_legislative_earmarks_pork_and_backroom_deal_making_was_ugly.html.

Zajonc, Robert B. 2001. "Mere Exposure: A Gateway to the Subliminal." *Current Directions in Psychological Science* 10: 224–228.

Zaller, John. 1992. *The Nature and Origin of Mass Opinions.* Cambridge University Press.

Index

Affordable Care Act, 8, 25, 149, 172
Armey, Dick, 156
Army Corps of Engineers, 15, 16, 20

Bachus, Spencer, 127
bag of words, 186
Bernice-Johnson, Eddie, 60
Boucher, Rick, 41
Burton, Dan, 40, 41
Bush, George W., 32, 140

Camp, Dave, 56
Cantor, Eric, 159
Cardin, Ben, 127, 128
Cassidy, Bill, 159
cheap talk, 23
Citizens Against Government Waste, 152, 154
Clinton, Bill, 155
Coble, Howard, 159
Coburn, Tom, 171, 173
Cole, Tom, 171
Congressional Budget Office, 161, 162, 164, 165
consequentialist, 146, 147, 176, 180
content analysis, 36
Cornhusker Kickback, 150, 172
Costello, Jerry, 127
Cramer, Bud, 61
Crenshaw, Ander, 157, 158
cross-validation, 38, 187
Cuellar, Henry, 59
Culberson, John, 156, 157
Cummings, Elijah, 127

Davis, David, 127
deception, 12, 30, 119, 120, 122, 123, 126, 144–147, 176, 178–180, 182
deliberative representation, 146, 179
demand effects, 69, 107
DeMint, Jim, 173
Democratic accountability, 12, 118, 145, 177, 178

Department of Health and Human Services, 143
Diedrich, Larry, 5
Duncan, Jeff, 123

earmarks, 19, 37, 46, 53, 118, 124, 145, 151, 170, 171, 180
ecological validity, 69, 76, 161
Edwards, Chet, 41, 159, 163
entity extraction, 60
Eshoo, Anna, 76
external validity, 13, 70, 115, 116

Facebook, 71, 72, 74, 76
Federal Emergency Management Association, 121, 130
Foxx, Virginia, 157

Hastings, Doc, 56, 61
Herseth-Sandlin, Stephanie, 5–9, 25, 49
Higgins, Brian, 58
Hinchey, Maurice, 59
Hoyer, Steny, 141
Hulshof, Kenny, 127

ideal points, 51, 52, 141
ideological alignment, 4, 177
implicature, 29, 125, 126, 178
incumbency advantage, 16, 64
institutional design, 123, 146, 176, 181

Jankalow, Bill, 5
Johnson, Tim, 7

Kantian ethics, 145, 146, 179
Kennedy, Ted, 61
Kerry, John, 5, 45, 61
Kline, John, 157

Landrieu, Mary, 150, 172
Latent Dirichlet Allocation, 55
LaTourette, Steve, 141
Lincoln, Blanche, 61
LoBiondo, Frank, 29, 41, 59, 126, 127

Louisiana Purchase, 150, 172
Lummis, Cynthia, 49
lying, 31, 126, 178

Malkin, Michelle, 172
McCain, John, 47, 48, 154, 157, 158, 180
McDermott, Jim, 61
McGroff, John, 40
McIntyre, Mike, 59
Mechanical Turk, 70, 73, 74, 107, 108, 129
Melancon, Charlie, 159
Mikluski, Barbara, 127, 128
Moore, Gwen, 59

Nelson, Ben, 150, 172
Noem, Kristi, 9

Obama, Barack, 5, 8, 12, 19, 32, 45, 47, 141, 148, 149, 154, 156, 158, 170, 183
Obey, David, 58, 128
Olver, John, 61

Pascrell, Bill, 141
Paul, Ron, 53
Pelosi, Nancy, 9, 41, 156
Pence, Mike, 41
personal vote, 23, 32, 64, 170
Pickering, Chip, 44, 45
Preibus, Reince, 164
Price, David, 141
Price, Tom, 45
principal-agent models, 118
Proxmire, William, 172
Pryor, Mark, 61

Rahall, Nick, 127
Reagan, Ronald, 155
Reid, Harry, 156
Rogers, Hal, 21, 28, 41, 42, 54, 62
Rogers, Mike, 58, 59
Ross, Mike, 56, 61
Royce, Ed, 159

Santelli, Rick, 149, 153, 154
Sarbanes, John, 127
Schatz, Tom, 152, 153
Schock, Aaron, 127, 142, 143
Sessions, Pete, 157
Shelby, Richard, 128
Shuster, Bill, 156
Slivinski, Stephen, 120
Specter, Arlen, 128
Stark, Pete, 53
stimulus spending, 8, 48, 148, 149, 151, 154, 156, 170
Stupak, Bart, 32, 33, 41, 42, 61, 127
Sullivan, John, 156
supervised learning, 36, 38, 39, 55, 186

Tea Party, 8, 9, 12, 47, 48, 123, 149–154, 156, 157, 160, 161, 170, 171
text as data, 34, 36, 186
Thune, John, 7

Udall, Tom, 58
unsupervised learning, 55

Visclosky, Pete, 15, 16, 127, 174

Wamp, Zach, 152–154
Wasserman-Schultz, Debbie, 164